1

Horse Kisses

365 Inspiring Stories and Devotions
for the
Enduring Horsewoman

By

Sheri Grunska

Edited by
Cindy Lambert

Book cover design by
Stoney's Web Design
www.stoneyswebdesign.com

You can find all of Sheri's books at www.probarnmanagement.com and also sold on Amazon and other outlets.

Dedication

This book is dedicated to my husband, David. He has been by my side for thirty-plus years and has always supported and encouraged me to follow my dreams. God blessed me when I met you.

A Special Thank You

Thank you to Barb and Roxy for being my book cover models. Barb, your wonderful relationship with Roxy is easy to see through this beautiful cover image. Also, I want to thank the extraordinary horsewomen who shared their stories for this book. You inspire so many and I am blessed to know each of you.

She is clothed with strength and dignity,
and she laughs without fear of the future.
Proverbs 31:25

Table of Contents

~January 1~
The Horse Phase

The heavens declare the glory of God;
the skies proclaim the work of His hands.
Psalm 19:1

If you were lucky enough to be bitten by the horse bug as a young girl, then you know after living several decades that it's not just a horse phase you were going through in your teen years. It never is for women who are absolutely crazy in love with horses.

I once dated a guy in my early twenties, and after a few weeks, he had the nerve to ask me when I would grow out of this "horse phase." Can you believe that? I stopped dating him quickly! I am in my sixties now and God sent a wonderful man into my life thirty-plus years ago who loved my passion for horses. And, of course, I married him. Years later, we started a horse boarding stable and never looked back.

Women fall in love with horses as young girls, and for many, those feelings just get stronger and stronger. The dream of owning their own horse may only happen once they have raised their children and are thinking about retirement, but the burning desire often grows deeper with every passing year. Women bring so much to the horse world with their sense of nurturing and care for these extraordinary animals. We love to gaze at them while they munch on hay in their stall or sit in a lounge chair and happily watch them just being horses out in the pasture. They bring a sense of peace and calm into our often crazy lives and can make us feel like young girls again who can't contain our excitement when we are near them. They take our breath away no matter our age.

What a passion these incredible equines stir in my soul and I can't help but smile when I think about how beautifully unique each one is. Thank you, Lord, for the gift of the horse.

~January 2~
Finding Courage

Be strong and courageous. Do not be afraid; do not be discouraged.
For the Lord your God will be with you wherever you go.
Joshua 1:9

For the woman who is crazy about horses and has always wanted to own one, it takes courage to jump in with both feet and purchase your first horse, especially when you are older. As a young child, I was brave and often reckless, riding my horse all over the city streets and open fields that hadn't been developed yet. Horses have always been a part of my life and it has always felt natural to me to be around them. But for the woman who has equally loved horses all her life but was never able to own one as a girl, the thought of buying her first horse later in life can be exhilarating and scary all at the same time.

As children, we don't think about the consequences of our actions, but as adults, we do, and the responsibility of horse ownership is much different. Once we take that leap and bring home our first horse, it is like having our first child. We sit for hours and gaze at him, and our hearts feel like they will burst with joy. There is so much to learn for the woman who ventures into horse ownership, and she jumps in and soaks it up like a sponge. She can't get enough.

Finding the courage to live out your dream is something to be proud of. For some, it is an easier leap than others, but we are all in it together and supporting each other as we learn everything we can about these animals entrusted to us. God gave us a beautiful strength inside that comes out many times throughout our lives. What a fabulous time to have that strength come shining through.

~January 3~
Marrying A Horse Girl

And we know that for those who love God all things work together for good,
for those who are called according to his purpose.
Romans 8:28

We went to many horse shows when my daughters were in high school. It was exhausting work at times but we had so much fun. Looking back, I don't know how I had all the energy to run a boarding stable, go to weekend horse shows, be a wife and mom, and take care of life's daily necessities. The one thing I remember from all the kids and parents who circled the same show circuit was that, often, there were young guys hanging around the young girls all day. I am smiling as I write this because my daughters were no exception. The boys would come around and if they wanted to be a part of our family's life, then they had to like horses and that meant going to horse shows. Some of the boys were into it and some were not.

All these decades later in my own personal life, nothing has changed. My husband knew when we started dating that I loved horses, and today, we care for many horses together every day! He stuck around and I am glad he did. Life can get crazy at times because you never know what a horse will get into, but I love working side-by-side with my husband on our farm. It can bring out the best and worst in a person, and you learn to forgive and support each other daily. It builds character even if you don't realize it at the time.

The Lord already knows that special person He has planned for your life. They may not know yet that their life will be filled with horses but God knows it's the perfect match. Marrying a horse girl can be wonderful.

~January 4~
A New Season

For I know the plans I have for you, declares the Lord,
plans for welfare and not for evil, to give you a future and a hope.
Jeremiah 29:11

Today is a new day. You might not be that twenty-year-old who rode her horse barefoot and carefree back in the days before helmets and cell phones, but you are ready to ride again all these years later. You never gave up your first love of horses. They were just tucked away for a few years while you went to college, got married, and raised your kids. And it's been a wonderful life but now you are ready to get back in the saddle and ride again.

Many women who love horses were lucky enough to ride often when young, only to set it aside as they became adults. You are not alone at all. The best is yet to come. Embrace this new adventure and fall in love again with these amazing creatures. Age is only a number, and sure, we are more aware of our physical shortcomings that often come with age, but that shouldn't stop you from living out your dreams.

Nothing is more beautiful than watching a woman ride her horse for the first time after many years of being an observer. Be intentional and take your time. Take the lessons and don't cut corners. Enjoy and savor every moment you have with your equine partner. For this is a new season in your life.

God has given us so many wonderful things to enjoy on this great earth, but the horse is a gift beyond compare. Thank you, Lord, for all your creation—especially the horse.

~January 5~
Looking For A Horse

So teach us to number our days that we may get a heart of wisdom.
Psalm 90:12

Things have sure changed in the last fifty years when it comes to shopping for horses. I can remember my parents buying my first horse when I was around ten years old before cell phones, the computer, or the internet! How did they do it? It was the good old-fashioned newspaper or, even better, word of mouth from a trusted friend.

Buying a horse for a young child is so much different than someone who has lived a full life. Age does play a part, and I think it only gets better as we age gracefully as horsewomen. We still get all giddy inside each time we go to look at a potential prospect as our new equine partner. Praise God that wisdom also starts to find its way into our heads as we gain a few years on us. It often helps keep some of the emotion out of the equation and lets our brain and commonsense do some of the talking.

As women who have hit the trail a few times in life, it may take longer to look at a horse and we are slower to mount and ride. We have learned to look closer at the feet, legs, and conformation, and now know that a good personality is paramount. We don't have time to deal with a horse with a lot of baggage, even though our heart breaks often because we wish we could take them all home. But that little voice inside of us tells us to stop and think it through. We are not so impetuous anymore.

For the woman who has endured a lot during her life, finding the right horse is a journey that she is thrilled to be able to take. She savors it all and wouldn't trade any of it for the world. Thank you, Lord, for the lessons and discernment you teach me daily. Guide me each day on this journey of life with horses.

~January 6~
Bad Choices

The prudent sees danger and hides himself,
but the simple go on and suffer for it.
Proverbs 22:3

If your equine veterinarian knows your number by heart, then you might be the proud owner of a horse that makes bad choices. I am smiling as I write today's devotion because I can think of a few horses that fit this description. Some might call these horses accident-prone. They end up with stitches or stall rest because they got into something they shouldn't have, or play hard with their herd buddies and come in with cuts, bite marks, and even hoof indentations on their bodies. And for some horses (usually geldings), it can be often! Lord, help the woman who owns a horse that likes to make bad choices.

When I think about the horse that seems to get hurt on everything, I often think about God looking down on his children, and I smile when I envision God shaking his head in disbelief as he watches us doing things that are not good for us and often unsafe. Some of us play too hard or try things we shouldn't, and then we call to the Father, asking Him to heal our wounds and mend our broken hearts. Sometimes, we learn from our mistakes, but often, we go down another rabbit hole again with turbulent results. As I have gotten older, I look back at my younger days and now realize that the Lord was right there saving me from the terrible situations I got myself into. I have a few scars from some of my bad decisions, but I have learned to make wiser choices these days. Praise God!

Dear Lord, if I may, I have a humble request. Could you perhaps guide my horse to make wiser choices? These vet bills are becoming quite a burden!

~January 7~
Wisdom Of Older Horses

I will instruct you and teach you in the way you should go;
I will counsel you with my eye upon you.
Psalms 32:8

There is something extraordinary about older horses. They have lived long enough to become wise from their younger antics, and if they have had a good life with kind hands, they are quiet and at peace. I love older horses, especially as I have aged, because they move a little slower and are not so unpredictable. They can be stoic, drama-free, and usually take everything in stride.

As a young girl, I wanted a fiery horse that could run like the wind and blow hot air from his nostrils. He needed to be fast and furious and make me feel invincible. Isn't that what most horse-crazy girls want? I am so glad those days are behind me and my wants are so much different now. The older horse has patience and is not so reactive. He wants to please and seems to understand the riding ability of each person on his back. I have watched older mature horses act differently depending on their mount and you can see in the horse's eyes that he is thinking about his next move.

If a horse has been treated well throughout his life the blessings he will bestow on his owner when he is in his twenties and thirties are something to behold. His nature will be sweet and he will bring joy to the people around him. He has worked hard in his younger days and is now ready to slow down, but he is still the leader of his herd and demands respect. Don't discard the older horse, for he brings something to the table that a young horse is not ready to do. That something is wisdom.

~January 8~
The Do-Over

But the wisdom from above is first pure, then peaceable, gentle,
open to reason, full of mercy and good fruits, impartial and sincere.
James 3:17

The things you wish you could do over in life become much
more apparent as you get older. The same is true with horses. I
have talked with many women in my barn who are around my age
about our first horses as teenagers. The one thing we all agree about
is that we made so many mistakes with our horses as young girls,
and looking back, we see that our horses were the recipients of
some of our mistakes. Oh, how I wish I could do it over, but I
can't. But I can help the next generation to think about things
differently.

As a stable owner now, I see the same cycle with the young girls
riding and showing at my barn. They are intense and want
perfection but don't have the maturity to stop and think through
what they are doing to their horse. The good news is that many
equestrians look at the horse in a much better way than they did
forty years ago. Our training techniques are easier on the animals,
and we are learning so much about how intelligent horses are and
that they never forget. I wish I had known someone who could
show me a better way when riding as a teenager. We may not get a
do-over with our first horse, but we have a chance to teach the
younger riders so much more than we were ever taught. Don't miss
the opportunity to share your wisdom with the next generation of
equestrians. You have so much to offer as an older horsewoman.
Don't ever forget that.

Lord, thank you to the women who are willing to share their
knowledge with the young equestrians who are just learning, for
that is how we can improve the horse's life in the future.

~January 9~
New Priorities

He will tend his flock like a shepherd; he will gather the lambs in his arms; he will carry them in his bosom, and gently lead those that are with young.
Isaiah 40:11

The world seems to stop when our horse gets injured or sick. Nothing else matters at that time except to get the help needed as soon as possible. Our priorities change instantly and what seemed important just a few hours earlier has faded away. At that moment, we would do anything to help our equine partner.

A new horse owner is never mentally prepared for the first time their horse gets injured or shows signs of pain or illness. We may have experienced it through a friend's horse, but it becomes very real when it is your baby and it hits painfully deep in your soul. As women, we are nurturers, and our mothering instincts often come out when we see a horse that is struggling. Our senses seem to hit high gear and we find ourselves doing numerous things simultaneously to help the situation. And at that time, nothing else matters.

My daughters learned young that if one of our horses became sick or injured, it would become our top priority, and things might be canceled and plans disrupted because the horse came first. What a wonderful lesson for our children to learn. Teach them to put something before their needs no matter what. It is a great lesson about putting other's (including animals) needs before our own. It is teaching them that they are not the center of the universe and that God created the horse for us, and we are to be good stewards of these amazing creatures. What a wonderful wake-up call to ensure our priorities are right. I pray that my children and their children learn this, for that is how we learn to love others more than ourselves.

~January 10~
We Worry More Now

Do not be anxious about anything, but in every situation, by prayer and petition, with thanksgiving, present your requests to God.
Philippians 4:6

Rusty was a wonderful first horse and you could do almost anything with him. He was definitely a child-proof horse. As a young person, I never worried about getting hurt or my horse getting injured. We just rode and everything seemed to always turn out. Things really change when you have children of your own and buy horses for them when they are young. Suddenly, I became very aware of all the things that could go wrong, and when my daughters rode, it was tough for me to watch them fall off. It turns out that I worry much more as I age, and horses and children are all part of it.

We understand that life is more fragile and we become these protective and sometimes hovering horse moms that I thought I would never be. But for a short time I did when my kids were young. My parents were not horse people or around me when I rode, so they didn't worry. It was also a time in our world when it seemed people didn't worry about as much but instead just went about their days. We took crazy chances that I know I never wanted my girls to take as young equestrians.

When I start to worry now, I need to give it to the Lord and ask Him to calm my soul. I also know reading the Bible daily is the best way to ease worry. If you find yourself worrying, I encourage you to give it to the Lord, grab a cup of coffee, and read the Bible. It never fails. And if you have young children just getting into horses, hang on for the most wonderful ride ahead. Children are a blessing from the Lord, and watching them grow as equestrians will be music to your soul.

~January 11~
How Things Have Changed

Every good and perfect gift is from above, coming down from the Father of the heavenly lights, who does not change like shifting shadows.
James 1:17

Often, you don't really start to appreciate your youth and how things were done back in the day until you reached mid-life. At least, that is how it was for me. In my mid-forties, I started to reminisce about my childhood and riding horses. At first, it was just occasionally, but as I reached my sixties, I thought about it often. When I talk to my horse friends around the same age, they do the same thing. Was it that times were simpler back then? Or was it that my life was all about horses and I didn't have a care in the world during my teens and early twenties.

For us women who have lived a few decades, our memories are filled with friends riding together who were at the same stable or who went to the same horse shows we did. But our world was much smaller because we didn't have cell phones to distract us, and we weren't on our phones trying to see what everyone else was doing. We enjoyed each other's company and played with our horses for hours.

Riding horses is still the best pastime for many horse-crazy girls, but nothing can replace picking pomegranates from the back of my horse and eating them as we rode home and watching the red juice drip all over my horse's neck. Nothing can compare to taking plums off the plum tree and putting them in the water trough to get nice and cold and eating them until our bellies were full. It's those memories that are some of the sweetest. Some things can never be improved upon.

~January 12~
Thousand-Pound Kites

Wait for the Lord; be strong,
and let your heart take courage; wait for the Lord!
Psalms 27:14

We had just had the first big snowstorm of the year and the horses were in the barn during the storm. The temperatures almost seemed balmy for January, which made me happy. There was nothing I could do but wake up early the next morning to see how much the storm had dumped and if we could get the horses back outside for the day. It turned out the storm wasn't as bad as expected and my husband got up at 2:30 a.m. and started plowing the drifts so we could get the horses back outside. With the fresh snow, I knew it would be beautiful outside and the horses would love it. After doing this for almost twenty years, I also knew that the horses would be full of themselves after being stuck inside the barn the day before. I prayed they would all be well-behaved.

We haltered and walked the horses out one by one and you could feel the excitement building with each step. Suddenly one of the horses had exploded and pulled out of my hands! He was loose and having a ball running up and down the fence line like he was set free from prison! He was stunning and irritating all at the same time. We quickly grabbed a bucket of grain, and since food is a great motivator, he trotted right over as if everything was normal. I quickly walked him into his paddock and took off his halter, and he ran even more and rolled in the snow several times. As more horses were being led outside they became more excited as they watched the others running around in the snow-covered paddocks. It was like holding on to a bunch of thousand-pound kites! After the last horse was safely in his paddock, I sighed in relief, thanked the Lord that they were all safe, and I enjoyed the beauty before me.

35

~January 13~
Another Winter

Come to me, all who labor and are heavy laden,
and I will give you rest.
Matthew 11:28

I have lived in Wisconsin for more than thirty years now and still dream about the warm Southern California weather. I love it here, but sometimes I find myself staring up at the sun with my eyes closed on a cold winter's day, trying to feel the sun's rays and remembering what it feels like to be warm. As we approach cold temperatures every year, I have to mentally prepare myself for it. I think to myself about the horses and all the chores that are part of my day, and I know after all these years that there are going to be some tough days again. There always are when taking care of horses.

Feeding grain and supplements takes longer with heavy gloves, feeding hay outside can be exhausting in itself, and walking the horses outside seems to take forever, especially when walking on snow-covered paths. I replay it over and over in my mind each fall, and then it is here, and I do it all over again.

The horses seem to know that the seasons have changed and do well as they settle into the short winter days. They adjust to the longer hours in their stalls when we are hit with below-zero temperatures or a snowstorm and they always seem to handle it better than I do. I am not as tough as I used to be, but I work smarter and know what to expect, and we always manage to make it through another winter. Praise God!

Today, I pray for all the women working with horses in frigid temperatures. I pray that the Lord will keep you strong and that you will find rest and peace to rejuvenate your soul each day.

~January 14~
The Queen

*And I am sure of this, that he who began a good work in you will
bring it to completion at the day of Jesus Christ.*
Philippians 1:6

She was 96 years old and still riding her favorite Fell pony, Emma. Queen Elizabeth II was born into royalty, but that didn't stop her from doing the one thing she loved the most. She loved her horses, and if she wasn't doing the royal duties bestowed on her, you wouldn't need to look much further than the stable because that is where she would be. Her love for horses began much earlier when her father, King George VI, bought her a pony when she was four years old. It was love at first sight, and horses became a deep-rooted part of her life.

Throughout the queen's reign, she rode many horses and became an excellent equestrian. Not only did she need to follow the pomp and circumstance of her time in the castle, but also when riding horses. She learned to ride side-saddle, and when called to participate in royal ceremonial events, she rode her favorite black mare, Burmese. She loved all horses and would rather be in the barn than anywhere else. She bred Thoroughbreds, Shetlands, Highland, and Fell ponies and took pride in naming all the horses at the Royal Mews at Buckingham Palace.

When Queen Elizabeth died, her pony Emma quietly stood on the side as the funeral procession drove slowly by. The longest reigning Monarch's pony was saddled with the bridle on, and across the seat of the saddle laid her majesty's riding scarf. Never was there a more fitting tribute to a woman who ruled her country with a crown graced upon her head and sugar cubes in her hand for the horses she loved so dearly.

~January 15~
Emeralds & Diamonds

May the God of hope fill you with all joy and peace in believing,
so that by the power of the Holy Spirit you may abound in hope.
Romans 15:3

Barb fell in love with horses as a child and her parents let her take a few riding lessons. Time went by fast, and as a young adult, life took a different path. Horses were now a fond memory. She got married and was blessed with two beautiful children and did all the things young moms do with their kids. But she never forgot about horses and tucked them deep inside her heart.

Many years later, her heart began aching for a horse of her own. Times had changed a lot since she was a little girl and horses were not cheap by any means. She spent months looking at horses while leasing a horse and learning as much as possible. But she had one major roadblock – the price. Horses were expensive, and the more she looked, the more she became discouraged because they were all out of her price range. Her husband was very supportive but they both knew they couldn't afford the horses she was looking at. She began losing hope that she would ever find the perfect horse. Then, one day, she had a thought. She had collected fine jewelry for years and it was all sitting in a jewelry box collecting dust. She rarely wore any of it and she realized that owning a horse was worth more to her than all the jewelry in the world. She started selling off her pieces, including a stunning emerald and diamond ring. Before she knew it, she had enough money to buy the mare she had fallen in love with, and her life changed forever!

She has never once missed the jewelry she sold because she knows that the beautiful little mare who waits for her to visit daily is worth more than all the emeralds and diamonds in the world.

~January 16~
Finally Satisfied

And the Lord will guide you continually and satisfy your desire in scorched places and make your bones strong; and you shall be like a watered garden, like a spring of water, whose waters do not fail.
Isaiah 58:11

As a teenager, it seemed as if I was never satisfied with what the good Lord had given me. I wanted to show my horses, and even back in the late seventies, I would go to some of the larger horse shows and many of the riders and horses were dripping in silver saddles, bridles, and very expensive show clothes. I couldn't afford those things and it was hard to go up against all that money. Looking back, I realize I was learning valuable lessons about life and what is truly important. I just didn't figure it out until much later down the road. I am so glad that those days are behind me, and it is such a wonderful feeling and gratifying when you are content with what you have.

The horse world is fickle, and for many years the trend was still silver inlaid show saddles and bridles that would break the bank, but times are changing. Finally, many judges are looking at the rider's ability more and the silver less. That is wonderful news!

I still love to go to horse shows and watch all the amazing riders and the horses perform, but I always focus on the rider who quietly comes in on the horse without all the flash. Those are the riders and horses to look out for. They are pure grit and have nothing to lose, and you can tell they worked hard. The horse world is still crazy but I LOVE it and all that goes with it.

Growing older has its benefits. You learn that not everything is paved with silver and gold, and true riches are the simple things in life, like God, family, friends, and horses. I pray that you find contentment and a beautiful satisfaction in the simple things in life.

~January 17~
Great Ride

Give thanks in all circumstances;
for this is the will of God in Christ Jesus for you.
I Thessalonians 5:18

"Today was a great ride," I heard the woman say. It made me smile inside because it is a phrase rarely said. Young riders, especially older teens, can be hard on their horses and themselves, and they miss the joy of the ride and what they can learn from every ride. Older people can be riddled with uncertainty and even fear as they grow into equestrians and they miss the joy and all they learned from spending time on their horse. This is nothing new and part of growing up and older as we experience different emotions of horse ownership.

The nice thing about being a little older is that you can look back and see things much clearer. I now see all the great rides I had that I never gave a thought to when I was younger. Those rides molded me and I didn't even know it. Even the challenging days on my horse taught me patience and to reach deeper for a way to correct a situation, and most importantly, how to read what my horse was trying to tell me. Sometimes, I just wasn't listening and made things worse.

Today, I encourage you to think of every ride as a great ride, no matter the outcome. There are so many lessons to be taught and experienced, both good and not-so-good, and each one will help you grow and become a more confident equestrian. If your horse is having a "lost his brain kind of day," then make it short and sweet and enjoy the groundwork, for everything that happens on the ground will resonate in the saddle. Today, enjoy the ride and all that it brings.

~January 18~
Trying To Love Again

Fear not, for I am with you; be not dismayed, for I am your God; I will strengthen you, I will help you, I will uphold you with my righteous right hand.
Isaiah 41:10

Your first horse will always hold a special place in your heart that no other can replace. It is like your first crush or first love. You never forget it.

I didn't know how to ride very well (even though I thought I did), and my father didn't know anything about horses when he said he would buy me one. My first horse (Rusty) was a beautiful grade roan. He was perfect for me. Then, the day finally came when I outgrew him both in size and experience, and it was time to sell him and find a new horse. I was heartbroken but I knew we couldn't keep two horses. My next horse was a two-year-old Quarter Horse mare that was very green and had to be taught everything. She was absolutely stunning but I couldn't act crazy around her. I needed to be calm and aware of my actions and she helped me grow into a much better rider. I was excited to have her, but I would often think about Rusty and compare both horses. Two completely different horses, but I loved them both.

Years later, I still think about Rusty the most. I could never find another horse to replace him in my mind. Sometimes, we compare what we have now with the past and have difficulty moving forward. It can slow us down and stop us from growing if we let it. Horses are great teachers and each one will teach us something different throughout our lives. We may like some memories better with certain horses, but ultimately, we loved them all.

Thank you, Lord, for the lessons horses teach us daily. I pray I will always be a good student willing to learn from these amazing animals.

~January 19~
Honest Expectations

And it is my prayer that your love may abound more and more,
with knowledge and all discernment.
Philippians 1:9

If you take the time to watch the horses in their herds, you will quickly learn they are sincere creatures. They expect consistency and safety from other horses and the humans around them daily, and they don't play mind games. They will never forget if a human sends conflicting messages or is cruel to them. Horses are amazing to interact with and we can learn so much from them.

I admit that when I was young, I did things to my horses that I now cringe at. I expected too much out of my horses when they were not ready to give it mentally, and the consequences of those poor decisions were frustrated animals. I was too young to understand what was happening at the time and didn't have a good trainer or mentor to teach me a better way. What is nice about growing older is that you become more in tune with realistic and honest expectations. This often makes for happier horses that are mentally much more grounded and eager to please.

Growing older does have many perks, and for horsewomen, it gives us a chance to learn from our past mistakes. Today, I expect certain behaviors from my horses, but I also know when they are ready for what I am asking. And if something seems amiss with a horse I am handling, I can look at the whole picture to see what is going on with him. He is trying to tell me something and now I am ready to listen. I pray that I will have eyes to watch and ears to listen daily to the equines in my care and be honest in my expectations for them. Thank you, Lord, for creating such an honest animal. What a blessing and gift from Heaven above.

Rest Is Good

*Come to me, all who labor and are heavy laden, and I will give
you rest. Take my yoke upon you, and learn from me, for I
am gentle and lowly in heart, and you will find rest for your
souls. For my yoke is easy, and my burden is light.*
Matthew 11:28

I have always needed a lot of sleep even when I was young, and
I know that if I don't get enough rest, I start to feel worn down and
sick. Can you relate? Working on a horse farm can be exhausting at
times. It's very laborious and the work never ends, especially with
horses, because the chores need to be done daily. On top of that,
horses love to break things!

Our day begins early and ends late, and even though the days are
busy, I love the life we have created. And since the horses need to
be fed, watered, taken out in the morning and brought back inside
later in the day, it becomes a split shift. That means the best time
for me to catch up on my rest is during the middle of the day when
everything is quiet and calm.

It seems as if today's young people don't know how to rest.
They are extremely busy then come out to see their horse and rush
off just as quickly. But as older women, we have learned the fine art
of resting and enjoying our horses to the fullest. We pace ourselves,
and if we need a nap, then so be it. Then we go to spend quality
time at the barn.

It is a blessing to be able to rest and rejuvenate our bodies and it
clears our mind. I have read articles that say that women who take
naps live longer. I don't know how true that is, but I do know that
women who take naps and then go out and spend time with their
horses will definitely have more fun! Horses are good for our mind,
body, and soul.

~January 21~
Fear Of Falling

*Trust in the Lord with all your heart, and do not lean on
your own understanding. In all your ways acknowledge him,
and he will make straight your paths.*
Proverbs 3:5-6

As horsewomen, a change occurs in our minds as we age, and
for some of us, it begins earlier than others. It is the fear of falling
off of a horse.

The summer temperatures in Southern California were often
sizzling, so we rode bareback as much as possible as kids just to
beat the heat for us and our horses. I remember being a teenager
and falling off my horse too many times to count. We also did some
really silly, and probably stupid, things with our horses, and falling
off was part of it. It was no big deal. We just shook it off and got
back on. Those were the days when we threw caution to the wind.

I am not sure when the feeling of fear or maybe wisdom came
into play but I think it was around my forties. I realized I wasn't
getting any younger and I became very aware that I could seriously
get hurt. I guess you could call it self-preservation. The fear is real,
and for some older horsewomen, it can cripple them to the point
mentally that they stop riding. It can be challenging to work
through those emotions, especially if you have had a fall that was
hard on your body.

My prayer is for the woman who has developed a fear of riding.
It is nothing to be ashamed of or embarrassed about. If every
equestrian was completely honest, they could all tell you a time in
their life when they feared riding a horse for one reason or another.
I encourage you to go slow, take your time, and enjoy your horse.
God is working on your fear and waiting for you to trust Him.

~January 22~
Sweet Destiny

Only let each person lead the life that the Lord has assigned
to him, and to which God has called him.
I Corinthians 7:17

Some call them an obsession. Others call them a money pit. I call them sweet destiny and thank God that He would put the love of horses in my heart. Women who are absolutely crazy about horses know exactly what I am talking about. You can't run from it. It may start with a pony ride as a little girl at the local fair, but it can quickly turn into much more. I always knew horses would be a part of my life, but when I was young, I thought I would be a barrel racer or horse trainer. Those dreams fizzled quickly, but I still rode as much as I could. I eventually grew up, got married, and moved to Wisconsin. I worked at a show barn for a while but couldn't take the cold, so after almost two years, I quit. I thought horses would be out of my life for as long as I lived in the frozen tundra but God had other plans for me.

When our daughters were young, we bought each of them a pony. Then, one day, David brought up the idea of boarding horses as a business. He wanted to work from home. We just needed to build a barn with an indoor riding arena. Since that dream popped into our heads, we have never looked back. We have had many ups and downs but have made it through the bad times and trusted God with all of it. God had a plan for my life that would include horses (many horses!), and I now know it was my destiny to be a boarding stable owner for many reasons, not just the horses.

Sometimes, we get to a point where we don't know which way to turn, or we have a hard time envisioning what our future is supposed to look like. I encourage you to pray and stay in the Bible. There, you will find your answer.

~January 23~
A Clear Path

Blessed is the one who finds wisdom,
and the one who gets understanding,
Proverbs 3:13

There is something about new bridles, halters, and horse accessories that make us feel all giddy inside. The smell of soft, well-made leather with the finest stitching is enough to send our senses reeling. It definitely is a horse-crazy girl thing, and often, we can never just have one but instead want a few of each in different shades or colors. You would think this is how young teenage girls act, but the truth is us older ladies do the same thing, and I'll tell you a secret – we probably enjoy it and appreciate it even more because we know how much fine tack costs. Not to put down the youngsters who may read this book; after all, I know they are just learning themselves and experiencing so many things for the first time. But when you have lived a few decades, the finer things in life are enjoyed to the fullest because we know the value and cost.

Over the years, I have watched well-meaning people buy beautiful new bridles only to buy a second or third during the year. I am the first to admit I have done this a time or two in my life. The horse looks fantastic in the new bridle and accessories and adorable in pictures and selfies, but the owner has many frustrating rides on her horse. The most important thing that was overlooked was the horse and rider. There will always be the latest fashion in bridles and accessories, but the horse doesn't change. He still needs clear instruction and consistency, just like we need in our personal lives.

Today, I want to encourage you to consider what is important in life and to ask for guidance. For the Lord is waiting for you to call on Him and will make your path clear.

~January 24~
The Second Chance

As far as the east is from the west,
so far does he remove our transgressions from us.
Psalms 103:12

What is absolutely amazing about horses is that they are so forgiving when we are dumb and do things that negatively affect them. They offer us a chance to do it again and think through what we are doing so that the end results are positive for the horses entrusted to us.

I know at times, I had a "brain fart," as I call it, and did something that I regretted instantly when it came to my horses. It could be that I was in a hurry, talking on the phone, or just being lazy. As I have aged, I have learned to read my horses and I can tell immediately if I did something that scared them and made them nervous. I also can tell now when I am sending mixed messages to them and they don't understand by their response. To the new horse owner, it might seem confusing as they learn.

The same is true for those of us who had horses when we were young and thought we knew it all. We did lots of dumb things to our horses and never thought anything about it. What a beautiful gift to be given a second chance as an adult and to look at past mistakes and tell yourself that you will not do that again. Sadly, some people never learn this or are never given the chance to do so.

If you are given a second chance to do it over and make it right with your horse, don't miss that opportunity! It is a beautiful gift from God. After all, you are his caretaker and he deserves the best from you. Second chances make us better horsewomen because we are willing to learn from our mistakes. Praise God for second chances.

~January 25~
Winter's Glory

As the rain and the snow come down from heaven, and do not return to it without watering the earth and making it bud and flourish, so that it yields seed for the sower and bread for the eater.
Isaiah 55:10

There is something mesmerizing about heading out of the house on a cold morning to do chores. The world becomes much quieter when the ground is frozen and covered with snow. Wintertime on the farm has its own perfect beauty. When I am up early and outside, it still takes my breath away even after all these years. The horses are quiet and waiting for their breakfast, and you can still see some stars and the moon in the sky as they quickly fade away, and a glimmer of sun rays peak over the horizon. That view only lasts a few minutes, and then it's gone, but it always reminds me of God's greatness and all He has created on the beautiful earth.

I am always amazed at how well the horses do in such frigid temperatures. They often will have snow and bits of ice on their whiskers, and the steam is coming out of their nostrils as they breathe, but they look happy and quiet and are warm under their heavy coats or blankets. I am not crazy about getting out of bed and putting many layers of clothes on just so I don't freeze, but once I go outside and see the vision before me and hear the nickers when I walk into the barn, I am glad for the life I have chosen. It doesn't mean it is easy, but it is a piece of heaven right here on earth.

When I was younger, I was much more in a hurry than I am now. I missed so much of the beauty that was right before me. I am glad I have slowed down, and now I will take the time to witness the birth of a new day with the sun glistening on the snow and watching the horses munch on their hay. It doesn't get better than that. Praise God!

~January 26~
A Quiet Spirit

But let your adorning be the hidden person of the heart with the imperishable beauty of a gentle and quiet spirit, which in God's sight is very precious.
I Peter 3:4

A horse with a quiet spirit makes it a joy to be around them. They may not be the flashiest horse that holds his head high in the air as he runs out in the pasture, but his quiet demeanor has so much to offer if you are willing to look deeper.

Years ago, a mother purchased a horse for her daughter. It was a stunning horse with a lot of forward motion and high energy, but very temperamental. You really had to be aware of what you were doing when you were around the horse because he was constantly moving around with this nervous energy. When the little girl rode the beautiful horse, you could see in her anxious expression that she was just trying to hang on. Quickly the little girl lost interest in riding. The mother asked me what my thoughts were and we talked for a while. After thinking about it, she decided to sell the horse and look for a quieter horse for her little girl. The next month, a new horse walked off the trailer. It was a sweet little mare. She looked around at her new home and gently lowered her head to the little girl. It was love at first sight. That same little girl began riding her new horse and soon they were riding all over the farm, and you could see her confidence blossoming. The little girl grew up into a woman and even though she went to college and eventually got married, she never sold her little mare. She took her wherever she moved, and eventually, her children learned to ride on her.

It is so easy for us to become blinded by all the glitz of fancy things that we can miss the incredible beauty that often comes wrapped in something less brilliant. I will forever be thankful for the horse that is clothed in a quiet spirit.

~January 27~
Time To Learn

Teach me your way, Lord, that I may rely on your faithfulness;
give me an undivided heart, that I may fear your name.
Psalm 86:11

Horses come in all shapes and sizes, each with their own unique personality, and one size does not fit all when it comes to these incredible animals. You will learn so much if you are willing to take the time and watch horses both under saddle and out in their herds. I had to learn this, and it took me many years to figure it out. I have gone to look at a horse and purchased it quickly, only to find out a month later that he was too much horse for me or my daughters. Let's face it, it's emotional and exciting, and as women, sometimes our feelings overtake us when we see those eyes looking at us from over the fence. We fall in love fast and hard without asking the important questions, and sometimes we find ourselves in a hard situation where the horse isn't working out. It breaks our heart and it's not easy on the animal.

I want to encourage you to learn as much as you can about horse behavior and care before you take that leap into horse ownership. Horses can teach us so much if we are willing to watch them and listen to others who know more than us. A horse needs the right human as much as you need the right equine partner. The Lord teaches us so much through the animal kingdom and when He created the horse, it was perfection wrapped up in four long legs, a flowing mane and tail, and a personality to fall in love with. The perfect horse for you is out there just waiting for you to find him and bring him home.

Today, I ask the Lord for discernment as I begin my journey of finding my forever equine partner.

~January 28~
Here It Comes

Whatever you have learned or received or heard from me, or seen in me put it into practice. And the God of peace will be with you.
Philippians 4:9

Life teaches us many things as equestrians, and if we are patient and willing to learn, then as we become seasoned horsewomen, our time with horses becomes that much sweeter.

Running a stable with my husband for almost twenty years has taught me countless lessons. They have usually come at times in my life when I needed them the most. Each lesson has taught me how to do things better the next time and deal with stressful situations a little easier. Being on a horse farm in the Midwest means that each day can bring many surprises, and the weather is a huge factor in what that day will look like. I used to panic inside when a snowstorm or possible blizzard was heading our way. I worried about the horses in the barns and how they would handle being inside for a few days. I have learned that the horses do just fine and, in most cases, do better than the humans who own or care for them.

I am glad my days of panicking are few and far between. I am learning to take things in stride and I have learned that each season will bring its own special challenges. From sub-zero temperatures in winter to mud in spring and blazing hot days in the summer, each teaches me to lean on the Lord.

As each new season comes, I am ready for it, and I know deep down inside that the horses will do just fine, and we will all get through it—we always do. The cycle never ends, and there is always a time to teach and a time to learn for all of us.

Thank you, Lord, for all four seasons and the lessons to be learned from all of them.

~January 29~
She's The Farrier

She opens her mouth in wisdom,
and the teaching of kindness is on her tongue.
Proverbs 31:26

The one occupation in the equine industry that I truly admire is the job of the Farrier. I have often said that if you find a great farrier, you spoil them with respect and kindness because they have a tough job. Not only do they have to deal with a thousand-pound, sometimes over-reactive animal, but sometimes they have challenging clients as well. It is a physically demanding job and I often wonder how their backs hold up because they are bent over as they work on the horse's hooves.

Now, let's talk about women farriers. They are a breed apart and I am in awe of them for their chosen profession. We have a couple of lady farriers who work on horses at our stable. They are resilient, not afraid to get dirty and have this natural beauty that shines through. They can be just as tough as the men but still have a feminine side, and the horses know not to fool around with these ladies!

There are many amazing women working in the equine industry, and women farriers are at the top of my list. They may not always receive the recognition that trainers or champion riders get, but they are an integral part of a group of equine professionals who keep the industry strong. Today, we celebrate these ladies whose passion is keeping our horses sound.

Today, I pray for the lady farriers who keep our horses going no matter the riding discipline. Your days are long, you work in all kinds of weather, and you always have a smile on your face. You are a blessing in every way.

Bad Habits

*Do not be conformed to this world, but be transformed by the
renewal of your mind, that by testing you may discern what
is the will of God, what is good and acceptable and perfect.*
Romans 12:2

Horses are gregarious animals and we love everything about
them. They are also creatures of habit, and it doesn't matter if the
habit is good or bad; once it gets into their head, it is hard to get
out. We love that we can teach a horse something with repetition
and he will figure it out quickly. This is especially wonderful for
good ground manners and riding, but once in a while, a horse will
pick up a bad habit that starts out small and soon escalates.

Many of the bad habits a horse learns come from us. We love to
spoil our horse with carrots and apples, and we give him samples of
different equine treats so we can buy his favorites. But then
something happens. Suddenly, he starts nipping at us. He becomes
obsessed with getting treats, and soon, we find ourselves
disciplining him for biting too hard on our arm. We finally figure
out that if we stop feeding treats from our hand and put them in his
stall feeder instead, his nipping will stop. Crazy, isn't it? But it's true.
We had to break the bad habit we created and I am just as guilty of
this as the next person.

This made me think of my own personal life. I have gotten
myself into habits that were not healthy for me, both mentally and
physically. During those times, I needed to shake things up and get
rid of those damaging habits, and I could only do it with prayer and
the power of Jesus Christ. If you are struggling with a habit that is
hurting you or your loved ones, I encourage you to pray and seek
the Lord, for He makes all things new time and time again. Praise
God!

~January 31~
It Was A Mistake

Guide me in your truth and teach me, for you are God my Savior,
and my hope is in you all day long.
Psalm 25:5

"It was an honest mistake!" Haven't we all said those words a time or two when it comes to horses? We may have left the gate open only to watch the horses take off down the road running as if they were wild beasts, or we forgot to close the stall door and our horse cleverly made his way to the grain room to an ample indulgence of his choice. We hold our breath until the horses are safely back in their paddock or stall, and then we lose our tempers for no reason. Then, a deep regret hits us hard inside as we watch his eyes lower with a sad withdrawal. Those are some of the most painful mistakes we can make because we see how our horse reacts and it hits us to the core. Often, our mistakes are because we are learning and don't know any better, and sometimes, our errors mean the veterinarian needs to be called. Those are some of the greatest learning moments we can have as equestrians if our heart is soft and willing to learn from our errors.

What an incredible animal the horse is. So big and powerful yet willing to take what we have to dish out with little resistance. The balance between doing things right for the horse and doing it wrong sometimes hangs by a thread, and we need to make sure it doesn't break. Love your horse and learn as much as you can about this extraordinary animal entrusted to you for everything from his mental well-being to his physical health. It's all equally important for his care. Today's mistakes are tomorrow's successes. Praise the Lord for creating an animal so willing to forgive us.

~February 1~
Could It Be...

Let the morning bring me word of your unfailing love,
for I have put my trust in you. Show me the way I should go,
for to you I entrust my life.
Psalm 143:8

I have often wondered why I am still so crazy about horses. After all, they cost a small fortune and often become a money pit (by our own doing!) after you bring them home. They have bad habits, poop a lot, and can sometimes be stubborn. They roll in the mud right after we have bathed them and then look at us proudly as if they just did a great thing. They seem to get hurt on everything, and I have learned that a special savings account is a must for vet bills. But then I looked much deeper and found many reasons to fall utterly in love with these animals. I love how they each have their own unique personality, and watching them with other horses taught me so much about their strengths and weaknesses. My heart melts when they see me coming into the barn early in the morning and they nicker with eyes wide open and ears forward.

I love horses because they don't play games and will tell you what is on their mind. But you need to be willing to study them, watch them, and listen. A horse will give you his all if he trusts you, but he will quickly take it away if he fears you. He will take you anywhere you want to go, but you must show him that you are there for him. Watching him grow from a clumsy and insecure youngster into a strong and confident equine is wonderful to witness. And then, as he ages, his beauty on the outside will fade, but the beauty in his heart shines like the brightest stars in the sky. The reasons to fall in love are vast and endless. Could it be that they are God's perfect animal? For many of us horsewomen, we would say yes!

~February 2~
Pain Is Temporary

But they who wait for the Lord shall renew their strength;
they shall mount up with wings like eagles; they shall run and
not be weary; they shall walk and not faint.
Isaiah 40:31

As time goes by and we age gracefully (or at least we try!), your body will start to ache in all sorts of places. There is no way around it. Riding horses or taking care of them daily is physical. We tell ourselves we will never be like those "older people" who walk a little slower and ride quieter horses.

When I was a young forty-something and we had just started our horse boarding stable, I had unlimited energy and was ready to take on anything that needed to be done. I would throw hay around during the harvest, and do the chores both morning and night by myself while my husband did other things on the farm. Nothing was too heavy for me back then.

Then, one day, years later…the first ache happens, and then another. Boy, it caught me off guard, but one of the best things about caring for horses daily is that it keeps you strong and in good shape. These days, I definitely get out of bed slower and have arthritis in my fingers, but I wouldn't change a thing about it. After all, I know that the pain is temporary, and one day, I will have a new body when I am in heaven with the Lord. Just knowing that keeps me going, and while I am still on this earth taking care of horses on our farm, I will take my time and do the best job I can. For we can do anything, knowing it is temporary and the best is yet to come.

Today, I want to shout out to all the enduring horsewomen who still get up and head out to the barn to feed the horses, muck the stalls, and so much more. You are more precious than fine gold.

Wrinkles

I praise you, for I am fearfully and wonderfully made.
Wonderful are your works; my soul knows it very well.
Psalm 139:14

I was born in Southern California in the early sixties (that should give you a hint of my age!), and life back then was about sun, more sun, and the beach. That was until I fell in love with horses in elementary school. Then my life became all about horses, horses, and more horses. I was outside more than I was inside during those early years. There weren't any video games or computers, and watching television was something you did only when the special shows came on in the evening, and even then, it was limited. It was the perfect life for a kid. I would ride my bike to see my horse as much as possible, which meant I was in the sun a lot. Back then, no one put on sunscreen, and baby oil was all the rage. Riding my horse out in the sun, hosing him off daily and hanging out with him lasted throughout my teen years. Even after buying a different horse and getting my driver's license, I was still outside often.

Well, as you can guess, it played havoc on my skin, and now that I am much older, I have wrinkly hands and skin to show for it. But those wrinkles are proof of a life well lived, and I am thankful for that. In fact, it is a wonderful reminder of the opportunities I was given as a child.

Beauty is only skin deep, and for us older horsewomen who have spent much of our lives outside in the sun, it has left its mark on each one of us. But I have never met an unhappy horsewoman because she was weathered a little bit. In fact, it is quite the opposite. Most of us are thankful for the life the Lord has given us.

Thank you, Lord, for reminding me of a good life well lived when I look at my hands.

~February 4~
Silver Linings

May the God of hope fill you with all joy and peace as you trust in him,
so that you may overflow with hope by the power of the Holy Spirit.
Romans 15:13

Taking care of horses on your own property is wonderful but it does have its drawbacks, especially if you live in an area that snows. It's during these times that Satan really does tempt us to have a bad attitude or feel defeated when the weather is horrid and we have livestock of any kind to care for. I have learned over the years that with every hard day, there are just as many silver linings that are God's way of showing me He is right by my side.

There is something magical about a new fallen snow. The horses are just like kids and they absolutely love it. They lay down and roll as if they are making snow angels and many of the geldings would rather play than eat their morning hay. The horses don't realize all the work that needs to be done to clear the paths just to feed hay and get them outside. They are only concerned with playing and enjoying the snow. It always makes me smile even though I am exhausted from walking all of them to their paddocks. I could also say that walking horses through the snow is great exercise and has helped me stay healthy. YES, that is a giant silver lining! And even on the hardest of days, the sunrise glistening against the snow takes my breath away. For a few moments, the world is quiet except for the sound of hoofbeats and it feels like God is looking down and showing me his most wondrous creation in all its glory.

Today, Lord, I pray for the women working at stables in the dead of winter. There will be exhausting days and they will second-guess why they do what they do. Please shine down upon them and show them your glory in all that you created. Let them know that they got this and you will be right by their side. Amen.

Be Their Voice

And whatever you do, in word or deed, do everything in the name of the Lord Jesus, giving thanks to God the Father through him.
Colossians 3:17

Standing back and watching someone make mistakes with their horse can be excruciating, but often, those mistakes are great lessons. Standing back and watching someone be abusive to their horse is evil! Yes, you read it right. It is cruel and evil, and we are at fault if we don't step in and try to stop the madness. After all, the horse doesn't have a voice, and most horses will not try to fight back but instead take it and slowly sink into a deep, dark, silent spot where it may be impossible to ever bring them back out. I have seen in the hollow eyes of a horse that has had a horrible life and has given up.

What can you do as an observer? So much! Start with your children and grandchildren, for they will be the next generation of equestrians, horse trainers, stable owners, etc. If we start now teaching new horse owners, no matter their age, about these incredible animals and how sensitive they are, we are paving a road to better care both on the ground and in the saddle. Standing back is not an option. If you have the knowledge and tools to help a new horse owner become a great horse owner who is kind and understanding, then you are changing the equine world one person at a time, and that is a beautiful thing.

It's never easy to speak up, but you will never regret doing the right thing. When God created the animals He gave us dominion over them. That is an awesome gift but it comes with a huge responsibility. We are to be their caretakers and their voice when need be.

~February 6~
Old Cowgirls Are Too Cool

Wisdom is with the aged, and understanding in length of days.
With God are wisdom and might; he has counsel and understanding.
Job 12:12-13

I found myself mesmerized by a horsewoman being interviewed on a television show. She had been a huge deal in the horse industry for decades and was going to participate in this year's New Year's Day parade. She was petite, with grey hair pinned neatly under a creme-colored cowboy hat and she wore western clothes to match. Her smile was contagious and drew you in as she talked, and I found out she was 90 years old! What a life this old cowgirl has lived.

She had been involved with horses for many decades and accomplished so much, and I thought to myself how I would love to meet her and talk to her about her life and how things have changed with horses. This woman was such an encouragement to me, and just listening to her talk for a few minutes told me she had taken risks in her life because of her deep passion for horses. She may not ride much anymore but she had so much wisdom to share and teach the younger generations. I realized just how cool this old cowgirl was and what an inspiration she had been to so many.

What a gift to be able to share stories and wisdom with the younger generations so that the days of old are never forgotten. If you know someone who has been involved with horses for a long time, talk with them and glean from their words. They have riches to teach that will last a lifetime.

The Lord gave us wise older women to teach us about life (and horses) so that our trials might be easier. God bless the older cowgirl, for her wisdom is a treasure trove waiting to be opened.

~February 7~
Scars

Therefore encourage one another and build
one another up, just as you are doing.
I Thessalonians 5:11

Horses can do a lot of damage to themselves and to other horses by playing, fighting, or just not thinking! If you are around them long enough, you will eventually see the equine veterinarian making a visit to stitch up a cut. Unfortunately, many of the cuts will leave some sort of scar when they heal.

Horses can also have emotional scars that can manifest itself in their behavior. People can do a lot of damage to horses and leave mental scars that last a lifetime because they don't forget. The incredible miracle is that if you care for the wound diligently, the scar usually becomes very minimal, and sometimes, you won't even see it. If you are patient and gentle with a horse that has been abused, in time, the horse will learn to trust you and open his heart again, and you will see an animal willing to do anything for you.

Women are no different. Some of us have been around horses for a long time and will have some scars to show from it. I have a few scars on my body from different horses and I am okay with that. The more difficult scars to deal with are the emotional scars from hurt feelings, which we tend to carry deep down inside of us for a long time. Those emotional scars can be much harder to erase. Life can get messy and people say things that hurt, and if we are not grounded in what really is important in life, it can wear us down.

If you have been hurt by others and struggling inside, I encourage you to pray and give it to the Lord. Only the Lord can bring a peace that is deeper than anything on this earth. He keeps my ways straight and my heart strong and heals the wounds in my heart.

~February 8~
Better Than Yesterday

Therefore I tell you, whatever you ask in prayer,
believe that you have received it, and it will be yours.
Matthew 11:24

The wonderful thing about the gift of tomorrow is that when tomorrow comes, it allows you the opportunity to be better than yesterday. That is so true with horses. How many times have you gone to see your horse and things didn't go as planned? You might have lost your temper with your horse or done something without thinking which caused your horse to spook or experience pain. We have all been there. I have made stupid choices that impacted my horse and it took me a few days to reverse what I had done.

Don't beat yourself up! Instead, learn from your mistakes and tell yourself that tomorrow will be better than yesterday. That is all anyone can ask. Look at each day as a fresh start and new beginning with your horse, and you will quickly find out how forgiving they are. They want to trust you and feel safe around you, and you can make it happen.

It reminds me of my walk with Christ. When I have had a bad day at the barn and lost my temper with people or a horse, the Holy Spirit convicts me right away and I had to stop in my tracks and pray for forgiveness. The wonderful news is that I can move forward and make sure tomorrow is better than the day I had today. What a great feeling to have the weight of guilt lifted off of me and the freedom of knowing each day is a new beginning.

Today, I encourage you to take each day with horses as a new day and remember that they are learning as much about you as you are learning about them. You will learn about each other together and soon make a great team. That is healthy horsemanship and it is so much better when you are guided by the Lord.

~February 9~
I'll Be Home Shortly

With all humility and gentleness,
with patience, bearing with one another in love.
Ephesians 4:2

"I'll be home shortly" are words I have heard spoken countless times throughout the years from women at our stable. It makes me smile every time because those same women will often be with their horses for a few more hours before finally heading home.

It's something that starts at a very young age with horse-crazy teenage girls. They come out to ride right after school, and before you know it their parents call them and ask when they will be home to do their homework. Quickly, the girls rush around, putting everything away including their horses, and off they go. Then, the boyfriend comes into the picture. He may come out a few times, but soon, he is calling her and asking when she will be done riding. She quickly says, "I will be done soon and I'll call you after." She finally calls him a few hours later. I always smile because I know she can't help herself and this is how it will be for the rest of her life if she owns horses. It is a crazy kind of love that graduates from teenage girls to adult women, and then as we become much older and have more time to do the things we are passionate about, our time at the barn grows even longer. The good news is that by then, our husbands will know this also, and they will smile because they see us doing something we absolutely love.

"I'll be home shortly" are words that should never be taken too seriously when you are in love with a horsewoman. She will try her best to honor those words, but in the end, there will be one more carrot to feed and one more hug and kiss to give to her favorite steed, which could take at least another hour!

~February 10~
Fountain Of Youth

Rejoice in hope, be patient in tribulation, be constant in prayer.
Romans 12:12

If you are going to be involved with horses for a long time then you learn fast how hard it can be on your body. Everything about horses is heavy except when you are riding them. Taking care of these large and amazing animals is a dream come true for many women, including myself, but my body shows some of the signs of the daily life of living on a horse farm and dealing with the weather during all four seasons. It may not be the fountain of youth for the outside of a woman's body by the time a few decades have passed, but it sure is the fountain of youth for the inside.

Your mind will become clearer when you are around horses daily and they seem to take the stress out of our lives. As I head out to the barn, my thoughts lighten up as I gaze upon the horses in my care and see their beautiful differences. All these years later, it still takes my breath away when I watch the horses playing or sometimes having disagreements and doing what horses do. They keep my heart young and my mind content.

Worldwide, women are trying to find the fountain of youth, hoping to look like they did when they were twenty or even thirty years old. I think they have the wrong idea of what the fountain of youth looks like and where it comes from. It doesn't come in a pill, bottle, or shot. It comes from something created in the heavens with long legs, flowing mane and tail, and a nicker that makes your heart skip a beat. It doesn't matter what the world calls the fountain of youth. What does matter is how I feel when I am around horses. Thank you, Jesus, for this gift that keeps me young at heart. There is nothing better.

The Buckle

But Mary treasured up all these things,
pondering them in her heart.
Luke 2:19

As a young horse-crazy girl, I felt like I had to have a belt buckle to fit in with the other kids. Well, I finally did get a large heart-shaped buckle with intricate designs etched into the silver and a Quarter Horse head on the front. I proudly wore that buckle all the time and rarely took it off.

As a young adult, I was busy with work and doing other things and that buckle I loved so much got put away in a dresser drawer, not to be pulled out again for almost thirty years. Life went on, and I got married and had children. Then, when our kids were young, we decided to start our own horse boarding stable. It was a long road but opening day finally came and we invited the public to the open house. Then, we had a dance in the arena that evening with food and cake. It was a day I'll never forget. As I dressed for the open house, I thought about that belt buckle that my father had bought me so many decades earlier. Believe it or not, I had saved it all those years and decided to wear it for the grand opening. But when I pulled it out of the drawer I saw how badly tarnished it was. I looked around and found some silver cleaner and soon that buckle shined up like it was brand new! My kids giggled as I put it on and my husband smiled, unsure what to think. But the thing I remember most about that buckle wasn't the cowboys I had crushes on when I was young or the "in-group" I wanted to hang out with. What I thought about the most was my father and how he had been there throughout my horse journey that started when I was just a kid. I am so glad I kept that buckle because it will forever remind me of his love for a horse-crazy little girl.

Character Building

Consider it all joy, my brethren, when you encounter various trials,
knowing that the testing of your faith produces endurance.
James 1:2-3

Horses build character whether we want them to or not. They often will test and see right through us if we don't know what we are doing. They teach us that fancy clothes and boots will still get covered in mud, and the brand-new saddle may end up in the dirt if we do not cinch it correctly. Horses will teach us that cutting corners never works with them, and in the end, they will force us to rethink how we do things. They will teach us what humility looks like and humble us when they show us their strength. When such a large animal (that could kill us in a moment) is willing to do whatever we ask, it should bring us to our knees in gratitude for the incredible gift we have right before us.

Character building comes from late nights with a sick horse or missing a party because your horse has been injured. It comes from being exhausted after a long day at a horse show, but you know your horse needs to be taken care of first before you crash on the couch for the evening. It comes from making sure his hay looks good and topping off his water bucket to ensure he has enough to drink throughout the night. It comes from cutting back on designer coffee and jeans so your horse has his grain and supplements. It means rethinking what was really important to you before your horse walked off the trailer and became yours.

Lord, help me to put my horse's needs before my selfish wants and desires. He depends on me to make sure he is safe, has plenty of good food and water, and has shelter when the weather gets bad. He is always there for me and I need to be there for him. Thank you for this beautiful animal you have entrusted to me.

You've Come So Far

I have said these things to you, that in me you may have peace. In the world you will have tribulation. But take heart; I have overcome the world.
John 16:33

It doesn't matter your age, background, or experience. When it comes to horses, there are no shortcuts and no freebies. You go at your own pace and take your time. The one thing I have noticed is that some women can't see how far they have come with their horses, especially during the first year. I have the pleasure of watching from the sidelines as they learn to halter and lead a horse, brush and pick their feet, and bridle and saddle them. Soon, they are riding at a walk and trot, and eventually, they graduate into a canter. I have also witnessed the frustration of a bad ride or when things don't come as easily as envisioned. Many of these good-hearted women can't see the big picture and how far they have come. They can only see what is happening at the moment.

If you are a horsewoman with some experience under your belt and you see another woman struggling and hard on herself, hug and encourage her. We all need that occasionally, no matter how long you have been around horses. Be her rooting section so she doesn't give up. Let her know that those baby steps she takes daily with her horse are the foundation of making a great horsewoman. The truth is, we never stop learning and that is a good thing. As my dad told me when I was young, "Try to learn something new every day." I still believe that today.

Our walk with Jesus is no different. When we give our life to Christ, from there on, it is baby steps daily. We are learning how to live a life for Him. Some days go smoothly and other days we struggle, and that is okay. It is good to be with women who will walk through life with you and pray for you when needed.

~February 14~
This Is For All The Girls

I wait for the Lord, my soul does wait,
and in His word do I hope.
Psalms 130:5

This is for all the young girls whose first horse wasn't a show horse, but he was safe. This is for the teenage girls who wanted a fancy show horse, but their parents couldn't afford it, so instead, they bought you a horse to love and show locally. The lessons and character-building were worth more than all the world championships, for they made you dig deep inside your soul and learn to be content with what you have. This is for all the young women who had to sell their horse when they went to college and got a job. It is never easy, but one day, you will enter the horse world by storm and never look back. This is for all the women who have put their horse dreams in a box on the shelf and embraced marriage, motherhood, and life head-on. You still strain your neck to see the horses in a pasture as you drive by, but you know your time will come again to saddle up one day. This is for all the women who have raised their children, attended every sporting event, chaperoned school dances, and volunteered for the booster club. You enjoy every moment because time is short and your children will soon fly away to live their own lives.

Today's devotional is for all the girls who never got the horse when they were young but loved them fiercely from afar. God knew your time would come. Don't give up on your dreams, for your love for horses will be something you share with the next generation. And when that time comes, find the horse and hit the trails. God will be smiling down from above. You did well. Now enjoy!

~February 15~
The Second Half

*I will praise the name of God with song
and magnify Him with thanksgiving.
Psalm 69:30*

There is something absolutely wonderful about owning horses as an older woman. Some of us may have been around horses all our lives, but many women don't become horse owners until their "second half" of life or what many would say the golden years. When we finally take the leap and become a "horse mom," it is something to celebrate. What a gift to embrace.

I have had the privilege of watching many women who are in their golden years become first-time horse owners. It tickles me inside because I see their eyes light up, and they are excited to do everything and anything to help me at the barn, including cleaning stalls and doing chores. What a joy to be a part of their new adventure. They come out to the stable and will stay for hours as they watch which horses have bonded with their horse and take it all in like fresh air. Being a horse owner during the second half of life makes us feel like we are just teenagers again.

As a boarding stable owner, my life is somewhat different because I am around the horses daily, either taking them outside for the day or bringing them back in, along with all the other chores that need to be done. I sometimes forget to stop and just take it all in and see the remarkable beauty the Lord has created right before my eyes. So when I see one of our clients enjoying their horse to the fullest, it is a great reminder to enjoy the moment and thank the Lord for all He has given us on this earth. What a playground of beauty and wonder right before my eyes in an array of colors, shapes, and sizes. It doesn't get any better than that. Praise God!

~February 16~
Wild Horse Annie

For you have need of endurance, so that when you have done
the will of God you may receive what is promised.
Hebrews 10:36

Velma Johnston was born in 1912 and had endured a tough childhood due to having Polio. She couldn't do many of the things other children would do, so she educated herself and as an adult went to work as a secretary. On the way to work one day, she saw something that would change her life forever. As she was walking down the street, she saw a large trailer filled with half-dead horses being hauled away. She had never seen such sad-looking horses in all her life. The horses were wild Mustangs and they were being taken to a slaughterhouse where they would be killed and made into pet food. From that moment on, Velma made it her mission to help as many Mustang horses as possible.

As Velma started learning about the Mustang's fate, she found herself sneaking into places where the horses were being held and she witnessed firsthand the cruel treatment the horses were forced to endure. Velma became a voice for the Mustang horses at a time in history when women were to be quiet, but she wouldn't take no for an answer. She took on the government and the powerful ranchers and began a campaign encouraging children from all over America to draw pictures and write letters to Congress. More mail from this campaign was delivered to D.C. than any other issue besides the Vietnam War. In 1971, Congress passed the Wild Free-Roaming Horse and Burro Act due to her endless dedication. Soon, Velma became known as Wild Horse Annie, and she proved to children and adults everywhere what one person can do if they don't give up. God bless the woman who sees injustice and stands strong even when it gets tough.

~February 17~
No Divas Allowed

You make known to me the path of life; you will fill me with joy
in your presence, with eternal pleasures at your right hand.
Psalm 16:11

Much has improved for the horse's well-being over the last thirty or forty years, but I also believe we may have swung the pendulum too far and become over-saturated with stuff for our horses to the point where it can be overwhelming and sometimes even harmful. It almost feels like some have forgotten that horses are animals that like the dirt and even mud at times, prefer their own smells to ultra-clean bleached floor mats, and need to be turned out daily for fresh air, sunlight, and playtime.

When we first opened our boarding stable, I had already decided that all the horses would go outside daily, no matter what. Show horses and trail horses went outside together, and if a show horse got muddy, he could be hosed off as easily as a trail horse. All horses were equal no matter their accomplishments, and there were no divas allowed at our barn! The horses each had their individual jobs but they were also allowed to be horses daily.

After many years, I still believe it is much healthier for the horses to be turned out daily. Just like children playing in a mud puddle, they will do the same thing and love it. Yes, so much has improved for the horses in the last few decades, but I pray that we never forget that they are horses first.

Lord, help me remember that you created this majestic animal to run, play, and be with his own kind daily. When we see the horse in all his glory, we see God's creation at its finest.

~February 18~
Different Needs

For this is the will of my Father, that everyone who looks on the
Son and believes in him should have eternal life.
John 6:40

The one thing that really opened my eyes at our stable was the difference in the individual needs of the horses, especially when it came to their ages. Young horses have their own special needs, and the horse in his twenties and thirties will keep you on your toes. That alone taught me so much about horse care that I couldn't have learned in most books. It's funny to me now when I think about it because I thought I knew horses well until I started caring for many of them all at once.

Learning that your horse may have special needs regarding diet, turnout, or seasons and weather can be a real learning curve for the new horse owner. The same is true for the horse owner who has an aging horse, and suddenly, his weight, hair coat, eyesight, and eating habits start to change. The aging horse, whom we have grown to love so much, has sent us into unfamiliar territory and we find ourselves worrying often and learning many new things daily to improve his health and well-being. If you are blessed to own a horse with special needs, you will fall in love even more with this wonderful animal that looks at you with his soft eyes as if he is saying thank you for taking such good care of him.

We are all learning what the Lord wants for our lives, which will look different for each of us. God sees what you need long before it enters your mind, and He will give you strength to help you overcome the hurdles that come your way. Praise the Lord!

Mama Bear

Cast your burden on the Lord, and he will sustain you;
he will never permit the righteous to be moved.
Psalm 55:22

If someone dares to criticize our children, our mama bear claws come fast and furious. It is a natural response of any mother and I would have to say the same would be true about our horses. I have watched people over the years say something with critical tones about a horse that sends the hairs of the horse owner up on end, and you can see her mama bear claws start to inch their way out. The truth is sometimes we need to hear those honest words if we are having issues or our horse is putting us in danger. But it is never easy to hear. No matter how gently a trainer, barn manager, or another boarder says it, it still hurts. How we deal with it after is a whole other story.

Many people take the advice or gentle criticism well and put in motion a plan to correct the issue. But I have also had clients leave our stable or fire a trainer because they didn't like what they were hearing. Sometimes, the mama bear comes out for a good reason, but sometimes, we must step back and think about what was said before reacting. It is a balancing act and is never easy because we love our horses just like they are our kids.

If you find yourself in a place where you need to talk to someone about their horse, and it may not go well, take it to the Lord first and ask for guidance. If you are on the receiving end of critical words, my prayer is that you step back and think about it before you say anything or act upon it. It is never easy, but giving it to the Lord is the first step in keeping your heart in the right place and not allowing bitterness to take root.

~February 20~
I'm Not Adulting Today

The Lord is my shepherd; I shall not want.
He makes me lie down in green pastures.
He leads me beside still waters.
Psalm 23:1-2

I first saw the phrase, "I'm not adulting today," on a meme on Facebook a few years ago, and instantly, I could relate to it! As an adult who has raised her children to young adults and tried to do all the things a wife and mom should do to keep her house in order over the last few decades, the words were freeing. Even if it was for just a day or weekend, it sounded like heaven to me, especially after taking care of horses seven days a week for almost two decades.

Sometimes, you just need a break from the routine, do something entirely different, and have no responsibility for a short time to rejuvenate the body and soul. For the woman who loves horses, the barn is your place to go. She comes out to the stable to refresh, rejuvenate, and have no responsibility but her horse. The moment she drives up to the stable she feels giddy inside as she sees her horse looking at her from out in the pasture. She has flashbacks of her childhood when she first fell in love with horses and quickly rushes to grab a halter. There is no better feeling for her and all the cares and responsibilities of the day disappear for a few hours.

One of the best things about growing older is that we know how to enjoy life and it can be something as simple as just being with our horse. We don't need much as we age. We need to know our family loves us, is healthy, and that our horse is happy. That is the cowgirl way for so many of us and we wouldn't change a thing about the life we created. Praise the Lord for this wonderful life He has blessed us with.

~February 21~
Pebbles

Let love and faithfulness never leave you; bind them around
your neck, write them on the tablet of your heart. Then you
will win favor and a good name in the sight of God and man.
Proverbs 3:3-4

I have a confession to make. I bought a horse without my husband knowing about it! When my daughter was young, her pony had gone completely blind. The autumn season arrived with brilliant leaves on the trees and it was also the hunting season in Wisconsin. My husband had planned a few days away to go hunting with friends. All was good after he left, and shortly after, I got a call from a friend who had a lovely pony for sale. He was a loud-spotted Appaloosa, and he was adorable. They called him Pebbles and my friend thought he would make a great kid's horse.

We didn't own cell phones then, so there was no way to reach my husband and I didn't want to miss a chance to find a good pony for my daughter. So, we jumped in the truck and went to see this little horse, and of course, we fell in love with him. The next day he was delivered to our farm and quickly bonded with the other horses. Now, I had to wait for David to come home a few days later and I was praying he would be okay with it, especially since we really didn't have the extra money. Three days later, he pulled in and I watched him slow down as he went by the paddock where Pebbles was now living. I knew I was about to face the music. To my surprise, he handled it all pretty well and all these years later, I still smile about that day.

It's not something I would ever recommend doing, but I think many married women can share similar stories of buying the horse and telling their husbands later!

~February 22~
Burned Out

And let us consider how we may spur one another on toward
love and good deeds, not giving up meeting together,
as some are in the habit of doing, but encouraging one another
and all the more as you see the Day approaching.
Hebrews 10:24-25

It is easy to get burned out when taking care of horses daily, especially when the temperature is below zero! What a winter we have had with the frigid temperatures. It shouldn't surprise me because we have been running our boarding stable for almost twenty years, and every winter, midway through, I say the same thing—"Why do I do this for a living?" Then, as soon as the thought enters my head, it leaves again and I remember why.

Today's devotion is for all the women who work hard taking care of horses daily, no matter the weather or time of year. There are going to be those days when it is painfully hard and you wonder why you do this. I want you to know that you are not alone. Horses are a gift from God and I wouldn't change anything except the weather. But many things in life come with hard work, which keeps us humble, grounded, and seeking the Lord when we can't take it anymore. And that is a good thing. Today, if you feel burned out from the life you have chosen with horses, take a step back and give it to the Lord. Reach out to Him and ask for direction and the way you should go.

Dear God, I humbly ask for peace in my troubled heart and strength for my weary body. I feel like the waves are crashing upon me daily, and I can't seem to find a healthy balance between work and family. Please give me clarity on finding the purpose you have for my life. I believe through your grace, I will find the strength to keep going. In Jesus' Name, Amen.

~February 23~
The Promised Land

For God gave us a spirit not of fear
but of power and love and self-control.
II Timothy 1:7

We start as young girls who reach out to touch a horse's nose for the first time and quickly fall in love. Our young and naive mind tells us that we can do anything without fearing consequences, and for some, it lasts longer than others. As a young woman, I never worried about what could go wrong while riding. For better or for worse, I took chances and kept going. God gives us this incredible boldness and courage when we are young, and we race off into the sunset on our horse without a care in the world. One day, we will look back and remember those fearless days of our youth.

But what happens when the things you once did naturally seem to slip away, like riding bareback or without the parameters of an arena fence? Those are huge obstacles for some women. I have been blessed to watch many women find their confidence and do something with their horse that was completely out of their comfort zone. When this happens, it is like they entered the Promised Land! They are beaming inside and you can see their confidence sky-rocket. The feeling they get from accomplishing something new will last a lifetime.

God gave us this incredible mind and body to try new things and step out in faith. My prayer is that you will find the courage to step out of your comfort zone when your heart urges you forward. When it comes, seize the moment and take the chance. Thank you, Lord, for those sweet moments of success in our lives.

~February 24~
Unleash Your Imagination

Now faith is the assurance of things hoped for,
the conviction of things not seen.
Hebrews 11:1

When I was young, I followed the crowd regarding horses and what I could do with them. Partly because I was insecure but also because I wanted to be with the "cool" kids—or at least I thought they were cool when I was a teenager. Looking back, I missed so many opportunities to do some really fun stuff with my horses because it was different, and I didn't want to be different.

I am so blessed to have a daughter who looked "outside the box" when trying different things with her horses. She had a lot of fun growing up with them and learned so much more because she attempted many disciplines and loved them all. Don't get me wrong, I have wonderful memories of riding and doing 4-H, but I wasn't a chance taker when trying different riding disciplines. Now, decades later, I love watching different riding disciplines and equestrians who do things outside the box. They are inspirational in so many ways.

When I meet a new horse owner, either young or older, who is unsure what riding discipline they want to learn, I encourage them to try what is on their heart and not follow the crowd. There is no limit to what you can do if you are willing to try something new. With horses, anything is possible.

That is what God is telling us every day. He asks us to be brave, use our imagination, and try something new for His glory. You never know—you might just find yourself sharing the love of Jesus Christ while at a horse show, on a trail ride, or herding cattle on the wide open range!

~February 25~
Forgiveness

Be kind to one another, tenderhearted, forgiving one another,
as God in Christ forgave you.
Ephesians 4:32

They say that the horse community can be cruel and leave many people disenchanted and with very hurt feelings. I don't believe it is just the horse world, but since I am involved in the horse community professionally, I can say that I have had my feelings hurt and so has every single person I know. It has not swayed my feelings for horses or equestrians, but it is a process of reaching down deep and learning to forgive.

Until you forgive the unkind words or actions of another, you will never be free to enjoy your horse and all you plan on doing to the fullest. In fact, not forgiving someone will steal any joy you have with your horse even if you move to another stable because it will always be on your mind. You will still go to shows, go on trail rides, or just hang out with your horse, but it will still be there deep inside. I can say this from experience because I was hurt deeply years ago and it was extremely hard to get over. In fact, when I think about the situation that transpired it made me sick to my stomach for a couple of years. That is when I had to ask God to help me release the bitterness taking over my life. I had to learn to forgive the person just like I need forgiveness daily. Praise God, for He did just that! It was a work in progress, but I finally was able to let the pain and anger leave my body, and compassion replaced bitterness. For the first time, I felt how freeing it was to forgive and to be forgiven.

If you are struggling to forgive someone in your life, I want to encourage you to pray and ask for help. With the Lord by your side, anything is possible, even when it seems impossible at the time.

~February 26~
For The Horse

Love bears all things, believes all things, hopes all things, endures all things.
I Corinthians 13:7

The alarm went off at 5 a.m. and she reached over to shut it off. As she hit the button, the alarm flew off the bed stand and she lay there wondering if she should go back to sleep. Then she realized she had horses to take care of this morning. She put her legs over the side of the bed a little slower than she had just a few short years ago and could feel the stiffness in her body as she made her way to the bathroom. Her body reminded her that she was getting older, but she pushed that thought out of her head and made a fresh pot of coffee instead.

She looked outside and saw the wind howling and the snow starting to come down. She was glad the horses were snuggled inside the barn and it gave her a few extra minutes because they would not be going outside today due to the impending storm. She walked downstairs into the basement and put her barn clothes on. Each layer made her feel big and heavy but she knew the routine and refused to be cold while doing the chores. She remembered for a minute the woman she was years ago, working in an office and dressed to the hilt daily with the finest shoes and work clothes. Those days were behind her now, but she was glad for the new life she had chosen with horses. She was content and the hard work didn't bother her most of the time. She headed out the door and could only think about the horses waiting for her in the barn, and this sense of peace flowed over her. She was where she was supposed to be.

When God sees you doing your part and giving it your all, even on the hardest days, He is there to carry you through. When it all feels like it is too much, He will be your strength.

~February 27~
A Wise Friend

Oil and perfume make the heart glad,
and the sweetness of a friend comes from his earnest counsel.
Proverbs 27:9

When I started as a boarding stable owner I was younger and very naïve to the business world, even in the horse industry. I had a lot to learn and I made many mistakes along the way. I will be the first to tell anyone wanting to start their own horse business that it is not easy and can be equally hard on your spouse and children. But all these years later, I have learned a lot and I am thankful for those challenging but fruitful lessons because they helped me rely on God more and myself less.

There is something special about coming through the fire and finding out a couple of decades later that you are still standing. You might be singed from some of the flames that flared up during tough times in your business but you made it out the backside and became a much stronger woman. Nothing can teach you more about life, horses, and running a business than just doing it daily.

If you feel discouraged and are beginning to question why you got into this crazy life with horses and people, take a step back, pray, and rest. Pray to the Lord for guidance and ask Him to unveil what He is trying to teach you. Then, I encourage you to dive deep into His Word and soak up the wisdom on the pages like a sponge. There you will find peace. Then, after you have had a moment to reflect on everything, call your best friend and meet her for lunch. I have had many lunches with my bestie just to clear my head, eat good food, and laugh out loud. It works every time!

Praise God for the friend who will listen to your every word, not judge, and give you wise advice.

~February 28~
Trusting Your Decision

The Lord is my strength and my shield; my heart trusts in him, and he helps me. My heart leaps for joy, and with my song I praise him.
Psalm 28:7

Learning to say no to peer pressure gets easier as you get older. That is true in our personal lives and definitely true with the horses and people you come in contact with at your stable, campsite, or any other equestrian activity.

The truth is, if you are a new horse owner and are just learning everything for the first time, you will be bombarded with numerous opinions about horse care, groundwork with horses, and, of course, riding. You will be given opinions and views on farriers and whether your horse should be shod or not, and the subject of vaccines will lead to long, lengthy discussions. The list can go on and on, BUT there is one thing for certain. Time is a wonderful gift and wisdom is a diamond among jewels.

If you are an older horse owner, you will navigate this easier than a young person because life will have taught you so much about the world and following the crowd too quickly. You will have learned how important it is to do your homework and then make a decision that is best for you and your horse. It is okay to say no to good intentions and views and follow your heart for you and your equine partner. And above all else, give it to the Lord in prayer. Ask Him to send people into your life who can give you solid advice, honest feedback, and encouragement when you need it.

Dear Heavenly Father, I ask for clarity in the decisions I need to make for my beloved equine partner. Sometimes, I feel bombarded by all the opinions being thrown at me, so I will wait quietly and listen to your voice of discernment with everything in my life. In Jesus' Name, Amen.

~February 29 (Leap Year) ~
Horse Kisses

But the fruit of the Spirit is love, joy, peace, patience,
kindness, goodness, faithfulness,
Galatians 5:22

Sometimes when I am on social media, I will scroll through the horse groups I am part of and see image after image of little girls all the way up to silver-haired women kissing their horses. It always makes me smile because I understand their feelings and desire to be as close to their horse as possible. What is it about the horse and his long nose and soft muzzle that makes even an older woman feel like a little girl again?

We do the silliest things with our horses and love every moment. When it comes to our horses, we don't worry about catching germs and we don't worry if they have just had their nose to the ground nibbling for pieces of hay through the manure and dirt. We are completely unaware of anything that would normally seem unclean to us. In fact, most horse-crazy women can clean their horse's stall and eat a jelly doughnut at the same time and never think twice about it! The horse has transformed us into something our non-horsey friends would never understand.

So, to all the women who want to kiss their horse-GO AHEAD! He will look at you with those big eyes and wonder what you are doing. And without realizing it, he will transform you into that young girl who loved watching horse movies and going to the fair just to see a horse up close. It is truly wondrous.

Thank you, Lord, for the gift of this beautiful animal that gently nuzzles up to me when I am near him. I can't help but smile when I look into his eyes and kiss his nose. I know I am not a child anymore, but it sure is fun to feel like that little girl I was years ago, even for a moment. I'm abundantly blessed. Amen

~March 1~
The Goliath In Front Of Us

Be strong and courageous. Do not fear or be in dread of them, for it is the Lord your God who goes with you. He will not leave you or forsake you.
Deuteronomy 31:6

The other day, I saw a saying on Facebook that said, "God will place a Goliath in front of you to bring out the David inside of you." When I read it, I thought how true that is. Sometimes, the only way to make us step out of our comfort zone and face our fears is to be forced to face them. That is true in all areas of our life, including with horses.

Every equestrian I have ever known has had fears of some kind regarding horses. It could be the fear of falling off and getting hurt or entering the show ring and making a fool of themselves. It could be trying a new riding discipline and looking silly or failing at a new horse business. It doesn't matter the age or experience; every horsewoman has been there, and some jump in both feet first, while others stick their toes in to feel the temperature before slowly going in. But for all of us, the fear of the unknown is huge and can become overwhelming if we allow it. I have even seen it mentally cripple women to the point where they don't even try. It is as though they have a giant Goliath in front of them and they can't get past it.

Today, I pray that you will find your inner David, take that little pebble out, and aim straight ahead. God already knows your fears about horses and the obstacles in front of you and He is just waiting for you to call upon Him for help. He loves you and wants you to be successful, and will be right by your side if you trust Him. God's love is never-ending, and He will see you through.

~March 2~
My Poor Horse

*Call to me and I will answer you, and will tell
you great and hidden things that you have not known.*
Jeremiah 33:3

Horses pin their ears, bite, kick, and chase other horses at times, which can be hard to watch, especially if your horse is at the bottom of the hierarchy. In a horse's natural setting, the strongest survive and the weakest unfortunately live shorter lives. Don't worry, good news is coming.

When we domesticated the horse, there came with it a huge responsibility to ensure they were cared for. We made them dependent on us for food, water, and shelter, but also equally important, we decided who their herd mates would be. It's a responsibility that shouldn't be taken lightly and it is up to us to ensure that they are well-fed, have water and shelter, and feel safe with other horses and humans. Over the years, I have heard many horror stories and my heart aches for these people as they are frantically trying to find a new stable for their horse. Life is never going to be perfect but we can try our best to make our horses feel safe. God gave us dominion over the beasts of the ground and to care for them the best way we know how.

What an awesome responsibility filled with so much return if we do it right. Today, I encourage you to learn your horse's personality and watch for anything that is causing him stress. If your gut is telling you things are not right, take control of the situation and do whatever you need to for your horse. You will never regret it. The last thing you want to think about is "my poor horse" and feel like you can't change anything. Pray about it and be proactive. You're his voice, and when he is in a good situation you will see him come alive like never before.

~March 3~
Good And Faithful Servant

His master replied, 'Well done, good and faithful servant! You have been
faithful with a few things; I will put you in charge of many things.
Come and share your master's happiness!
Matthew 25:23

If you are lucky enough to have owned your horse for his entire life, you have been part of something rather extraordinary. After all, horses can live well into their thirties and even their forties! That is half our lifetime and it takes true commitment.

During the horse's life, you will watch him grow into a strong and full-size horse full of piss and vinegar. And even though his body is big, you can still see his baby brain come out loud and clear by his actions. Then, as he approaches the age of double digits, he has matured and doesn't overreact as much, but instead, executes precision when being asked to do a job. He is physically and mentally strong and even though he is fully grown, he is still your baby. Your rides are wonderful and you feel as though they will last forever until one day he slightly trips, and you find yourself asking what just happened. In your mind he is still fifteen, but when you start counting the years on your fingers, you quickly remember he is nearing twenty years old!

As your life changes, so does your horse. He doesn't compete anymore but he has a much better job. He carries your children on his back and has become their gentle giant. His days consist of short, easy rides, and once in a while, you enter him in the lead-line class and he gently carries the precious cargo.

Today marked his thirtieth birthday and everyone came out to celebrate with carrot cake and apples. What a true privilege it is to care for a horse for such a long time. He is a good and faithful servant to all who have known him throughout the years.

~March 4~
The War Effort

Even though I walk through the valley of the shadow of death, I will fear no evil, for you are with me; your rod and your staff, they comfort me.
Psalm 23:4

With the start of World War 1, Great Britain was void of men. Every man who was fit enough now donned a uniform and was headed to unknown places to fight. This meant that the country needed every horse possible. Hundreds of thousands of horses were being made ready for the war effort. With so many men gone, many women stepped up to help care for the horses and get them fit before they shipped off to battle. The women came from all classes but had one thing in common – they loved horses.

These ladies volunteered to muck out stalls at remount depots and proved they could offer an invaluable service for the war effort without knitting blankets or socks. These ladies were drafted into the Land Army in 1915 and became grooms and stable managers at remount centers housed at former racing stables. In three army remount stations, not one man could be found. The entire operation was being run by "gentlewomen," as they would call them, but today, we would call them horsewomen!

These women did things that were never before allowed in society. They fed the horses, groomed them daily, and clipped the ones that would pull heavy artillery. They even became farriers and took care of any sick or injured animals. It was often said by the inspectors who would check on the readiness of the horses, "They have never known horses to be so well attended to by men." For many of the ladies it was a far cry from their pre-war lives and they embraced every minute of it. Little did they know they were also changing how society viewed the role of women, and their war effort opened the equestrian doors of opportunity for the future.

~March 5~
This Too Shall Pass

I will not cause pain without allowing something new to be born.
Isaiah 66:9

Okay, so it was a less-than-stellar day with your horse. It started with him running away from you in the paddock and you spent the next twenty minutes trying to get close enough to put his halter on. You thought to yourself, "Well, this is strange." Then you take him in the barn to brush and saddle him, and you think, "What a lucky girl I am to have you." Soon, you have your saddle cinched up and you plan on riding outside because it is a beautiful fall day. And even though it is a bit breezy and cooler than normal, you say to yourself, "I am sure my boy will be good out on the trail." So off you go. Ten minutes later, a horse comes running back to the barn without its rider! You're not hurt, just embarrassed as you slowly walk back to the stable and say to yourself, "Wow! He has never done that before," as you recall him spooking at the blowing trees. You decide not to let him win, so you take him to the indoor arena, get back on, and take a slow walk around. After five minutes, you say to yourself, "I believe I have shown him that his silliness is not allowed." Then you dismount, untack, and lead him back to his paddock to be with his herd mates. As you get in your car, you see him staring at you from the paddock and giving you those eyes that say, "How come you left so fast? I miss you." You tell yourself that this day will pass and tomorrow will be much better.

Less-than-stellar days always pass, but with each challenging day, we gain a little more wisdom and knowledge, and incredible lessons are taught to us about these amazing and sometimes frustrating equines that we love so much. Thank you, Lord, for the lessons you teach us about life through the horse.

~March 6~
Other Plans

You can make many plans,
but the Lord's purpose will prevail.
Proverbs 19:21

Since the day we opened our horse boarding stable, life has changed for me in ways I never expected. One of the biggest things I have learned from taking care of horses is that things don't always go as planned. I have had many days (too many to count) where I had the day perfectly planned out in my head of everything that needed to get done and then a horse gets sick, injured, or breaks something that needs fixing. Sometimes, the things that get damaged can wait (or my husband will take care of it), but when a horse is sick or injured and the owner is not there, then I need to step in and help the animal. I have to be honest and tell you that my attitude was not the best once in a while since horses seem to get hurt at the most inopportune times. Sometimes my plans were with my daughters and they had to wait or cancel completely. But it taught all of us so much about what is truly important in life and it has helped mold each of us, hopefully in a good way.

I have learned to lean on the Lord when the day starts to fall apart and things don't go how I envisioned. I know He has other plans for me that are always better than mine. I just often don't see them while things are happening. Trusting God and being open to any situation that comes your way is challenging at times, but so many wonderful things can come out of it if we are willing to stop and wait upon the Lord.

Thank you, God, for the unexpected plans that pop up in my life, for they hold valuable lessons that will last a lifetime.

~March 7~
Twinkle In Her Eyes

A joyful heart is good medicine.
Proverbs 17:22

I looked at Carol from across the table and saw this larger-than-life smile emerge as she began to talk about her childhood. It was easy to see that her memories were good ones as she shared her horse stories with me. As I listened, I envisioned this fearless little girl who would do anything to be near a horse. She talked about how when she was very young, she would walk two miles down the road and when the owner wasn't around she would jump the fence and hop on this old sway-back mare in the field. That was where she fell in love for the first time. Soon, Carol was saving all her babysitting money for riding lessons at a nearby stable.

Horses consumed Carol throughout her childhood, but once she graduated high school, she got married and started having babies of her own. Life got busy being a wife and new momma, and the horses were tucked away in her heart for many decades. It wouldn't be until Carol retired and her children were all on their own that horses crept back into her life. She bought her granddaughter riding lessons as a gift and decided to take lessons as well, and all her sweet memories of riding as a child came rushing back. Quickly, her mind was made up. She was going to have a horse of her own, and she never looked back. Carol bought her first horse and began riding English, and soon, she started jumping. Then she purchased a horse trailer and truck and started horse camping with other horsewomen, and a new adventure began.

That day, I witnessed the twinkle in the eyes of a woman who truly loved horses. I began to realize how blessed I am by God to know such an amazing person who is so young at heart and has inspired many other women to ride and live out their dreams.

90

~March 8~
Learning Horsemanship

You enlarge my steps under me,
and my feet have not slipped.
Psalm 18:36

Nothing can compare to buying your first horse, especially if you are a little older. We become horse-crazed wild women consumed with learning as much as possible about our new equine partner. It is as though nothing else matters and we strive to be the best in everything regarding our horsemanship.

The hard part is it can take years to feel like we are mastering a skill, and once in a while, we need to give ourselves a pep talk because we are not picking up things as quickly as we did when we were younger. We have to learn to be easier on ourselves and slow down. As my daddy used to tell me when I was young, "Try to learn something new every day. One thing is enough, and then tomorrow will come, and you can learn something else." When he would tell me that as a young girl, I didn't get it, but now I do!

Take your time and enjoy every moment with your horse, even when you feel like things are not clicking. Learning is all part of it, and it is something you will do for the rest of your life with these amazing animals. You never stop learning, and that is a good thing. The horsewomen that I see struggle the most (and so does their horse) are the ones who feel like they know it all and don't want to learn something new or different. That is dangerous territory to be in.

My prayer is that you will gain new horse knowledge each day and learn to be easy on yourself. No matter the size of your accomplishments, remember that slow and steady is always best, and your horse will thank you for it.

~March 9~
Rest In This

For nothing will be impossible with God.
Luke 1:37

For every frustrating ride you have in the beginning as a new equestrian, you will have just as many good rides if you are patient. Those good rides are the cherries on top of the ice-cream when the day went perfect and your horse was an angel. You will walk a little taller and your smile will be a little brighter because everything seemed to go flawlessly. But when the day is tough and you start to feel a tear trickle down your cheek, don't lose heart, for those are the times when you are learning and growing, and that is only possible when things don't go as planned.

Embrace each ride no matter how easy or hard it is, for that is what is molding you into the horsewoman you want to be. There is no easy way around it regarding horses and that is the true beauty of horses and horsemanship. You can't rush the ride or try to find shortcuts because your horse will not allow it. He will see right through you and only respect an honest rider who is trying their best day in and day out. Remember, it is okay not to have a good ride for that was your classroom today, and tomorrow will be different. It is okay to shed a tear because we are emotional beings and tears are good for the soul. One day down the road you will look back at how far you have come with your horse and the bad days will slowly disappear and the good rides will be the norm.

Embrace it all, for it is the life of women and horses, and it is perfect. Every horsewoman has her struggles, but find comfort and peace in the knowledge that God knows what you are going through. Give all of your struggles to the Lord and ask Him to give you rest, for tomorrow will be a new day and you will be ready to have a better ride. You can rest in this promise.

~March 10~
The Balancing Act

We love Him because He first loved us.
I John 4:19

If you own a horse and are married, then you know that, at times, you will struggle to balance out your "horse time" with your husband. I see it all the time at my barn, where the women are having a great time leisurely brushing their horses and talking about life and then chatting some more as they ride together. Before you know it, the time has slipped away and everyone is hurrying to put their horses away and get home. It is sweet, and these ladies love their husbands, but they sometimes forget about the time when they are out at the barn with their horses.

There is something special about being with your horse. Time seems to stop, and nothing else matters for a few moments (or hours). Then you realize that you need to go to the market and get something to make for dinner, and it looks like dinner might be later than usual. Then, as you rush out of the driveway, you remember that your husband loves Chinese food and you want to make him feel special, so you stop and pick some up. You had a wonderful day with your horse and your husband is thrilled that you picked up Chinese food, and you were able to spend time with both of your loves today.

As women, we are good at doing many things at once and finding a balance so everything fits in. Sometimes, it can get a little crazy as you rush out of the stable and drive off wondering what to make for dinner, but in the end, you make it all work out and never break a sweat.

Thank you, Lord, for the wonderful man I married and for his understanding of this crazy love I have for my horse. You blessed me when you sent him into my life. Praise God!

~March 11~
Personal Best

He stores up sound wisdom for the upright;
he is a shield to those who walk in integrity.
Proverbs 2:7

I first heard the phrase "It's about your personal best" when my daughter started competing in Dressage at horse shows. She was around ten years old and the riding discipline of Dressage was entirely new for me since I grew up riding Western. I kept hearing that phrase at every level of competition, and I started to really love the idea of doing your personal best and not worrying about how others are doing.

Finding your personal best as a horsewoman can, at times, seem confusing. We are constantly striving to do our best when it comes to training horses, running boarding stables, competing in horse shows, and the list goes on and on. But if we took the time to stop and see how the day actually was, we might find out that it was a day that got high marks in our book. It might be that you had a wonderful breakthrough with a horse that has had a terrible life and is fearful to the point of being dangerous. It could be that your horse business is not making you rich, but you are paying your bills and have a small savings account started. Maybe you didn't get the blue or red ribbon in the advanced class, but you got a first in the walk/trot class, which is huge for your Thoroughbred since she is a nervous nelly and has a hard time just walking. Those little things make for unforgettable personal bests that you won't forget.

Enjoy the ride and take your time. Just remember, it's not a sprint; it's a marathon. Don't miss the incredible views and your personal best accomplishments that God shows you along the way.

~March 12~
No Power Steering

Getting wisdom is the wisest thing you can do!
And whatever else you do, develop good judgment.
Proverbs 4:7

It becomes very apparent when a horse comes with no power steering! The horse that is hard to turn left or right feels just like driving a vehicle where the power steering is not working. It can be frustrating, but the woman with some experience and wisdom will look deeper to find out what is wrong, especially when this is not normal for the horse.

I remember watching an instructor years ago with a horse that suddenly would not turn left or right. This horse was always well-behaved for the children who rode on his back, but this one day was different. He refused to turn and the students were becoming frustrated. At first, he was strongly encouraged to try and make him move, but still, he refused. Then the instructor got on, and still, the horse refused. As I watched, a little voice inside told me something serious was going on with the horse. It was as if his power steering was completely broken. It was realized quickly that this sweet horse was very sick. Not only did the instructor feel terrible, but the students were also devastated. The horse only lived a few more days and we all said goodbye with tears in our eyes.

As women, we need to understand that there will be times when we don't see things as they really are. We often look at the moment and forget to look at the big picture. Today, Lord, I ask for wisdom and discernment regarding the horses in my care and the people in my life. Help me see the big picture and not get fixated on what is happening at the moment. Open my eyes so I can properly care for the animals you have entrusted to me. In Jesus's Name, Amen.

~March 13~
Harmony

He does great things too marvelous to understand.
Job 5:9

The horse's power and strength are incomprehensible unless you have felt and watched his strength in action. I have watched a horse drag a person while they are on the ground hanging on (I highly do not recommend this!) like they are a rag doll. If a horse becomes frightened, his power is magnified as he tries to get away from that plastic bag blowing in the wind. And when you watch two horses either fighting or playing, their strength comes out in full force and their precision of what they are aiming at is remarkable. It reminds me that they could seriously hurt me in a minute if they really wanted to.

Yet horses will let us do unimaginable things to them and they will surrender willingly. How do these two worlds of power and surrender live in harmony? I truly believe it is because of how God created the equine. What makes the horse so beautiful is not only his physical beauty or strength, but his willingness to trust and give to the human who is in his life daily. If done correctly and slowly, the bond will become unbreakable and the trust will be like no other. They are a gentle animal that is curious and playful, loves a job, and when he understands what he is supposed to do, will try his hardest. His heart is big and he will forgive but never forget.

Lord, help me always strive to create harmony with my horse and listen with my eyes to what he is telling me each day. I will work to ensure his needs are taken care of and he always feels safe. You have entrusted me to care for this extraordinary animal and I am honored to answer your call. Thank you, Lord, for the gift of the horse.

~March 14~
Out Of Hand

The heartfelt counsel of a friend
is as sweet as perfume and incense.
Proverbs 22:9

If truth be told, we are often the creators of bad habits in our horses. Some of those bad habits initially seem adorable because our emotions get involved. We know our horse can be nippy as he is looking for treats, but we ignore it sometimes because it makes us feel good and it gives us a sense that we are bonding with him. Our horse can be pushy as we lead him, but we love being close to him so we look the other way as he forgets his boundaries and knocks us off our feet. We even watch our horse run away from us in the paddock, only to admire his strength and beauty instead of dealing with the issue. Don't get me wrong, I have done all those things too! But eventually, a time comes when we realize that our sweet boy has turned into a naughty monster and undoing the behavior can be challenging.

Admitting that your horse has some behaviors that need fixing is the first step in moving forward with your equine partner, and it is a humbling experience. It's not easy to admit it, but once you do, your horsemanship will really start to grow. The same would be true in our own life. We create these bad habits that quickly get out of control, and often, we can't even see we are doing them. That is when a loving friend or spouse will tell us the truth and help us to change and live a better life. It won't be fun getting back on track, but that is when the Lord does His best work, and that is when we grow the most.

Thank you, Jesus, for surrounding me with people who love me and help me when I need it the most.

~March 15~
The Stillness

My voice you shall hear in the morning, O Lord;
In the morning I will direct it to You, And I will look up.
Psalm 5:3

There is something wonderfully calm and breathtaking about early morning chores on our horse farm. My first steps out the door often wake my senses to everything around me. The horses are quiet and all I can hear is the sound of an owl on our barn roof. I look up in the clear sky with the last remnants of a beautiful moon that is now fading away quickly. As we inch closer to summer, the moon will often be fading in the background as the sun starts to rise, and for a few brief moments, the two worlds come together. I see the greatness of God in the light projected from both and it is beautiful.

I turn on the light to the barn and I catch a few of the horses still lying down sleeping, and my heart melts. But as with all animals who are fed by humans, once they see me, they quickly wake up because I am the "grain lady," and I bring good stuff for them to eat. The quietness has now become a rousing ruckus as some horses do not have the gift of patience. The soft nickers have now turned to more demanding whinnies, and a few will paw, pin their ears, show their pearly whites, and even kick a little at their neighbors to say, "I'm next!".

The stillness I felt earlier is now gone for another twenty-four hours as the horses head outside for the day. Then, the same thing will happen all over again tomorrow, and for a few brief moments, I will look up into the sky and see the incredible beauty, hear the perfection of silence, and give my prayers to the Lord before the busy day ahead. I long for your presence, Lord Jesus. Please grant me the serenity to face the day with a calm heart and peaceful spirit.

~March 16~
Independence

It can be hard as a mother to watch your kids become independent on the back of a horse. They take off galloping down the path and your heart skips a beat as you watch. We worry, and it is all part of motherhood. There is nothing new under the sun and it was the same for mothers hundreds of years ago who watched their daughters ride off on the back of a horse when it was still relatively new for women to ride. The wonderful thing about horses is that they have given women independence ever since they were domesticated. For various reasons, many cultures did not allow women to ride horses. However, once riding a horse (even if it was sidesaddle) became more acceptable, there was no stopping those incredible horsewomen of the past. Not only were mothers watching their daughters hop on the back of a horse in a long dress and jump fences sidesaddle, but these brave women were doing everything the men were doing without hesitation. I can only imagine what those mommas were feeling. All I can say is we've come a long way baby!

The horse was more than just a mode of travel; he was a friend and protector. He gave many women the courage to try new things and the freedom to live life outside the culture's norm at the time. When I think about the horse and his contribution to the world, it always takes me back to the Lord and His love for us. Only a loving God would create such a perfect animal that would allow a woman to ride on his back sidesaddle, which I am sure was uncomfortable for the horse! I pray I never take for granted all the horse has done for women throughout the centuries.

The Need For Speed

Jesus said, "Let the little children come to me, and do not hinder them,
for the kingdom of heaven belongs to such as these."
Matthew 19:14

When I was a young girl, all I wanted to do was gallop as fast as my horse could run. I had this need for speed and I would often pretend that I was a jockey coming down the homestretch to the finish line. My friends and I would run our horses on every patch of dirt or grass we could find, and since we often rode in the city, open dirt lots were few and far between, so we would take whatever we could get.

Boy, how things have changed a lot for me over the years. My need for speed has diminished greatly and I am happy with a gentle walk and jog. I often think back to my younger years and I wouldn't trade them for the world. We may not have had the miles of trails to ride on, but we did our best with what we had.

I often smile now when I see the young kids riding horses. So many of them want to barrel race or do other speed events, and they are fearless. You can see the intensity on their faces as they round the barrels and head back for the finish line and my heart always skips a beat. I think to myself, what wonderful memories they will have when they are older.

Dear Heavenly Father, thank you for the next generation of young equestrians. These courageous kids will learn to rope and ride, run like the wind on their horse, and jump whatever is in front of them. I ask for their safety no matter what they do on horseback, and I pray that their memories will be sweet and last a lifetime. Please watch over them as they saddle up and ride on. Amen.

~March 18~
Confusion

And the Lord, He is the One who goes before you. He will be with you,
He will not leave you nor forsake you; do not fear nor be dismayed.
Deuteronomy 31:8

We are good at sending mixed messages and commands to our horses. We do it without realizing it but they are creatures of habit and love consistency. They feel safe when they know what to expect, and if the routine changes, they are looking to you as their "herd leader" to get them through it safely. That is why when you see a calm and well-adjusted horse at a show, trail ride, or at home, he has learned that his human will take care of him and everything will be okay. But, if our messages are inconsistent with our horse and he becomes frustrated and confused, then it will spill into the rest of his life, whether at the stable or elsewhere.

We try our best to create a place where our horse feels secure and content, but we make mistakes, which sometimes leads to unpleasant behavior. That is when we start to wonder what is going on. It is a journey that all horsewomen will go on for as long as they own horses and we are constantly learning as we take two steps forward and one step back.

God bless the woman who is trying her best each day with her horse. She knows she has a lot to learn and realizes that she can sometimes be inconsistent with how she handles her horse on the ground or in the saddle. I pray that she finds confidence and consistency as she discovers new strengths about herself. She is already an amazing horsewoman and she doesn't even know it yet. Praise God for her willingness to learn.

~March 19~
Kingdom Bound

But seek first the kingdom of God and His righteousness,
and all these things shall be added to you.
Matthew 6:33

When I was young, I gave my life to Jesus Christ, but that was as far as it went for many years. After I got married, my husband and I decided to start a large horse boarding business, and I had no idea what lay ahead for me both mentally and spiritually. Starting a new horse business with two little girls almost seemed crazy back then, but twenty years later, God revealed His ultimate plan for our lives. Through many trials and errors, I would learn that I needed the Lord more than ever to see me through those tough years. The worse things got financially and with clients, the more I became desperate for the Lord to walk beside me. My faith was being tested, and I believe God was teaching me about horses and clients and learning to let go and let Him take the reins. It was a walk of faith unlike anything I had ever experienced, and God was showing me that anything is possible if I was just willing to live my faith outwardly with love and compassion. I praise God for those hard years because they forced me to look deep inside myself and to live with truth and hope in Jesus Christ.

Things look much differently when we are kingdom-bound, including our journey as horsewomen. We love our horses and everything related to them, but once we understand that all of this belongs to the Lord first and that we are caretakers of these beautiful equines that God has entrusted to us, everything looks much different.

Lord, teach us to be kingdom-bound in everything we do, and when we feel like giving up, take the reins from our hands and lead us out of the darkness and into the light. Amen.

~March 20~
Like Riding A Bicycle

For we are God's masterpiece. He has created us anew in Christ Jesus,
so we can do the good things he planned for us long ago.
Ephesians 2:10

For women who rode horses when they were young and then took off several decades due to life circumstances, getting back in the saddle for the first time can be an emotional roller coaster. In our mind, we remember riding as a fearless teenager, bareback and barefoot, on any available horse and we threw caution to the wind. The thought of falling off back then almost seemed inconceivable, even though it happened to me a lot! But years later, something changed deep down inside of us. A small voice inside us tells us to put on a saddle, proper riding boots, and a helmet, and above all else, the horse needs to be very calm. You think to yourself, it has been almost thirty years since I have ridden a horse. Will I remember what to do? Am I going to look stupid trying to post or sit the trot? Am I going to remember how to ride the canter? That is huge for many women who return to riding after a long hiatus.

The good news is it all comes back like it was yesterday, but with a few parameters in place before we start to feel that comfort level again. After all, we are older and don't bounce as easily as we used to. The fun part is now we can take our time as we learn all over again, and often, the second time around is even better!

Today, my prayer is for the woman who wants to start riding again but is a little nervous. I pray that the right horse will come into her life and be a safe horse for her to grow and become all she can be as an equestrian. And remember, it might be like riding a bicycle all over again, but this time, you might be riding a cruiser instead of a racing bike, which is okay!

~March 21~
Last Wish

Be still and know that I am with you.
Psalm 46:10

She was young by medical standards to have such a rare cancer. She had also lived a very full life by human standards for someone in her forties. But here she was, back in the house she grew up in with her parents by her side. She had never married or had children and that was okay with her. She had spent the last two decades barrel racing, traveling from rodeo to rodeo, teaching at clinics, and spending time on the ranch with her horses. She had become quite the horsewoman and she felt it all slipping away, but she had a profound peace that some of her friends could not understand. She had given her life to Jesus Christ years earlier and it changed her from the inside out. She knew from that point on that she would take any opportunity to share His love and message of salvation, and what better place than the horse world.

Her parents knew she only had a short time left and she was now getting weaker by the moment. She clutched her bible and prayed silently. Then, she opened her eyes and asked her mother if she could see Rambo one more time. Her mother knew exactly what to do.

Soon, her mother was driving the horse back from the ranch and unloading him off the trailer. Her father carried her outside, laid her down on a cot and covered her with a blanket. The fresh air felt pleasing to her senses but what she felt next was like heaven. She could feel the breath of her horse as he looked down at her. Rambo gently lowered his head and came close to her. She was too weak to sit up but she slowly raised her hand and touched him. With one hand on her bible and the other touching her horse, she went to be with the Lord. Her last wish had come true.

~March 22~
When It's Time

*The Lord is close to the brokenhearted
and saves those who are crushed in spirit.
Psalm 34:18*

It is never easy to say goodbye to your equine partner. Over the last two decades, I have watched quite a few horses be euthanized for numerous reasons and very few were from old age. Some had severe injuries or colic, and I have witnessed two horses in recent years die of a heart attack. Those were especially tough on me because I never saw it coming. No matter the horse or his age, it is always heart-wrenching, and sometimes, it isn't easy to know when it is time to say goodbye because our emotions overcome us.

I have struggled with this as much as other people because we love our horses so much and hope and pray that if they had just one more day, they would turn a corner and recover. Unfortunately, most of us at one time or another have kept our horse alive a little too long, and we have come to regret it later on down the road when we see things much clearer. It is only natural to want to keep the animals you love the most near you for as long as you can.

Lord, today, I ask for discernment when dealing with a sick or injured horse. Guide me and help me make the right decisions regarding the care of these animals entrusted to me. I pray that I will be wise in making decisions regarding their quality of life. I know my heart will ache but I need to put their needs before my own personal feelings.

My prayer is that I will be strong for the horses in my care and always do what is best for them. In Jesus' Name, Amen.

~March 23~
Hay In My Lexus

Our mouths were filled with laughter,
our tongues with songs of joy.
Then it was said among the nations,
"The Lord has done great things for them."
Psalm 126:2

The one thing I love about running a horse boarding stable is meeting people from all walks of life. Some are business owners, doctors, and lawyers, while others are high school or college kids. You will have retired clients living their best lives with their horses and others just starting families but still making time to ride as much as possible. The one thing in common is that they all love being with their horses. The other thing that many have in common (and I absolutely love!) is that their once pristine vehicle is now used to haul horse tack, horse supplies, horse supplements, grain, and even hay. Even the nicest of vehicles have now become the barn car that often has the residue of manure from dirty boots on the floor mats and an assortment of horse goodies on the back seat.

The woman who is crazy about horses is just waiting for the first opportunity to own a horse. At that point, her car will have a new purpose and job. It is no longer a status symbol but, instead, a means to get her to the different tack shops (which could be an all-day trip!) and then straight to the barn. And if her husband is not careful she might soon be trading in that Lexus for a truck and trailer! Oh, what a wonderful life with horses!

May you believe with all your heart and soul that the Lord is writing a great story in your life. He knows the things you once valued have gone by the wayside for something that makes your heart swell with joy. He knows your passions and will move mountains at just the right time for you. Amen.

~March 24~
Barn Sour

For everything created by God is good, and
nothing is to be rejected if it received with thanksgiving.
For it is made by the holy word of God and prayer.
I Timothy 4:4-5

"He is barn-sour" was a phrase used to describe a horse that didn't want to leave the stable, and it was often used for the rental horses that the general public (often very green riders) would pay to ride. The horse would stop, plant all four feet, and not move unless motivated with a crop, and even then, he would drag his feet. But when it was time to return home to the stable, you would see the same horses trotting and even galloping fast and the novice riders were transformed into cowboys for a few short minutes.

That ride home made up for the other forty-five minutes of turtle speed and everyone had a smile on their face. Once in a while, we will have a horse at our barn that acts a little barn sour. It could be because the owner has brought a friend out to ride and her horse senses that this person doesn't know anything, or herd separation anxiety might be the cause. But sometimes, the horse is just being naughty. Learning to decipher which one it is takes experience and keen observation. The one thing for sure is that horses are always teaching us. If we want to grow as equestrians, we need to be observant of what our horse is doing and surround ourselves with other more knowledgeable people who can teach us.

Thank you, Lord, for the barn-sour horse. I know that even when I am frustrated, there are lessons to learn. Praise your name for loving me when I am being difficult and even a little "barn-sour" because I am dragging my feet and don't want to leave the comfort of my surroundings. Your love is always patient and you gently encourage me to put one foot in front of the other. Amen!

~March 25~
All It Takes Is...

There is no greater love than to lay down one's life for one's friends.
John 15:13

You really begin to see a horse's personality come out in full force when he is with his herd mates. The interaction between horses still gives me goosebumps all these years later.

We had a young and very small horse come to our barn years ago, and for some reason, I was having difficulty placing him in a herd. No matter where I put him, he was picked on to the point that I became fearful that he was going to be seriously injured. He wouldn't fight back and you could tell he was a nervous little guy. I placed him in a different herd of geldings (this was the third attempt) and watched to see what would happen. It didn't take long for some of the boys to start picking on him, and I was about to pull my hair out, wondering why this horse was having such a hard time fitting in. All he needed was one horse to buddy up with, and to this point, I had no success. Then suddenly, out of the blue, one of the older geldings started going after all the other horses that were picking on this little guy. He would spin around, double-barrow at them with both hooves flying, and charge at them with teeth aiming to bite deep! Then, he would run over to the little horse and stand in front of him with his body. It quickly became evident that he was protecting the little horse and wouldn't let anyone pick on him. As I watched all of this taking place, I felt like I was watching a miracle unfold before my eyes, and I began to tear up.

From that day forward, that little horse hung out with that older gelding and no other horses ever chased him again. All it takes is one horse to change an entire herd for the better. Praise God for the miracles we witness every day.

~March 26~
Taking Lessons

For He will command his angels concerning you,
to guard you in all your ways.
Psalm 91:11

Taking riding lessons is definitely the best thing you can do, especially during your "green years" of horse ownership. As a young girl, I quickly caught on during my lessons. I usually understood what the trainer was trying to teach me, and even if I was struggling with something new, it soon came around. I guess that is one of the blessings of youth.

Decades later, I decided that I wanted to learn how to ride English, which I had never done before. I was going to ride my daughter's horse which was trained in Hunt Seat and he was a pretty steady boy. I was super excited, and I remember those first few lessons very well because so much of what the trainer told me did not sink in! The verbiage was different, and even how I cued the horse made my mind dizzy. I found myself laughing out loud because I was a newbie all over again when riding in an English saddle and bridle. The trainer had to go slower and do a lot of visuals, and I thought to myself, things sure are different when you start talking lessons again after forty years!

We may grasp things quicker when we are young, but there is something special about learning to ride all over again when you are older. We are often more relaxed and we know how to laugh at ourselves a little easier. Today, I encourage you to take the lessons, learn something new every day and, above all else, enjoy the ride! It is a journey worth taking. God made you for this moment.

~March 27~
Babies

Work willingly at whatever you do, as though
you were working for the Lord rather than for people.
Colossians 3:23

Women love babies, and the babies with four legs are especially adorable. We have had many young horses here at our stable over the years and when they are only around four months old, it's hard not to be smitten. They are small, curious, and melt in your hands when you scratch them on the neck, withers, or butt. They also can be a handful! I give so much credit to the women who breed horses and do it well. They have the patience and calmness that a young horse needs. They understand that this little creature will quickly become a big horse with power, and the first year is critical in teaching him to mind his manners around humans. It is a big job, especially when the youngster has a mind of his own.

Over the years, I have come to learn that some women have a natural gift for breeding horses and all that it entails. It's like they have a sixth sense that can read what type of horse this baby will grow up to be in a very short time. They can tell if a colt will be fearless or timid, and if he will be at the top of his herd or the bottom as he grows up. These unique horsewomen can see fairly quickly if they have a baby that manages to get into trouble easily or stays clear of it (which means a lot when it comes to accidents and vet bills!).

Today, I want to give praise to the horsewomen who breed horses and have been there during the late nights and early mornings, easy births and heartbreaking ones. It is a labor of love like no other. The Lord has given you a passion that helps bring new life into this world. What a blessing you are among horsewomen.

~March 28~
Wing-Tipped Boots

God has given each of you a gift from his great variety of
spiritual gifts. Use them well to serve one another.
I Peter 4:10

I went to a school with many girls who wore the latest fashions in the 1970s, like maxi shirts, long dresses, and bell-bottom jeans with high heels. All I wanted to wear were my wing-tipped Justin cowboy boots. I wore them every moment I could with my Wrangler jeans. I often felt like I didn't fit in with my girlfriends, but they accepted me just how I was, even if I didn't dress like them. My style was my own and you could say that I was country when country wasn't cool.

It takes time for teenage girls to figure out who they are and find their passions. For me, it came easy. I was a country girl stuck in the city, trying to figure out how to get out of the city and into the country. Little did I know that God had already planned who I would marry, and a decade later, He answered my prayers.

I often see young girls trying to figure out who they are and being torn in several directions all at once. But the girls who love horses already have a sense of who God created them to be. You can see the hunger in their eyes, just like I had when I was their age. They don't know how it will happen but they are already planning on having horses for the rest of their lives. They are focused young equestrians who have a deep passion for this incredible animal, and it makes my heart happy to watch them grow.

Thank you, Lord, for the horse-crazy girls who live and breathe these wonderful animals. They are the next generation of equestrians who will change the world from the back of a horse.

111

~March 29~
A New Freedom

I can do all things through Christ who strengthens me.
Philippians 4:13

Buying a truck and horse trailer and hitting the open road is a freedom like no other. I love it when I see horsewomen packing up everything they need for horse camping because I see the excitement in their eyes. They are bubbling over with energy and enthusiasm and throwing around bales of hay like they are cotton candy. Soon, I see these women loading their horses, saying goodbye to their husbands, and driving off into the sunset. Their destinations might be different and their idea of hitting the open road might mean just driving an hour away, but either way, it is a freedom that makes them feel like they did as a teenager when they got their first car. For some women, driving their trailer to a horse show all by themselves is bold and courageous and the determination these women have is amazing. The feeling of not being dependent on anyone to get them and their horse from one place to another gives them strength to persevere as horsewomen. It's something that can't be explained but if you ask any woman who has her own truck and trailer, she will tell you that it is true.

Today, Lord, I ask for safety for all the women traveling with horses in small and large trailers to their destinations. They might be horse camping, moving to a new location, or going to a horse show. Keep them safe out on the road and fill them with peace and confidence as they pull the trailer with their precious cargo inside. Thank you for all the new things we are experiencing because of the horse. The learning never stops with these incredible animals and that is a wonderful blessing.

Also, Lord, I pray that one day I will learn to back up a trailer as well as my husband!

~March 30~
The Perfect Horse

God is my strong fortress, and he makes my way perfect.
II Samuel 22:33

King Henry VIII had a vision of the perfect horse and he did everything in his power to create a flawless equine for wartime. This horse needed to be huge and powerful and carry the heavy weight of the armor that would protect him and his Knights.

The cowboy also has his idea of the perfect horse. This horse needed to be agile, fast, and have the endurance to travel long distances and drive cattle. Size was less important, and the cowboy found that the smaller horse seemed to do better over rough terrain than the long, lanky horse. He also needed to be surefooted and dependable.

The racehorse breeder's idea of the perfect horse was long-legged, lean, and high-spirited with a powerful hind-end. He needed the speed of lightning and a strong heart that could push through the exhaustion to win the race, even when the odds were against him.

The mother's perfect horse is gentle and quiet, patient and willing. This horse will carry precious cargo several times a week and she wants to make sure her child is in good hands with this gentle equine. This mother is not looking for blue ribbons or excellent bloodlines, but instead, she is looking for a horse that will be perfect for her child to ride. In her daughter's eyes, this little horse will be her first love. She will pretend to fight the bad guys from the back of her horse and help move cattle across the plains, and she will always win the Triple Crown race on her horse. At the end of the day, she will go to bed with sweet dreams of riding through open fields with her best friend – her horse. It doesn't get any more perfect than that.

~March 31~
Everyone's A Critic

Do not grieve, for the joy of the Lord is your strength.
Nehemiah 8:10

How does a person get past the criticism and break away from the negativity when it comes to anything regarding horses? These are questions many new horse owners and equine professionals ask themselves after they have had enough from all the critics and haters out there.

When I was learning to ride my first horse as a young girl, I remember other kids teasing me because my horse (Rusty) was slow and they called him a "plug." Little did those kids know that Rusty taught me so much and kept me safe while I was learning to ride. Then, decades later, my husband and I decided to build a large boarding facility, and suddenly, I found myself on the receiving end of criticism for how our facility was being run. It brought back memories of when I was a young girl just trying to figure out everything, and I won't lie, it was very hard at times.

My saving grace was that during both those situations, decades apart, I had the Lord in my life and my confidence came from Him. When I started feeling insecure about what I was doing, I prayed and looked to Him for strength. All these years later, I still search the Lord out first before the anxiety sets in, and that is where I find my peace.

Today, Lord, I seek refuge in you. As I learn all that I can about horses and horsemanship, I pray that I will keep my eyes on you and not lose my confidence when I hear negative talk about my skill level. Please send positive mentors into my life so that I can learn more through truth and encouragement. Lord, you know I am trying my hardest and have a long way to go, but I know all things are possible with you by my side.

~April 1~
Second Time Around

And he gives grace generously. As the Scriptures say,
"God opposes the proud but gives grace to the humble."
James 4:6

You wake up and your heart is pounding because your forever horse is coming home today. Your palms start to sweat and you lose your appetite for breakfast, which is unheard of! You can only think about driving to the stable and watching the trailer pull up. Your mind flashes back to when you were young and you are flooded with memories of your first horse and all the fun you had. And then you stop and ask yourself, "How hard can it be to own a horse again?" You know you haven't ridden in a few decades except for the occasional invitation from friends to ride with them. Quickly, any negative thoughts get filed away.

Owning a horse the second time around for most women is a humbling experience. It was for me. I thought I knew a lot about horses because I owned them as a child, but the reality was that I would be learning all over again. This time I would be the one calling the vet if he was sick or injured, making the farrier appointments, running to the feed store to pick up grain and supplements, and I would be the one paying all the bills.

I appreciate everything associated with horse ownership so much more, probably because I understand the cost and sacrifice involved in caring for these extraordinary animals. I have to say that owning a horse after a long absence is much more rewarding and sweeter the second time around.

God bless the woman who is ready to own a horse for the second time in her life. She knows that the responsibility is all on her this time and she gladly embraces it. I pray her life is filled with horse kisses and wonderful horsewomen to share new adventures.

~April 2~
Barbed Wire To Blessing

From his abundance we have all received one gracious blessing after another.
John 1:16

I remember my friend's mother getting the call from her trainer that her horse, Molly, had been seriously injured in barbed wire. Back in the day, it was more common to see barbed wire for fencing than electric fencing. Molly was quickly trailered home to get all the care she needed. The deep fleshy cuts from the barbed wire had caused some severe wounds. When Molly got off the trailer, I remember feeling sick to my stomach as I looked at all the cuts on her body. It was as if someone had taken a knife and cut the horse up everywhere including her face. She slowly walked to her stall and the owner began a recovery regimen that would include gently cleaning her wounds twice daily.

Molly got a little better each day and she began to perk up as her wounds slowly healed. Over the months, everyone began to notice how fat she had become. She was normally a very athletic but she looked more like she needed to be put on a diet. Since she couldn't be ridden due to all the cuts that were still healing, Molly was turned outside in a paddock daily, hoping she would get some exercise.

Almost a year had passed and Molly had healed completely. It was indeed a miracle. Then, one morning, the owner went out to feed the horses and she saw something that stopped her dead in her tracts. Next to Molly stood a newborn colt! You could see he was only a few hours old but he was up and nursing. No one could believe what had happened, especially since the mare had been sent to a trainer for competition. She must have gotten loose, found a stallion and, in the process, got hung up in the barbed wire. What started as a terrible tragedy became the most wonderful blessing and miracle anyone could ask for.

~April 3~
After Three Years

Finally, be strong in the Lord and in his mighty power.
Ephesians 6:10

You never know when something is going to happen that will change you in ways you never thought possible.

Three years ago, I was walking a horse outside for the day and he ran into me and knocked me over. In the process, he stepped on my ribs. I knew instantly that I was seriously hurt and yelled to my husband to call 911. Hours later, I was recovering in a hospital bed after surgery. I had five broken ribs, four more that were fractured and a punctured lung. And, you know, I don't remember any of it.

Three years later, I still handle horses daily and do everything I did before, but the accident took me a long time to get over mentally. The hardest part of the whole thing was dealing with the fear of getting run over again. It was as if I was having flashbacks and they seemed to appear when I was walking horses. I became frustrated because I had always been very confident handling any horse on the property, but now I felt embarrassed and weak as a horsewoman because I struggled with some of the horses. After all, what kind of horsewoman was I if I couldn't handle all the horses in my care? After a long inner battle, I needed to give it to the Lord and pray for my mental recovery and, above all else, learn to be patient with myself. I kept hearing this voice say, "Take your time and go slow. It will come back when you are ready." This wonderful peace would flood my mind and I knew God was talking to me.

Today, I want to pray for the woman who is struggling after an accident with a horse. The struggle is real and the fear can overcome any of us. I pray that she will find the peace and comfort that only the Lord can give during trials like this.

~April 4~
Growing Up Together

Thanks be to God for his indescribable gift!
II Corinthians 9:15

Growing up with your horse is a gift that most children never experience. But if you were lucky enough to be one of those young buckaroos, then your memories will run deep when you look back years later.

I knew a woman years ago who was one of those lucky girls. Her parents had horses and they did a little breeding for fun. When she was young, one of the mares gave birth to a beautiful little colt but the birthing was very difficult and the mare died suddenly from complications. The colt was left without a momma and the little girl became the colt's best friend. They bottle-fed the colt and he grew big and strong. The deep bond between the little girl and the colt was undeniable and the parents knew they couldn't sell him. So they kept him and the little girl learned to do everything on the little horse. It was as if they were made for each other. They took care of each other and that horse trusted her more than anyone else.

That little girl grew up into a woman, got married, and had children of her own. Soon, her children were learning to ride the horse their momma had known all her life. They were growing older together and the woman saw signs that her favorite horse was slowing down. The thought of his last days would immediately bring her to tears but she knew that when it was time, she would never allow him to suffer.

Growing up and growing old with your horse is a gift like no other. You learn together, make mistakes together, and have beautiful successes together. The Lord gives us remarkable gifts and sometimes they come with four tiny hooves. Praise God for the gifts that come in small packages.

~April 5~
Changing Careers

Ask and it will be given to you; seek and you will find;
knock and the door will be opened to you.
Matthew 7:7

If you were born with the "horse gene" (yes, I made that up!), you probably started out at a very young age trying to figure out ways to make money with horses. I know I did. My dreams were much more elaborate when I was young, and I envisioned being a famous horse trainer or equestrian. Then, when I grew up and reality set in, I had to get a job that had nothing to do with horses. I am sure you can relate. The crazy thing is that it never left my mind. Years later, my husband and I opened our boarding stable. It is much less glamorous, but after two decades of boarding horses, I know I am where the Lord wants me to be.

It wasn't until I was forty-something that I changed careers and jumped in with both feet, and I found that to be true for many women. Often, what the Lord asks us to do is not on our radar until later in life. But when you hear His voice talking to you about His plans for you, it may shock you. It did for me at first, and it often wasn't easy in the beginning.

Now, years later, I am still boarding horses as a business but that is only a small part of it. It has opened doors to writing horse books and helping others in their horse businesses. These new careers are not glamorous, but they are a way to help others and share the love of Jesus Christ through my work.

If the Lord is calling you to try something new with horses you have never done, I encourage you to pray about it and see where it leads. The Lord opens doors, and if you are willing to walk through them, He will provide the promise of provision. Amen!

~April 6~
The Sick Horse

Do not withhold good from those to whom it is due,
when it is in your power to act.
Proverbs 3:27

My heart breaks when I see that a horse is not feeling well. Over the years, I have seen many different illnesses in horses and what I found so interesting is that they all handle the illnesses differently. Some horses are very stoic, and you might not even know they are sick except that they are unusually quiet. Some horses are much more dramatic no matter how small the issue is, and it would be safe to say that the geldings are bigger babies than the mares in many situations.

As women, we want to fix everything and make our horses feel better quickly. That is what we do. We take control, make a plan, and then execute it so our horses are as comfortable as possible. We will sleep in the barn if we need to just so we can be by our horse if he needs us.

I often look at how the Lord designed women and men, and we each have our strengths and weaknesses. When it comes to our horses, though, we become very emotional and protective and want to control every aspect, just like a mother would do with her child. We are on autopilot and don't slow down until we see that our horse has turned a corner for the better. It is never easy for us or our families when a horse is sick.

Dear Lord, please give me strength and discernment to make good decisions regarding my horse. It has become hard for me to think clearly and my emotions are getting the best of me. Please keep me strong and clear-headed. I will trust you, Lord, no matter the outcome, and know you are in control. In Jesus' Name, Amen.

~April 7~
Springtime

For behold, the winter is past, the rain is over and gone.
The flowers have already appeared in the land;
The time has arrived for pruning the vines,
and the voice of the turtledove has been heard in our land.
Song of Solomon 2:11-12

Everyone looks forward to springtime, especially after a long, cold winter. The horses are no different and you can see signs all around you that it's getting close. The horses start shedding their long shaggy winter hair and the mud is in full force (at least it is at my farm). The mares start getting squirrely next to the geldings, and of course, the geldings feel like they are youngsters again and look for every opportunity to play and roll in the mud. The sun becomes more robust and you can feel the warmth from its rays. Around midday, you will see many horses taking naps out in the paddocks while enjoying the long overdue warm temperatures. Before I know it, the barn swallows are back and as loud as ever as they begin their daily job of building nests in our barn for the arrival of their babies. Quickly, they grow big enough and huddle together on the edges of their nests just like little soldiers, as they wait for their next meal from their parents.

It is a rebirth of the land, and soon, the tractors will be out plowing the fields and planting seeds for another season. It is also a time for baby horses to be born. The veterinarians become increasingly busy with each new foal that arrives, and you can feel the excitement in the air everywhere.

With its vibrant renewal, springtime always reminds me of the Lord and his perfect creation, which I see all around me. For everything, there is a season and a time for every matter under heaven. Thank you, Lord, for springtime and all its wonder.

~April 8~
That Beautiful Sound

Splendor and majesty are before Him,
Strength and beauty are in His sanctuary.
Psalm 96:6

If you ask any woman who loves horses, they will all tell you the same thing...they love watching and listening to horses munch on their hay. They admire how each horse puts his nose down deep in a pile of alfalfa and moves it all around to find the sweet crunchy leaves on the bottom. Feeding our horses makes us feel like we are an essential part of their life. We buy the best hay possible and inspect it as if we were feeding our own children. We spend time studying the different types of forage to ensure it is top quality and then we watch our horse eat it with pride because we know we are taking good care of our equine partner. When the evening comes and the barn is quiet, we softly open our horse's stall and check on him one more time like we would have done with our own children when they were sleeping.

It's a crazy kind of love we have for this animal that you won't find with any other creature on earth. I believe one of the reasons we love to watch our horses eat is because we understand and respect the hard work they have done for humans for as long as they have been domesticated. The horse gives his entire heart with ease to those who treat him kindly, and as long as we have the ability to take care of him, we feel a sense of duty to ensure he has the best hay possible to keep him healthy and happy.

At the end of the day, the sound of a horse munching on hay is about so much more than just eating food. It is about the relationship and the give-and-take these animals have with their owners. It's pretty extraordinary, to say the least, and that beautiful sound is music to our ears.

~April 9~
Curious Creatures

And hope does not put us to shame, because God's love has been poured into our hearts through the Holy Spirit who has been given to us.
Romans 5:5

Horses are curious creatures almost to a fault. They get themselves into situations that they sometimes can't get out of. I was on social media scrolling through the horse groups one day and a woman posted a picture of a horse that had gotten himself stuck inside a metal round bale feeder and could not get out. When I first saw the picture, I laughed for a second and then realized how challenging it would be to get the horse out safely. Metal bale feeders are heavy, and this one was full of hay, so the horse was wedged between the feeder and hay! Thank goodness the horse looked calm in the picture.

As I began reading a few of the comments, some very opinionated people were giving this poor woman a hard time. I started to feel bad for her because this could happen to any of us. It may not involve a metal round feeder but it could be hundreds of other crazy things that horses seem to get themselves into, and sometimes we have no control over it. Horses are such curious creatures and it doesn't matter how safe you make your stable; they have a way of defying the odds and getting themselves in trouble. They are always thinking, and even though some of their choices are not the best, we will always love them.

I will forever think about that post on social media. My heart hurt for that woman and I will never know how the story ended with the horse, but I pray that I will always be an encourager and try to lift people up as much as possible. And if I am called to help someone by telling them the truth, Lord, please show me how to be gentle and kind with my words.

~April 10~
Jeans

May the Lord smile on you and be gracious to you.
Numbers 6:25

I am glad the days of tight jeans are long behind me. It was the 1980s, and we wore our jeans tight. It didn't matter if you couldn't breathe as long as you looked good in them and could get on the horse. I will admit I was pretty vain and self-absorbed back then, as I think many twenty-something young adults are, and I wanted to make sure I looked good at any cost. Can you guess where this is going? So I put on my favorite jeans, boots, and tank top (this was Southern California, and it was a hot day) and drove to my friend's place to ride one of her horses. I was so excited and thinking to myself that I looked pretty good. I knew my jeans were tight, but really, what could go wrong?

When I got to the stable, I found my friend and we brushed and saddled up the horses. During that time, I began to feel very uncomfortable because my jeans were so tight and it was hard to walk in them! Anyways, we put the bridles on and were ready to mount the horses. As I put my leg up in the stirrup and pulled myself up, I felt a weird sensation right down the center of my crotch to my leg. My pants had split wide open! And what made it worse was that my friend's trainer was there when it happened. I was mortified! I decided not to say anything and off we went riding.

It was the worst ride of my life because all I could think about was how I was going to get from the horse to my car without anyone noticing the massive split in my pants. It was indeed a humbling experience, and all these years later, I laugh when I think about that day. The moral of the story is that beauty doesn't come from tight jeans but from a pure heart. Thank you, Lord, for the lessons you teach me daily.

~April 11~
A Little Wisdom

And after you have suffered a little while, the God of all grace,
who has called you to his eternal glory in Christ, will himself
restore, confirm, strengthen, and establish you.
I Peter 5:10

The truth is wisdom does not come from having an easy life, and it doesn't come from having an easy horse, either. I believe we learn the most through experiences that force us to think and make choices, and those choices have consequences, whether they are good or bad. The same is true with horses. The easy horses teach us some great things about horsemanship, but the challenging horses force us to get to the root of the problem and correct it. Having a push-button horse is fantastic, but you will learn only so much. The rider with a challenging horse will learn to ride with a better seat and balance and have to reach deep inside to find out how to connect with her horse. Having a horse like this is much more frustrating, but if you can connect with that horse, the bond will become unbreakable and your skill level and knowledge will go through the roof.

The next time you ride a difficult horse, thank the Lord for giving you a horse that will force you to do some soul-searching and see what you are made of. There is so much to glean from those challenging days with horses that make you work for it. Then, thank your horse and end the ride on a good note. For one day, the wisdom you gained from your youth will be passed on to the next generation. The Lord teaches us so much through the horse and what an honor to be able to help the young equestrians who will be the movers and shakers of the horse world in just a few short years.

~April 12~
Horsewomen By Grace

My grace is sufficient for thee,
for my strength is made perfect in weakness.
II Corinthians 12:9

There is an extraordinary feeling you get when you realize that the Creator of the Universe also designed each breed, color, and personality of every equine that has ever been born. Even more remarkable is that these amazing animals will bond with their human as long as we are willing to show them the respect and love they deserve. For horse-crazy women, it is what we have always longed for when searching for a horse to call our very own. The horse forgives our shortcomings and mistakes and shows us grace every time. It doesn't mean they forget situations we may have put them in but they are willing to trust us never to make the same mistake twice.

I sometimes ponder what God was thinking when He created the horse. After all, He is omniscient, "The state of having total knowledge, the quality of knowing everything." So, what horses have endured over the centuries has come with no surprise to God. But then I realized that God already knew the blundering mistakes I would make with my horses, and He created an animal that would set aside the stupidity and wait patiently for me to mature in my horsemanship. When I look at it with that understanding, it leaves me speechless and in awe of the horse that God made.

The horse teaches us so much, but grace is one of the top things we can learn from these brilliant animals. My prayer is that I will learn to have as much grace as my horse has shown me, and I will never stop learning to forgive, just as I need forgiveness every single day. The Lord gave us a wonderful gift when He created the horse, and we are indeed horsewomen by grace. Praise God!

~April 13~
Falling Off

Her ways are ways of pleasantness, and all her paths are peace.
Proverbs 3:17

I remember growing up and hearing someone say, "You aren't a real cowgirl unless you have fallen off your horse at least once." Well, I must be as real as they come because I have fallen off too many times to count! It's an unfortunate rite of passage that almost all equestrians have had to go through. The good news is if you fall off when you are young, you bounce back much faster than in your fifties or sixties. In fact, as a kid, falling off was just part of the fun and then you hopped back on and kept riding. It's the beauty of youth.

As we add years to our life we become more cautious with everything. We know our old bones and everything else in our body need extra care and doesn't need to be banged up. Yet we keep riding and loving every bit of it, but we also have a new respect for the sport we didn't have when we were young. We are on the other side of youth and self-perseverance takes over and keeps our head screwed on straight.

As women, the best thing we can do is encourage each other, share our experiences, and be there for one another when someone hits the ground. We are all in this together, each at our own pace, learning to be the best equestrians we can be. That is what is so special about horses and horsewomen. We are there to help wipe the dust off and lend a hand up, to hug and laugh with each other, and to support and bring meals to our home if we get hurt. Falling off may be a rite of passage for the new equestrian, but sharing good and not-so-good horse experiences is what makes a true cowgirl. Thank you, Lord, for the wonderful horsewomen you have sent into our lives.

~April 14~
Crooked Fence Posts

And let endurance have its perfect work,
so that you may be perfect and complete, lacking in nothing.
James 1:4

When I was a little girl, I would ride the bus with my grandmother from Los Angeles to Sacramento to visit relatives. I remember seeing open fields with lots of horses and cattle and crooked fence posts everywhere. Since I was a city girl, I never understood why all the fence posts were crooked and wondered why anyone would do such a sloppy job.

When my husband first put up our fencing, the wooden posts looked straight and beautiful and we were so proud of how nice everything looked. It wasn't until we went through our first winter that my eyes were opened to why so many fence posts are crooked on farms and ranches. The harsh weather, constant thawing and freezing, waterlogged mud, and electric fencing pulling tight in one direction eventually wears down the strongest posts. And over time, they begin to move. Over the last twenty years, our fence posts have warped and bowed, and now, they all lean in one direction. They are no longer straight but I have a whole new understanding of how much these posts have endured throughout the seasons.

In some strange way, I now admire the crooked fence posts on our horse farm. They are a symbol of many years of housing horses and wonderful memories. They symbolize all the hard work we have done to keep our business afloat throughout the harshest of winters and the hottest of summers. I now have a newfound respect for the farmers and ranchers who have worked a lifetime to grow food for our tables and raise horses for our enjoyment. Each crooked fence post reminds me now of a life well spent taking care of the animals God has entrusted to us.

~April 15~
Sizing Us Up

Examine me, Lord, and put me to the test;
Refine my mind and my heart.
Psalm 26:2

Dogs love us no matter what. They see us coming through the front door and start wagging their tail, spinning in circles, and acting like they haven't seen us in a month. Their excitement makes our hearts melt and they don't question why we were gone all day. Horses, on the other hand, are a whole other beast. They are flight animals, which means they are always prepared to take off if danger is near, which can be hard for us to understand when we are the ones approaching.

As women, we drive up to the barn and are excited to see our horse. We quickly grab our halter and head out to the pasture to find our true love. As we spot him out in the pasture, he looks at us with his ears forward and stands like a statue. He doesn't move. He doesn't wag his tail or spin in circles, but instead, he looks cool, calm, and collected and watches us closely as we approach him. He is sizing us up as he has done every day since we have owned him.

It can be hard to keep our emotions in check and not take it personally if our horse isn't jumping in circles to see us. That is how God designed them, and once we learn this, it will open our world to how their mind works. The good news is if your horse slowly starts to walk towards you and lets you put the halter on him, he is telling you he trusts you and that you can lead him anywhere. What an awesome thing to experience from a thousand-pound animal. And that is his way of telling you he is happy to see you.

Dear Lord, help me to gain the trust of the horses in my life. Teach me gentleness and patience and to be mindful of how you created these beautiful animals. Amen

129

~April 16~
Stop The Pressure

Cast all your worries and cares to God,
for he cares about you.
I Peter 5:7

As women, we can put a lot of pressure on ourselves with everything. We want our homes to be perfect, and, of course, our children must never misbehave. We know in our heart that it is impossible to be flawless and we can't control some of the things our children do or say, but we often blame ourselves when things are less than stellar.

When it comes to our horses, we often put crazy amounts of pressure on ourselves and them. We have high expectations for how our horse should behave every single day, and we are easily embarrassed when our horse acts up in front of others. We stress ourselves out because our skill level is not where we think it should be and we start to feel like we are falling behind compared to other riders. Sometimes, we entertain the idea that we need to be trending with the latest riding clothes, saddles, or trailers to fit in. The reality is that none of it matters, and once we learn it's not a competition or race, we will start to enjoy riding and horsemanship like never before. The freedom it brings is immeasurable. Not only will we be happier but our horse will probably notice a difference as well and relax more.

I pray for the woman who has put mounds of pressure on herself. May she refuse to be diminished by her insecurities and instead embrace the perfection God created in her. I pray that she learns to enjoy the ride even when the trail seems steep and rocky, and she searches for peace from the Lord above. There she will find it.

~April 17~
The Newborn

You are the God of great wonders!
You demonstrate your awesome power among the nations.
Psalm 77:14

The little girl looked in amazement at the foal's soft hooves. Her grandmother told her that he still had his "foal slippers" on but they would disappear soon, and it was God's way of protecting the mother while the foal went through the birth canal. Within the hour the baby horse was standing and taking his first steps with his mother watching very closely. The little girl asked her grandma, "How long did it take for me to walk?" The grandmother looked down at the sweet child and told her that she didn't start walking for almost a year. Then the child asked, "Then why does the baby horse walk so soon?" The grandma looked at her and told her that God created the horse to stand on his own feet and walk very quickly so he could run from danger. This was God's way of protecting the young foal. Soon, the foal was taking his first steps and without anyone showing him how to nurse, he latched on and ate for the first time. The child looked up at her grandmother again and quietly wondered how the baby knew where his food came from. The grandmother could see the question floating around in her grandchild's head. She gently told her that when God created this little foal, He gave him the ability to know how to find his food. Then she told her that she had just witnessed God's most perfect and amazing miracle and that we were entrusted to care for these animals the best way we knew how.

That evening, the grandma tucked her beloved grandchild into bed and said goodnight. The little girl never forgot that special day, and when she grew up, she became an equine vet whose mission was to love and care for God's horses as best she could.

~April 18~
Someone Else's Prayer

He answered their prayers because they trusted in Him.
I Chronicles 5:20

I walked into our barn one evening and one of our boarders was letting a friend brush her horse. The woman was softly brushing the mare and you could see the joy illuminating her face as she took each stroke across the horse's neck. A few days later, I asked the boarder who the lady was, and she told me it was a friend she hadn't seen in a long time. They had reconnected and she invited her out to see her horse. The woman was going through a difficult time and her horse seemed like the best medicine.

I have had the privilege of watching similar scenarios play out at our barn or a horse show over the years and it never gets old. In fact, it has been such an encouragement to me and a reminder that if we open our hearts and share what the Lord has graciously given us, we will find ourselves feeling the same incredible joy as the person on the receiving end. I also need to remember that I was just like that woman when I was a little girl, just waiting for someone to let me touch their horse. I had that same yearning and I would stand by the fence praying that a horse would walk over to me and grab the bits of grass in my outstretched hands.

Answered prayers come in many different ways, and sometimes, they are disguised with four long legs, a long flowing mane and tail, and a very soft muzzle. Someone long ago knew that I loved horses and answered my prayer. I pray that I will always be open to God's calling with horses. And remember, it might seem like a small gesture at the time, but to another person, it's an answered prayer.

~April 19~
So Blessed

Give thanks to the Lord, for he is good!
His faithful love endures forever.
Psalm 107:1

Today, as I sat down to have a cup of coffee after lunch, the rain started to come down, and it was a cold rain. I was hoping it would be short-lived, but as I looked at the radar, I saw it only intensifying. I felt instantly irritated as I knew I was going to have to start bringing horses in and I would be soaked when it was all done. I reluctantly walked downstairs, put on my muck boots and rain coat, and headed outside with a grumpy look plastered all over my face. As I walked into the barn a handful of ladies were laughing and having a great time, and suddenly, I was feeling sorry for myself. I should have told myself to grow up, but instead, I walked by, hardly making eye contact, and grabbed a halter. I couldn't even muster up a smile to be polite. The women all got quiet and I was instantly embarrassed of how I was acting, but I couldn't control myself and wallowed a little more. Then, as I went outside to bring the first soaked horse into the barn, I looked across and saw two more women helping me bring horses in. As I watched them brave the wind and rain I started to realize how blessed I am to have such wonderful women at our stable. Horse by horse, they walked each horse in, and before I knew it, all twenty-seven horses were back in their cozy stalls.

I thanked the ladies for their help and apologized for my grumpiness, and soon, they had me laughing. That is when I silently said a prayer to God and thanked Him for sending me such wonderful horsewomen who aren't afraid to get wet, have frizzy hair, and help a fellow horsewoman in need.

~April 20~
Ever Changing

Jesus Christ is the same yesterday, today, and forever.
Hebrews 13:8

I never realized how much the earth below my feet would play a part in the daily chores and how unbelievably difficult it could be during the springtime. As the frost comes out of the ground and the days switch from snow to rain and then back again quickly, the paddocks are either muddy or rock hard with deep divots created by the heaviness of the horses feet. Sometimes, the ground is so hard and rough that it can easily cause you to fall if you are not careful. Walking the horses outside for the day in these conditions is difficult for them and their handlers. They lower their heads as they walk and watch where each foot falls as they follow me. The one silver lining during this time of year is the ground may be frozen in the morning, but it quickly softens as the temps rise above freezing by mid-morning. That is when the mud arrives and the horses slop around, roll in it, and are relieved to have soft footing.

Even after all these years, I still look down at the path when walking the horses into the paddocks and it amazes me how different it looks every day. The hoof prints from the evening before are now cemented into the frozen dirt, but by the afternoon, they are gone. It always reminds me of how things never stay the same in life. We try to stay one step ahead of it but it often catches us off guard.

I pray for all the women caring for horses in places where the temperatures fluctuate like the wind. It makes things challenging and exhausting. I pray that they will stay encouraged and strong. And when they feel beaten down from the weather and footing, I ask that they be comforted by you, Lord Jesus.

When I'm Weary

He gives power to the faint, and to him
who has no might he increases strength.
Isaiah 40:29

Owning and managing a boarding stable has taught me so much about horses and life. I never thought it could be as challenging as it was when we first opened, but it was, and the horses were the easiest part. I didn't realize how much work it would be day after day until it became my life. And I never knew how weary I would feel at times until I experienced it. But by God's grace, I got through the hard years and managed to keep it all together, both mentally and physically.

I want to encourage the horsewoman who is feeling tired and defeated. Your situation might look different than that of the barn owner or manager. You might own just one horse, but that horse is your whole life, and you know he depends on you. But even with one horse, it can be stressful when he has gotten injured and the road to recovery is long.

Today, Lord, I ask for strength and perseverance for the woman caring for a severely injured horse. She goes out very early to treat the injury and then she heads to work, only to come back late in the evening to take care of the wound again. She does this religiously day in and day out for what feels like eternity. Tears flow because she is exhausted and it takes all she has to get up and do it all over again. Please comfort the horsewomen who have chosen a life with horses when the dreams envisioned come crashing down.

Whatever the day holds for you, remember that God is bigger than anything that you are facing at home or with your horse. When you are too weak to walk, He will carry you through. That is His promise.

~April 22~
Tune Out The Noise

The heart of the discerning acquires knowledge,
for the ears of the wise seek it out.
Proverbs 18:15

If you search the internet, you will find every opinion out there and sizing it up can be difficult, especially for the new horse owner. There are many opinions about horses and it can quickly become overwhelming.

When my daughter was twelve, it was time to buy her a bigger horse. We searched, and finally, after looking at many horses, we came upon a ten-year-old Paint gelding that had never been broke! He was beautiful and sweet but had never had anyone on his back. The one saving grace was that his ground manners and demeanor were perfect. So what did we do? We bought him. The next six months were spent with a trainer who taught him both English and Western, and I could see that he had a great mind. It didn't matter that he had never been ridden. What mattered was that he had been worked with all those years on the ground, which quickly transferred into the saddle.

I want to gently encourage you to use discernment when listening to all the noise out there regarding horses and riding. While young horses need to be busy and a job is good for their minds, there are so many valuable things you can do on the ground that keep their young minds learning. It's okay not to ride because the groundwork lays a solid foundation for when you are ready.

Dear Lord, help me to tune the noise out and acquire wisdom and discernment when it comes to my horse and his individual needs. Guide me in my decisions regarding his well-being. And when I become frustrated because of all the noise around me, I will get on my knees and listen to your calming words. Amen.

~April 23~
Bicycling To Shows

He will restore the hearts of the fathers to their children
and the hearts of the children to their fathers.
Malachi 4:6

One of the sweetest memories I have of my father is when he would ride his bicycle to my horse shows when I was a teenager. Of course, back then, I was mortified because he would ride in on his bike with his black spandex bicycle shorts (that showed too much!), his Donald Duck t-shirt, and a bike helmet with a rear-view mirror attached. This was the 1970s before bicycle gear was trendy and my dad definitely had his own unique style. He loved me so much and just wanted to watch me show my horse, and at times, I was a snot to him (which I regret now!).

Years later, the entire picture of my father and his rides to my horse shows all came together. You see, my father was a recovering alcoholic, and when he quit drinking, he started riding bikes for something positive to do. Soon, he was riding all over the place, and whenever I had a show, he would be there with his bike. Looking back, it now brings tears to my eyes when I think about him and all he overcame and later went on to achieve. He knew horses were a huge part of my life and wanted to be included in it. I rode horses, he rode bicycles, and memories were made that I wouldn't fully appreciate for many decades.

Not everyone in your family will love horses as much as you, and that is okay. What is more important are the memories made when two different worlds come together. That is where you find the best of times. That is what family is all about. Enjoy each moment, and if you see your father riding his bike to your horse show, hop off your horse and give him a hug. It will make his day!

~April 24~
Don't Compromise

So whoever knows the right thing to do
and fails to do it, for him it is sin.
James 4:17

History has proven over and over that if you compromise what is most important to you, in the end, you most likely will lose it all. Many equestrians, both young and old, have had to learn this truth sometimes the hard way, either by being selfish and pushing a horse too hard to where he collapses (which was commonplace throughout history) or by trying to achieve a certain behavior through harsh tools and aides whereas you mentally lose him forever.

The good news is that if we study the history and past practices used on horses, we can learn and do things differently so we don't break their spirit or compromise their life. As horsewomen, we have an incredible opportunity to improve the horse's life by learning as much as we can and putting it to good use. We can nurture while training, provide comfort and safety while housing and caring for the horse, and grow his confidence with praise when he understands what you are asking him to do. If we compromise on any of those things, we take a huge chance of not gaining the whole horse but, instead, only part of the horse, because he will not have given us his entire self.

Lord, teach me today to be my horse's steadfast in the saddle and out of the saddle. Help me gain his trust and not put him in unsafe situations. When I get the urge to cut corners, please wake me up before I make mistakes that will take us both backward and threaten his trust in me. Please help me to be wise in all I do with him daily. Thank you, Lord, for the incredible gift you have given me.

~April 25~
Complete

I wait for the Lord, my soul waits, and in his word I hope.
Psalm 130:5

When I hit my mid-fifties, suddenly, I found myself in unfamiliar territory. I wanted to be around horses, but my desire to ride was less strong than when I was younger. I couldn't figure out why since I loved being around them so much. I was content taking care of them daily and handling all the chores, and that became enough for me. I felt whole as a horsewoman and didn't need to be in the saddle to consider myself complete. After all, I wasn't around horses for anyone else but myself, and my love for them was pretty evident to the people that knew me. I also realized that, as women, we are not alone if we start to lose the desire to ride as we age. I have watched a few women over the years struggle with this and feel like they should be riding with everyone else and they put added pressure on themselves.

As women, we can be good at making excuses for why we can't ride. I have been there myself also! We try to talk ourselves into it but then look outside and tell ourselves it is too hot or cold, or too windy or rainy for our horse. We are good at finding reasons for something we don't want to do, but the truth is, it is okay not to ride and still be every bit of a horsewoman. The horse world is big and there are so many wonderful opportunities without ever putting a leg in the stirrup.

My prayer is that you find your passion with horses no matter the time in your life and that you feel every bit a horsewoman out of the saddle as you did when you rode earlier in life. Your validation doesn't come from the miles you ride each week or the horse shows you compete in. It comes from the Lord who wants the best for you always.

~April 26~
Losing Sight

But test everything; hold fast what is good.
I Thessalonians 5:21

Nothing can compare to the thrill of winning blue ribbons and making it to the top of your equestrian aspirations. But what about when we lose sight of what matters the most? What happens if we lose our way and forget about the animal we are entrusted to care for? What if our drive to win ends up causing stress or, worse, hurting our horse? It sometimes happens because we let our emotions, peer pressure, or other outside sources take us off the path we need to be on. Then the horse suffers.

I have watched new equestrians reach for the stars, but sometimes, as they work towards their goals and ambitions, the lines get blurry on how far to push their horse. Having the drive to accomplish great things in the horse world is an admirable trait, but it is so important to find a balance and not let the horse, your family, or your friendships suffer. Having success or fame on any level in the horse world is wonderful as long as those you love (both humans and horses) are there to enjoy it with you and you know in your heart that you did it the right way. You never lost sight of what is truly important for your horse's wellbeing.

Lord, please be there for the woman working hard to achieve her dreams and goals with her horse. I pray she will find time to rest, rejuvenate, and surround herself with wise people who will guide her along the way. I pray she never loses sight of what is truly important and keeps her focus on you, Lord. May she feel your love every step of the way. In Jesus' Name, Amen.

~April 27~
Outside The Arena

God's way is perfect. All the Lord's promises prove true.
He is a shield for all who look to him for protection.
II Samuel 22:31

For many women, riding outside a fenced arena can be scary. There is something about the absence of fencing that can make us feel vulnerable, especially if we are learning to ride. But for many women, it is absolutely liberating, and it gives them the feeling that they can go anywhere. Some were taught young to ride out in an open field on a feisty pony and never looked back. Others learned in an arena where even the naughtiest horses couldn't go too far. I grew up learning to ride in fields that hadn't been paved or built on yet and on city streets. It was not the ideal learning environment but that was all we had. Fear was not part of my vocabulary as a young girl, but as I got older, I began to feel much more comfortable in a riding arena with fencing, and when I had children, they learned to ride in an arena.

It doesn't matter where you ride your horse - just ride. Learn and grow, and as you gain confidence, you might decide to open the gate and head out to the fields one day. And if you don't, please don't be hard on yourself. You need to do what is best for you, and it is fantastic that you are riding!

Sometimes, the Lord asks us to do things out of our comfort zone, and it can be scary, just like riding outside the arena. But those are the times that we often grow the most. He doesn't push us. He waits until He knows we can handle it and gently nudges us forward. If the Lord is nudging you to do something you feel nervous about, pray and ask Him to guide you. He won't open the gate until you are ready to go beyond the fencing. That is His promise.

~April 28~
Ordinary Days

Jesus said to them, "I am the bread of life; whoever comes to me shall not hunger, and whoever believes in me shall never thirst.
John 6:35

Many young people feel like they are missing out if they are not experiencing their world through the latest and greatest technology. They want the newest cell phones and tech games, and movies must have the latest cutting-edge effects to keep their attention. I understand that because when I was young, we were excited about cassette tapes coming out after using eight-track tapes for years. That was our version of cutting-edge!

There is a simplistic beauty when it comes to taking care of horses and living on a farm. Things don't change much with the improvement of technology but if I am to be honest, I would love a faster way to clean stalls each morning or fill the water buckets each evening. But the horses still get fed the same way every morning and night and for them it is good that things are kept simple and pure. There is something extraordinary about walking out the door each morning to do chores while the world still sleeps. The stillness surrounds me as the animals are waking up, and the sun slowly rising in all its brilliance can never be improved upon. Suddenly, you find yourself wanting things to stay the same and you see the magic of ordinary days.

The horse will teach the young equestrian that you cannot speed things up or look for the newest gadgets to improve your horse's willingness, attitude, or performance. It is simply the organic relationship between you and your horse. It is nothing fancy, but instead, very ordinary and that is when the magic happens.

Thank you, Lord, for the gift of ordinary days. They keep us grounded and open our eyes to what is really important in life.

The Mare

Shepherd the flock of God that is among you, exercising oversight,
not under compulsion, but willingly, as God would have you;
not for shameful gain, but eagerly; not domineering over those in your charge,
but being examples to the flock.
I Peter 5:2-3

Mares have a reputation for being moodier than geldings, but mares have also had some very important jobs throughout history. Who knows, maybe their moodiness played a small part.

Before the days of gas-powered tractors, many farmers preferred mares for pulling equipment and working in the fields. The mares tended to be harder workers and didn't fool around. They had a job to do and they did it. Some female horses were called "Bell mares" and were very important to the trappers and cowboys who journeyed across the country with pack mules. The bell mare wore a large bell around her neck, and the mules would follow her and the sound of the bell. She was their herd leader and they went where she went. This kept the rider from having to hold numerous ropes for all the mules that were carrying supplies. Bell mares were also used for leading strings of pack mules to their destinations during World War I.

The nice thing about mares is that they tend to keep out of trouble. They are not players like the geldings, which means there are fewer injuries. They tend to keep their blankets cleaner and you rarely find a torn blanket on a mare! They know how to take care of their stuff, unlike the geldings. Mares have a lot of heart and sometimes get a bad rap, but if you find a sweet mare, don't pass her by without looking closer. You might have just found your dream horse. A mare can be very loyal when shown kindness and love, and she will give you her all.

~April 30~
Can't Ride Papers

For by grace you have been saved through faith. And this is not your own doing;
it is the gift of God, not a result of works, so that no one may boast.
Ephesians 2:8-9

I understand the importance of good bloodlines for certain equestrian sports and breeding, but I have always been one to root for the underdog.

When I wrote my historical non-fiction book, *On The Sixth Day God Created The Horse,* I was completely blown away by all the true stories about horses I came across. These horses didn't have registration papers or win huge races or competitions. But what they did was even more impressive. They carried their riders through war-drenched landscapes with bombs going off all around them, and they carried injured soldiers along miles of treacherous surroundings while keeping quiet and surefooted. The horse has walked quietly behind the casket as if he understood the importance of his job at that moment, while carrying the boots of the soldier who died in battle. They have raced through congested city streets pulling the fire wagons so that the firemen could get to the fire and do their job before it was too late. There have been great horses that have carried little girls on their backs for weekly riding lessons without hesitation. They have kept steady underneath little bodies that lean from side to side with legs flaring about and high-pitched squeals that could pierce an eardrum.

You can't ride papers, and in fact, many of the greatest horses throughout history never had registration papers. But they had heart. The Lord has always told us not to be impressed by fame or fancy things of this world but instead to look inside a man (or horse—my words) to see what he is made of. There, you will find your champion.

~May 1~
Hay In My Bra!

The Spirit of God has made me,
and the breath of the Almighty gives me life.
Job 33:4

Well, ladies, you can't write a horse-themed daily devotional without a bit of wisdom regarding hay in your bra. After all, if you are around horses long enough, I can guarantee there will come a time when you take off your bra and suddenly little stems and leaves from alfalfa float to the floor. You knew it was in your bra when you fed the horses because you could feel it and it was driving you nuts! But you had more important things to tend to with your horse. It is all part of being a woman and having horses.

I started thinking about my life and the things that annoy me that are much deeper problems than hay in my bra. As I have gotten older, I am much more patient than even a decade ago, but I sometimes still let the smallest of things drive me nuts in my personal life and business.

Horsewomen are incredible ladies who love horses and are not afraid of hard work, but we also know we can be emotional and overreact at times. We know we are not perfect and when something is not right we shove it deep down inside and wait until we are at home to let the tears flow.

Dear Lord, please guide the woman who feels her life is like having hay in her bra. She wants to eliminate the irritation but is too busy and puts it off. She might look fine on the outside but she is having a hard time on the inside. I pray that she will realize how much she is loved by those who know her and that she is beautiful and wonderfully made in the image of God. And every time she finds a sliver of hay in her bra, I pray she will be gloriously reminded of a well-lived life.

~May 2~
The Original Cowgirl

Great are the works of the Lord, studied by all who delight in them.
Psalm 111:2

At fourteen years old, she was performing tricks on the back of a horse, swinging a lasso while galloping in front of an audience, and beating the men in rodeo competitions. In fact, in 1900, at a Rough Riders Reunion, she performed in front of President Roosevelt and he told her that she could handle a horse better than many of his troops. Her name is Lucille Mulhall and she was known as the original cowgirl.

Lucille introduced her audiences to the idea that women could rope and ride and still be a lady. She wore a long split dress while riding and always felt more comfortable in the saddle than anywhere else. She was constantly learning new tricks to do with her horses, and during one performance, she roped eight horses at one time. Her favorite trick horse, Governor, could play dead, ring a bell, kneel, and sit back while crossing his forelegs.

Tragically, Lucille died way too young in an auto accident. The day of the funeral was cold and rainy and the roads were covered in slippery mud. Cars were utterly useless, so a friend's plow horse pulled the hearse that her body lay in. It was said, "A machine killed Lucille Mulhall, but horses brought her to her final resting place." Sometimes, we forget the incredible women who blazed the trail before us so that we have the freedom to choose what we want to do with horses without restrictions. These women were pioneers and faced many obstacles, but they never quit.

God bless the women who cleared the path for the young female equestrians of today. They are truly inspirations to every horse-lover, and today I pray they will never be forgotten. What a strength the Lord infused in these cowgirls of the past.

~May 3~
That First Step

For as high as the heavens are above the earth, so great is
his steadfast love toward those who fear him.
Psalm 103:11

Today, the house became empty as your last child moved out, and you wondered what you were going to do with all your free time. You spent the last year looking at horses on the internet and fell asleep at night reading everything about horse ownership. Now, it was time to take the first step that would change your life forever. You thought to yourself, "Am I crazy for wanting a horse at my age?" You even wondered if you were being responsible. You visited a few local boarding stables, talked with barn managers, and took tours. It was overwhelming, but you kept putting one foot in front of another until you met some nice women who made you laugh and introduced you to their horses. You knew right then that you had found the place where you wanted to board your horse once you found him.

You put your name on the waiting list and started seriously looking at horses. Mile after mile, you kept searching for the horse of your dreams until one particular day you came upon a small farm. As you drove up, you saw this beautiful little horse and goosebumps started running through your body. You hoped it was the horse you came to look at. Sure enough, it was, and after you led him around, brushed him and picked his feet, a saddle was put on his back and you rode him all over the farm. That same day you fell in love, and he became yours.

From that day forward you never looked back, and the best was yet to come. That first step will take you a thousand miles. Thank you, Lord, for the chance to own a horse and live out my lifelong dream. Praise God!

A Story To Tell

Gray hair is a crown of splendor;
it is attained in the way of righteousness.
Proverbs 16:31

You have chosen a life with horses and with that comes a few surprises that most women are not prepared for until the day they just show up. These surprises are not invited or welcomed initially, but they have beautiful stories to tell if you are willing to embrace them. I am talking about the wrinkles we acquire from being in the elements daily on horse farms, ranches, and stables, whether for pleasure or work.

We love our horses with this crazy passion but it requires us to be outside in all types of weather. I was so fortunate to have horses very young but that meant I was outside in the sun every day and that lifestyle has rarely stopped over the decades. Horses have been in my life for what feels like an eternity, and now that I am in my sixties the lines on my face are much more prominent from the years of caring for these animals I love so much.

I praise God for giving me this life and showing me that beauty is only skin deep and wrinkles are a sign of a life well-lived. Women far and wide understand what I am saying and we all know that the wrinkles we have, each have a story to tell. We have gained worry lines as mommas and horsewomen, and laugh lines now grace each of our faces as we remember all the fun times we have had on the back of our horses. We might be getting older, but with each new line, a memory is born that no one can take away.

Thank you, Lord, for showing us that each wrinkle we acquire as we age is a gentle reminder of all the wonderful experiences we shared with those we love the most. Thank you for the gift of family, friends, and of course, horses.

~May 5~
Bringing Him Home

Surely goodness and mercy shall follow me all the days of my life;
And I will dwell in the house of the Lord forever.
Psalm 23:6

Many horse owners have longed to buy a little place in the country and bring their horses home. They dream of getting up and enjoying a cup of coffee while leisurely looking out the window at their horses standing peacefully in their paddocks. The sunrise is breathtaking against the backdrop of your barn and fencing, and the horses wait patiently but never make a fuss. What!? I must be dreaming!

The truth is the sunrise is gorgeous and the coffee is excellent, but the horses we love so much can be like impatient children pounding at the fence, chewing the wood, pacing, and even calling continuously if they are waiting for food. The sound of pounding hooves on stall walls when the horses see lights come on from the house is enough to put me in high gear. The funny thing is I know exactly which horses are making all the racket. We even had one mare who would toss the halters hanging below her stall on the ground when she got impatient, and she did this until she was in her late thirties! She clearly communicated what she wanted, but I loved her sassy personality anyway.

If you get the chance to bring your horse home, then you are in for a treat. You will get to know your horses like never before. But just remember, if you plan on doing your bible study early in the morning before chores, you might need to leave your lights down low so your horses don't see you, otherwise they might start making lots of noise, and you just might find yourself searching the Bible for what God says about having patience. Praise God for the impatient horses in our lives, for they teach us so much.

149

~May 6~
Over And Over Again

*If we confess our sins, He is faithful and just to forgive us our sins
and to cleanse us from all unrighteousness.*
I John 1:9

One of the harshest realities I had to learn when I became a barn manager is that your boarders will hurt each other. Sometimes, it is intentional, and sometimes not. But even the more difficult truth to come to terms with is that I have terribly hurt some of my clients because of my temper or harsh words and jumped to conclusions before finding out the facts. Those are the times I made things much worse, and I went up to my house with great remorse in my heart.

The horse stable should be a safe place to learn and grow but we make mistakes and feelings get hurt. Learning to forgive each other takes work, and sometimes it doesn't come easily. When I have found myself feeling hurt or even angry, I know I need to get on my knees and ask the Lord to help me forgive the person I am struggling with. I need to remember that God forgives me for all the stupid and sinful things I do without ceasing when I come to Him in repentance. I have learned that a horse business run with a spirit of forgiveness for each other is much healthier. However, it will mean humbling your heart, looking deep within, and doing it over and over again each day as you interact with people and new situations come up that will test you.

I encourage you to create an atmosphere of forgiveness and watch how it spreads throughout the barn. We all make mistakes but if we learn to forgive each other, the blessings of kindness and love will blossom and grow. Seek the Lord in all you do and ask Him to give you a forgiving heart. It will change your life and free you from the chains of bitterness. It has for me.

150

Horse Or Human

But now ask the beasts, and they will teach you; and the birds
of the air, and they will tell you; or speak to the earth, and
it will teach you; and the fish of the sea will explain to you.
Job 12:7-8

Before World War II, horses were still considered an essential part of the workforce in every aspect. The automobile had been around for a few decades, but after the war, the horse quickly faded into the background as gas-powered farm equipment took over. Not long after, horses were reintroduced into society as the perfect animal for pleasure. We embraced the new world of horse ownership and horse-loving women were now riding horses for pleasure and competition. Then, something strange started to happen with each passing decade. Many young riders were not being taught the history of the horse and its role throughout the centuries, and as reality faded, a new view was embraced. Some had forgotten that this was indeed an animal and started to relate to it as if it were a human. The most beautiful and unique characteristics of the horse were being replaced by human traits, which in turn started creating confusion with these animals and their owners. Excuses were made to defend their often human-created poor behavior and some turned away from the truth of how these animals actually relate to us.

Fortunately, there are dedicated trainers out there teaching how horses think and even sharing the complete history of the equine so that the next generation begins to understand these animals in a much healthier way which is better for the animals.

Today, Lord, we humbly ask for our eyes to be opened to see horses as you created them. Guide us in learning their language of communication, and in turn, we will become better horsewomen.

~May 8~
Less Is Often Better

You say, "I am allowed to do anything,"
but not everything is good for you.
And even though "I am allowed to do anything,"
I must not become a slave to anything.
I Corinthians 6:12

As women, we love to buy and accumulate stuff for our horses. We smile at the sight of a new riding pad in a bright new color, and we happily place it on top of the other ten riding pads in the tack room (I am guilty as charged!). Buying new horse blankets makes us feel giddy inside and we can't wait to put it on our horse and admire him. We drive to the feed store and always come home with new horse treats and goodies. We love every minute of it and know deep inside that we should have curtailed our spending, but we didn't.

Women were created to nurture, and it is a wonderful gift, but sometimes we can overdo it. I am at fault as much as the next person. We can become so excited about our children, dogs, or horses that we go a little crazy, spoiling them with things they often don't need. Looking back at my own personal life, I realize that I spent way too much money on things for my horses that could have been better used for lessons to improve me or my daughter's riding skills. Years later, many of the things I purchased were sold for pennies at the local 4-H tack sale, or even given away.

I am smiling as I write this devotion because I am just as liable as the next woman when it comes to spending too much money on things my horse doesn't need. Today, Lord, I ask for self-control regarding finances and my horses. Help me to remember that less is better and to be wise with the resources you have blessed me with.

~May 9~
Friendships

Rejoice with those who rejoice; mourn with those who mourn.
Romans 12:15

When the world shut down due to the pandemic a few years back, I admit I was on social media much more. The one good thing about it was reconnecting with someone I hadn't seen in over forty-five years.

When my father bought me my first horse, I ended up boarding him at a private home due to unforeseen circumstances. The parents had one daughter who rode horses and she was the same age as me. We became fast friends and did everything together. The next few years would be filled with riding all over the place, eating plums that we put in the water trough to keep cold, and doing everything horse girls do. But as we grew up, life took us in different directions and we lost touch. Many decades later, I found her on Facebook and it was as if time had stopped as we talked on the phone. We became those two young girls again as we laughed and reminisced about all the fun times we had riding our horses.

It made me think about barn friendships and how they never change. As women, we still love to ride together and talk about horse stuff. We encourage each other and give helpful advice when needed. We talk about how dirty our horses are from the mud and we urge each other on as we try to overcome mental obstacles. We go to tack stores together and love showing off our new bridles, saddles, and grooming supplies. We cry with each other when the day was bad and we celebrate together when it was good. We spend hours enjoying our horses together and love every minute of it.

Thank you, Lord, for the friendships over the years. What a blessing to hang at the barn with ladies who don't mind a little mud and horse hair.

~May 10~
Wake-up Call

For the Lord corrects those he loves,
just as a father corrects a child in whom he delights.
Proverbs 3:12

For the new owner, grabbing a crop to gently correct a negative behavior can be hard. It can be even more challenging for us women because we let our emotions take control of us and we worry that we will hurt our horse. The truth is, it is hard to hurt a thousand-pound equine with a little crop when used correctly, and that should never be our intention. But sometimes they need some persuasion to change an attitude or correct a bad behavior. It's a wake-up call.

The good news is that horses are very smart. They learn quickly that the little crop in your hand can sting a tiny bit and they straighten up very quickly. Soon, it becomes a tool that you can put back in the tack room and rarely bring out because your horse has learned a better way to behave. Horses are intelligent and they learn from the consequences of their mistakes and they remember.

That little crop often reminds me of God and how He has to correct me when I am being bull-headed. I like to call them spiritual spankings, and at times, they sting because the Holy Spirit is convicting me of my sin. Like the young horse, I would test God often when I was younger but thank goodness I was a quick learner most of the time. It doesn't mean there weren't consequences for my behavior, but God was gracious and was always there for me even when I was rebellious.

The Lord teaches us so many things through the horse and daily I am reminded of God's love for me and his holiness. His wake-up calls help me learn, grow, and realize my sins. The wonderful thing is that His mercy is unending and His love is always just.

Part Time Job

She extends her hand to the poor,
and she stretches out her hands to the needy.
Proverbs 31:20

My very first job (it only lasted a day, but that is another story!) was working at a breeding stable near where I lived. I didn't have a horse of my own yet and I was very young. But I was willing to clean stalls and do whatever the barn owner asked just to be around all the horses. When I was older, I helped out at a small private home where my horse was boarded in exchange for board. I loved everything, including taking the old farm truck to the local feed store to buy bulk hay cubes. Working at a stable seems like a dream job when you love horses.

Decades later, we opened our boarding stable, and soon, I was looking for part-time help. I was so surprised at how many older women wanted to work at our stable, and still do to this day. We have women who board with us and muck stalls a few days a week and women who don't own a horse but want to be around them as much as possible. Many of these women are older and delightful to work with. They work hard, we have great conversations about everything (but mostly horses), and they can work circles around most of the teenagers.

Blessings come in so many ways, and today, I am privileged to have wonderful ladies who love horses and want to work at our stable. They make my job so much easier and I enjoy their company and great conversations. Horse people often say that most of life's problems can be solved while cleaning stalls and I think there might be some truth in that statement.

Thank you, Lord, for the incredible women who clean stalls and help with chores at horse stables worldwide. They are a true gift.

~May 12~
Horse Movies

Open my eyes to see the wonderful truths in your instructions.
Psalm 119:18

I have encountered one downside as I have gotten older and learned more about horses. I have a difficult time enjoying most horse movies. I find myself watching the entire film and noticing if they made any equine errors, and that often determines whether I will ever watch it again. Most women who know a few things about horses will agree that we spend so much time pointing out the movie's mistakes regarding the horses that it ruins the entire film! We are quick to point out if the rider is pulling on the horse's bit too much or riding poorly when they are supposed to be an excellent rider in the movie. We notice when they call a horse a specific breed in the film, but the horse clearly is not. When they switch horses for various scenes and they have completely different markings on their legs, it drives us nuts! And the list goes on and on. It is the dreaded curse of the horsewoman, and we wonder if we will ever find a well-done horse movie again.

The good news is that there are some fantastic horse movies out there. Those are the movies I can watch over and over and still get goosebumps during the racing scenes or cry during the war scenes. Those are the great ones. When we are new to horses as children, we don't see all the mistakes in horse movies. But as we grow up and our knowledge increases, we see things much clearer. That's how it is with life. The Lord reveals things to us as we grow and are ready to see things more clearly and the gift of discernment becomes a part of our life.

Thank you, Lord, for horse movies, both the great ones and the questionable ones, and for opening my eyes to life each day so that I can see the truth in everything.

~May 13~
Persistence

With my whole heart I seek you;
let me not wander from your commandments!
Psalm 119:10

I love watching the horses, and you learn very quickly which ones have a persistent personality and which ones do not. Most of the time, persistence pays off, but sometimes it can get a horse into trouble, like when he learns how to open the gate or stall door!

Some horses will work extremely hard to get every last drop of grain from their feeder and then scrape the bottom with their teeth as if hoping to find more. Some horses will not only eat all their hay but spend hours picking up the tiny specks of alfalfa leaves left on the ground. The precision used when eating the micro-size leaves with such a large head, nose, and mouth is amazing. We have a gelding at our barn that loves to play with a Jolly Ball and is constantly looking for someone to play with. He will grab the ball by the handle and bang it on another horse's head until finally the horse plays back. He is so persistent and will not give up until he has a buddy to play with.

Over the years, I have come to realize that there have been times when I was very persistent and refused to quit. I pushed and pushed until I made it happen, but looking back now, I see that some of those times came with a heavy cost. I didn't seek the Lord first and His will for me, and instead, I listened to my selfish heart.

Dear Lord, today I come to you on my knees and ask humbly for guidance in all parts of my life and daily decisions. Help me to clearly see your desires for me. I ask for strength to keep going when you ask me to and to stop when you tell me it's time to change direction. Today, Lord, I give it all to you. Amen.

~May 14~
Robots

When both my girls showed horses in high school, you often heard the phrase, "That horse is a robot." This phrase usually referred to a horse that had been in strict training and was taught never to make a move without permission.

Some horses are naturally born with a quiet personality and do what they are asked with little correction. But some horses are busybodies and want to look around at everything they see while you are riding them or doing groundwork, and the trainer spends a little more time getting the horse to focus. With the proper training for each type of horse, a positive outcome can be reached even with their distinctly different personalities.

It is hard to watch a horse being overcorrected while in training because the rider wants him to be perfect. They forget he is a living, breathing animal with good days and sometimes not-so-good days. As women, we can easily fall into the pit of wanting our horses to be perfect. We somehow have this idea that if our horse is perfect, then it is a positive reflection of us. The good news is as you age a bit, you start to realize that things don't have to be perfect, and it's okay. Once we understand this, it will make the time we spend with our horses so much better. Even on those less-than-perfect days at the stable, we learn to roll with it and know we can start again tomorrow and all is good   .

Lord, thank you for showing me the beauty in life's imperfections and teaching me that life is more fun when we relax and enjoy the ride.

I Was Reminded

Then the Lord God said, "It is not good that the man should be alone; I will make him a helper fit for him."
Genesis 2:18

Today, I was reminded of all the years my husband and I have shared working side-by-side on our horse farm. No, it wasn't our wedding anniversary or the date we opened our horse business. It was something much deeper.

After all these years, I learned to recognize when he has had enough and needs to step away to rest and rejuvenate. I have learned to see quickly when he is down, stressed, or worse, feels like giving up. Working together on the farm is not easy at times. The weather is brutal, especially during the winter, and the ground conditions will quickly exhaust any man. The days never stop and you learn to pace yourself so you don't burn out. Over the years, I have watched a strong man start to weaken by exhaustion or unmet expectations, and in the beginning, I couldn't see it or know what to look for. I had to learn as a wife and a helpmate. I needed to understand my husband on a much greater level.

Today, I am reminded that he needs encouragement when he has to fix the fence and it is only five degrees outside or quietly does the jobs on the farm that no one else wants to do but need to be done. I was reminded that he will have bad days on the farm and will want to retreat to his favorite chair and be alone. It might mean I need to take over his part of the chores and let him rest. Lord knows he has done that for me many times over the years.

Today, I was reminded that having horses is not always glamorous or easy, but having a husband to share in the work is the most precious gift a woman can be given. Thank you, Lord, for all you have blessed us with.

~May 16~
The Little Horse

*I will give to the Lord the thanks due to his righteousness,
and I will sing praise to the name of the Lord, the Most High.
Psalm 7:17*

We have come to a time in our culture where many people want larger houses, grander trucks and boats, and even bigger horses! The breeds of years ago were smaller and had a job to do. The Quarter Horse was a compact little horse with unparalleled speed for short distances. The Morgan horse was also smaller with a muscular build and could go for miles under saddle or pulling a carriage. Even many draft breeds, like the Belgian horse, were a little smaller but built like a brick house and could out-pull most other breeds at the time. Today, horses are larger, but it doesn't always mean bigger is better.

When my girls were young, I wanted them to each have a horse to ride. Then someone wise told me to find some ponies that they could learn to ride on and gain their confidence. I am glad I listened. They didn't have far to fall when they fell off their ponies, which was good. I learned over the years that some of the best horses come in smaller packages and they serve an excellent purpose. Each horse has a job that best suits him and once you learn what he will excel at, it is awesome!

Today's devotion pays homage to the little horse. Though he may be small, he comes with a huge heart. Thank you, Lord, for the horses that come in compact bodies, bursting with personality and drive, and will go the distance with a willing spirit. Your creation of these incredible animals is something I will never tire of.

~May 17~
Every Horse

I have loved you even as the Father has loved me. Remain in my love.
John 15:9

There was an expression going around on social media that said, "Every horse should be loved by a little girl once in his lifetime." It was a picture of a little girl hugging her horse along with the caption, and you couldn't help but smile when you saw it. It made every mother want to run out and buy their daughter a pony. Even though I agree with the saying and was lucky enough to be one of those little girls, you could easily say the same thing about the older woman who loves horses. In fact, I would dare to say that every horse should be lucky enough to experience the love of an older woman for the rest of his life.

Little girls and horses are pure joys, but nothing can compare to a woman who loves her horse. She is more grounded, has lived life a bit, and is not always in a hurry like her younger self. She can see the beauty through the mud on rainy days and has learned to be patient and not sweat the small stuff. She doesn't need ribbons and trophies to fill her bedroom but is touched by the soft nickers she hears when her horse sees her. She takes her time when brushing her horse because she's not in a hurry to get to the next big thing, and she notices when her horse is relaxed to the point where he lowers his head and sighs with contentment. She becomes keenly aware if her horse seems off or is not feeling well and makes him her priority until he feels better. Every horse should be loved by a little girl once in his life, but every horse should be loved and cared for by an older woman for the rest of his life.

Thank you, Lord, for the older horsewomen who will love and spoil their horses until they take their last breath. What a blessing these women truly are.

161

~May 18~
Racing Grandma

In you, O Lord, do I take refuge; let me never be put to shame;
in your righteousness deliver me!
Psalm 31:1

I was online the other day reading an article on paulickreport.com about a female jockey that was so inspiring I knew I had to share it.

In May 2013, Thistledown Race Track in Ohio had the honor of having the oldest female jockey to win a race on its track. Diane King was 67 years old when she rode the Thoroughbred across the finish line, becoming the oldest woman to win a race in all of North America. How's that for impressive! Diane has been a jockey for over fifty years, and even after all these years, she still gets up early and exercises horses on the track.

When Diane was fourteen years old, her mother helped get her a job exercising horses for a friend. She worked hard and caught the eye of a trainer who put her on some very fast horses. She learned a lot and was good at riding Thoroughbreds. From there, she met another female jockey who took her under her wing and taught her everything about racing. Diane had wonderful mentors who taught her well, and many years later, she has had the opportunity to help other young women get into the industry.

Today, Lord, I want to pray for all the women who work in the world of horse racing. It is a dangerous sport, and the closer you get to the top, the more pressure these women have to make a mark for themselves in this industry. I pray that they will be surrounded by honest and solid mentors who will help keep them safe, be an encourager to them, and help them pick up the pieces when things have fallen apart. Lord, let them know they are loved by an incredible God who created the horses with wings they sit upon.

Getting off The Fence

I will instruct you and teach you in the way you should go;
I will counsel you with my eye upon you.
Psalm 32:8

When a horse gets clear directions from the cues he is being given, you can see the easiness in his eyes. He looks happy while doing his job and he waits for confirmation and gentle pats to tell him he has been a good boy. Sometimes, a horse will be nervous as he is trying to figure out everything he is learning, but often, once they do, they gain great confidence. And the transformation from an unsure horse to a horse full of confidence as he does his job, is impressive to watch. That is why I love to watch ranch horses work cattle. They know their job and the rider just lets loose of the reins and hangs on while the horse does the work. You can also be sure that when he was learning how to work cattle, he was a bit apprehensive as he took a good look at this cow staring right back at him. It may have been a slow learning process, but once it clicks, there is no stopping a good cowhorse.

We love horses and want to be around them as much as possible, but jumping off the fence and getting in the saddle can be intimidating for some women. But if we are willing to trust our riding instructor, then we will soon be riding and smiling from ear to ear. I also think about my life as a Christ follower. I know there are times when the Lord is asking me to do something new, and to be honest, I can start to feel anxious. But the Lord also knows that if I sit on the fence and never get off, I will never grow or experience the incredible things He has planned for my life. Getting off the fence is the first step to fully embracing His blessings. Today, I pray that you will find the courage to jump off the fence and take a leap of faith. You will never regret it.

~May 20~
Always Laughing

A time to weep, and a time to laugh;
a time to mourn, and a time to dance.
Ecclesiastes 3:4

All I can say is you had better have a great sense of humor because horses will humble you in ways you couldn't have imagined, and laughter is the best medicine in most cases. I can remember a few shining moments in my life when I thought I knew what I was doing and BAM! I tripped over my lead rope and fell flat on my face or forgot to cinch up the saddle tighter and found myself on the ground with my horse looking down at me. You know the look a horse gives you when suddenly you are off his back and on the ground looking up at him. His eyes say it all.

The most beautiful thing about horses is that they will leave many wonderful memories, and you will find yourself smiling and even chuckling out loud as you tell your horse friends about your escapades. I have found that the women who can laugh at the dumbest mistakes and mishaps are the happiest because they understand that they are not perfect, and neither is their horse. These same women love their horses unconditionally and make great mentors because they can teach so much through their life experiences. Their encouraging presence makes you want to be around them even more.

God bless the woman with a sense of humor. She can light up the barn when she walks in and has "horse wisdom" beyond her years to share with those willing to learn. She has endured the rookie years of horse ownership and gives grace to those just learning the ropes. Her laugh is contagious, her smile comforts, and she is truly a joy to be around.

~May 21~
A Reason To Live

And my spirit rejoices in God my Savior.
Luke 1:47

You never know where life will take you, especially with horses. We start out on the road of adulthood in our twenties, but somewhere in all the craziness of our career and life, we finally stop long enough to see a whole other world out there worth more than all the money we could ever make. That is precisely what happened to Sarah.

Sarah went to law school, studied hard, and became a trial attorney. She was hired by an excellent law firm, became good at what she did, and was quickly on the road to great success. Her job was very demanding and she gave everything she had to excel at the expectations placed on her. But the job came with tremendous pressure and she began drinking heavily to numb it all. Her marriage started falling apart and she found herself in rehab and feeling like she had hit bottom. And then a miracle happened. A friend invited her to go horseback riding, and Sarah's life changed forever. She fell in love with horses and soon began leasing a sweet mare. She realized that her job wasn't her whole world anymore and she didn't need the alcohol to heal her pain inside. When the lease was up with the little mare, she decided to buy her first horse. Sarah was in love and spent every free moment at the stable. She was happy for the first time in a long time and felt like she had a reason to live.

Years later, Sarah owns two sweet Arabians. At sixty years old, she competes in 50-mile endurance rides with the goal of entering the Tevis Cup 100-mile Endurance Ride in the next few years. If you ask Sarah, she will tell you that her horses are the best therapy she has ever invested in and they saved her life.

~May 22~
Making Us New

For the wages of sin is death, but the free gift of God
is eternal life in Christ Jesus our Lord.
Romans 6:23

The thought that a human could hurt an animal is beyond comprehension to me. Praise God that there are incredible men and women all over the world who are rehabilitating horses that have been starved or physically abused.

One particular story will always stick out in my mind. A woman had bought a horse from a kill pen that she saw standing by himself. He was shivering with fear and his new owner prayed that she could get him home without either one of them getting hurt. The horse was unpredictable and had become aggressive due to the abuse he had endured. But this woman was willing to go as slow as her new horse needed. She knew it would take a long time for this horse to trust anyone again.

Every day the woman would come out and feed the horse and sit quietly near him so he would get used to seeing her. She gave him lots of good food and he slowly put on weight. When the horse had first arrived at the stable he would turn his butt towards her anytime she approached him. Then one day, he looked at her with his ears forward and didn't move. She slowly walked up to him and stroked his neck and he lowered it into her chest. She started to cry tears of joy because she knew he was learning to trust again. He was becoming a new horse.

I can't help but think about the work God does in our lives when we give our hearts to Him. He accepts us with all our baggage and ugliness, and slowly, He transforms us with love and makes us new people. Praise God for the women who have a passion for helping abused horses and praise God for saving a wretch like me.

~May 23~
Barn Girl To Working Woman

Let no one despise you for your youth, but set the believers
an example in speech, in conduct, in love, in faith, in purity.
I Timothy 4:12

Horse ownership changes dramatically for many women during their twenties and thirties. The young girl who rode horses without a care in the world has now grown into this beautiful adult. She is working, attending college, and living in a little apartment with roommates. She still loves horses but her mind is elsewhere as she discovers a new world. Then she falls in love and gets married, but in the back of her mind, she hopes to have horses again soon.

This is a time of growing, figuring out life, and trying to find a way to put horses back into the picture. The dream of getting back in the saddle never leaves us, and squeezing a horse into our busy lives can be a real juggling act. That is how it was for me, and I have watched the same scenario unfold for many young women who find themselves horseless after high school.

Lord, please guide the young women of today. Life is not simple anymore and often takes them far away from their roots. For many of these young equestrians, being without a horse is like missing a body part. Lord, please encourage them and help them to feel complete even if they are not in their element. The transformation from a barn girl to a working woman can be bumpy as they learn to find peace and strength in new things. I pray that they will find their peace and strength in you, Lord Jesus, and I hope that one day they will find their way back to the barn and the horses they love so much. Who knows, maybe it will be when they have children of their own. That is how it was for me and what a blessing it was!

~May 24~
Those Blustery Days

I thank him who has given me strength, Christ Jesus our Lord,
because he judged me faithful, appointing me to his service.
I Timothy 1:12

My husband and I watch the weather every morning before heading outside because the forecast will determine what we do with the horses, especially during the wintertime. I have come to believe that the wind is one of the horses' biggest challenges. They have difficulty keeping themselves warm when the wind howls against their bodies, and some horses start shivering almost immediately. When the wind is crazy on those frigid winter days, we often leave the horses inside. Thank goodness it doesn't happen that much during the winter months. After all, nothing is worse than a bunch of pent-up horses anxiously waiting to go outside.

The rest of the year is different in terms of very blustery days. The horses are outside and the wind seems to rev them up. After boarding horses for a long time, I have learned to predict how the horses will behave depending on the weather. If the wind is howling, you can be sure a few of the horses will be a handful. Nothing is more unnerving than trying to walk a horse out to the paddock when he has come unglued because of the wind. My heart starts to race, but once I get inside the paddock, close the gate and take off his halter, the first thought is, Thank you, Jesus! He may be running around like a wild beast, but he is safe, and that is all that matters.

It makes me think of God as he looks down on us. He knows when the weather is perfect, we often (especially when we are younger) go off the rails as His wild children. Thank you, God, for keeping hold of me and helping me get my head back on straight, especially when I feel the wind and my mind starts to wander.

They Are So Young

So we fix our eyes not on what is seen, but on what is unseen,
since what is seen is temporary, but what is unseen is eternal.
II Corinthians 4:18

As you get older, it starts to feel like the riding instructors are getting much younger. Suddenly, the older horsewomen are taking riding lessons from younger horse trainers who could be their daughters and sons. I see it all the time at our stable and it makes me smile. It also reminds me how important it is to encourage the next generation of young women to go after their dreams. If they want to be a horse trainer, horse breeder, or a different equine professional, they should put their heart into it and try it. The worst thing that could happen is it doesn't work out. But not trying at all may lead to regrets later in life.

I was young and often carefree (careless would be a more appropriate word at times), and I didn't heed some of the sage advice from some of the older horsewomen I knew. I was still full of myself and thought I knew everything about horses. I am so blessed to have a wonderful group of young equestrians in my barn now, but over the years, there have been a few that remind me of myself when I was their age.

Today, I pray for the younger women who work in the horse industry as horse trainers and riding instructors. They will make mistakes, have good and bad days, and sometimes want to break down and cry. I pray, Lord, that wise women will come into their lives to mentor, encourage, and pray for these young ladies daily because they will need it. Trying to make it on your own can sometimes feel isolating, and they need to know they are not alone. God bless these incredible young ladies who are the next generation of professional horsewomen.

~May 26~
Your Partner

Two are better than one, because they have a good return for their labor.
For if one falls down, his companion can lift him up.
Ecclesiastes 4:9

There are hand-written letters from soldiers to their loved ones, talking about their equine partner in battle and how their bond is unbreakable. Soldiers have walked through hell on the back of the horse, cried while hanging on to their horse's neck, and had many long discussions with their equine battle buddy while making the long trek to their next destination. For the soldier, there was no better partner.

Things haven't changed much since the retirement of the horse from battle. He is still just as much a partner to his rider as ever. I have walked down our barn aisle and heard the sound of tears as a teenage girl sits in her horse's stall, crying over a broken heart. For the young girl, her horse is her best friend. I have watched from afar as a woman slowly heals from a bad divorce by coming to the barn daily and finding comfort in her horse and a reason to live again. And the relationship between the woman and her competition horse is a sight to behold. She has great trust in him to take her over the jumps safely, and he trusts her to guide him safely to the finish. No matter the battlefield, riding arena, quiet stall, or competition field, the horse has always been there for his rider, and the bond runs deep. It is a partnership that only horse lovers understand, and after all these centuries, it is still as strong as ever.

Thank you, Lord, for my equine partner. He consoles me without knowing it and helps me see things more clearly. His ears move back and forth as I talk out loud, and even though he doesn't understand every word I say, he can sense my mood and takes care of me. Thank you, Jesus, for the gift of the horse.

170

First Signs Of Trouble

*If you will receive my words and treasure my commandments within you,
make your ear attentive to wisdom, incline your heart to understanding;
for if you cry for discernment, Lift your voice for understanding.*
Proverbs 2:1-3

Over the years, I have watched a few people buy horses, and at the first sign of trouble, they are ready to send the horse down the road. Now I understand that some issues can be serious and downright dangerous, like an aggressive horse or a horse that won't stop bucking, after all, we don't want to get hurt and the thought of breaking bones (especially when you are older) doesn't sound like a good thing. But what about the person who doesn't give the horse a chance at all and instead sends the horse packing at the first sign of trouble? How do you learn the root of the problem? There is never an easy answer because so much will depend on the horse's history and the owner's experience. As they say, "Green on green can lead to black and blue!" But, once in a while, you find a woman who has a brilliant insight into horse behavior and can look deep inside their soul to see what is really going on. These horsewomen can see through all the garbage on the outside and that is when they find true beauty and a diamond in the rough on the inside.

We had a horse at our barn years ago that was a total mess when he arrived. He was extremely thin, had become food-aggressive, and was mixed up in the head when under saddle. The baggage he carried with him was heavy. But gentle hands from those working with him turned this horse around. His aggressiveness with food disappeared and he became an incredible horse to ride. Yes, he had some trouble when he was young but learned to trust again. With prayer and gentle hands, miracles can happen every day.

~May 28~
What Happiness Is

I pray that the eyes of your heart may be enlightened in order that
you may know the hope to which he has called you,
the riches of his glorious inheritance in his holy people.
Ephesians 1:18

I was as horse-crazy as they came and my heart felt happy every time I rode my bicycle to the stable. It was as if I was seeing my horse all over again for the very first time. Fast forward a few decades, and I still get excited, but I also have this profound peace when I watch them outside just being horses. My happiness has turned to joy when I watch them now and it is because I see them through the lens of the Creator. I have a much better understanding of how the horse has changed the world once we harnessed him and put him to work, and the horse has earned my respect like never before.

I often think about the women before me who worked the farms and ranches, carried babies on their hips while making dinner, and helped take care of the animals when their husbands were gone. They probably didn't have much spare time to gleefully admire the horses around them, but I am confident many of those women loved their horses as much as we do today.

Horses make us smile and leave us in awe as we watch them work. We get all googly-eyed when we see them lying down to rest and we want to squeeze their muzzle like a stuffed animal. Happiness comes in many different forms throughout our lives, but what a joy it is when we see the horse as this incredible animal full of personality and color and see the Master's creative hand in all of it. When I look at the horses on our farm each morning, I see God in every horse and my happiness turns to complete joy, and a sense of comfort fills my soul. Praise the Lord!

~May 29~
A Healthy Fear

*For wisdom will enter your heart and knowledge will be pleasant to your soul;
discretion will guard you; understanding will watch over you,*
Proverbs 2:10-11

A healthy fear of horses is a good thing. Unfortunately, as a young girl, I often threw caution to the wind, but I started to see that my behavior was not the smartest way to ride after I witnessed a friend get dragged by his horse when his boot got caught in the stirrup as he was falling off. He was fortunate. He only broke his leg. I have witnessed numerous accidents at our barn, and in most cases, no one saw it coming. I have also been the recipient of a few injuries in my life from horses and it reminded me of their power and, at times, unpredictability.

As women, we sometimes have unrealistic views about horses, especially if we are newer horse owners. We can tell ourselves that our "best friend" would never hurt us or do anything to put us in harm's way. But then something happens and our hearts become broken when our horse does something that sends us to the emergency room. It's a hard lesson, but some of those lessons are possibly the thing we needed so that we gain a realistic understanding of the horse and learn to have a healthy fear of them. When we gain a reasonable understanding of the horse, our horsemanship will become much more solid, and our skills will grow daily. And that is when we can start to enjoy our horse to the fullest.

The same is true for our spiritual lives. When we start to have a healthy fear of God, we begin to see the magnitude of His Holiness. My love, respect, and awe for our Lord in Heaven deepens with each passing day, and the peace He brings fully consumes me. Praise God for that!

~May 30~
Disentangling

For God is not a God of confusion but of peace.
I Corinthians 14:33

As horsewomen, we sometimes change things with the best intentions, only to discover they were done too quickly. We can bounce from trainer to trainer hoping to correct an issue, but it ends up confusing our horse even more. It could be that the trainer is moving too fast for the horse to comprehend what he is being asked to do, or the trainer treats every client and horse as a "one size fits all" fix. Since each trainer has their own philosophy about training and horsemanship both on the ground and in riding, it can lead to confusion for the horse and the rider. Some horses are mentally strong enough to handle the different cues and training methods, but for many, it becomes stressful, and they start to act out their frustrations by way of bad behavior both in the saddle and on the ground. Then we become frustrated and often make it worse by disciplining the horse because he doesn't understand. It can be a vicious cycle that leads down a path of frustration and tears. As women, we need to be patient and understand that there is going to be a lot of disentangling in the horse's mind. The baggage he carries might be significant.

I commend the woman who has fallen in love with a horse that has been through a lot and needs someone who will be patient and take things slow. His mind is full of junk and he needs someone who will gently untangle the mess in his head one strand at a time. I want to praise the horsewoman who can see that her horse has gone through a lot in life. She understands the challenge ahead of her but she faces it without fear. God has brought this horse into her life to heal, and He knows she is up to the task ahead of her. What a blessing she is.

The Horse Business

As each one has received a special gift, employ it in serving
one another as good stewards of the manifold grace of God.
I Peter 4:10

Starting any kind of horse business takes a giant leap of faith. After running our horse stable with my husband for almost twenty years, I have come to realize that there are parts of the business that we look at differently regarding the horses and clients. The differences are not bad; instead, they can complement each other and balance each other out when needed. Horses add a very unique element to the world of business because you are dealing with a very large animal and the owner of that large beast! Sometimes, it can be hard to tell who is in charge, and the lines can get muddied if we are not clear on our goals and expectations.

I tend to be more emotional and look at each horse and client through the eyes of my heart and emotions, while my husband is much more pragmatic. Finding a balance can take time and patience. I have had the pleasure of talking with many horsewomen over the years who are trying to find that balance in their businesses. They know things need to change, and the stress it can cause in a marriage is magnified when you disagree on how things should run. Sometimes, it can make you feel defeated and you start to regret that you ever started the venture to begin with. My heart is always heavy for the women who have opened up to me with brokenness in their voices.

Lord, I lift up the woman who bravely ventures into the business world with horses. I pray that she will find her strength in you Lord, and find the answers she seeks from your Word. Please send another woman into her life who understands her lifestyle and will fervently be her prayer warrior. In Jesus' Name, Amen.

~June 1~
New Passion

And now these three remain: faith, hope and love.
But the greatest of these is love.
1 Corinthians 13:13

Susan was a police officer and loved her career. She was also crazy about horses and hoped she could have one of her very own when the time was right. Then, one day, she was driving by a field in her patrol car and she saw something that made her slow down. As she got closer, she could see that it was a horse. His bones protruded everywhere and he looked very sad. She went to the owner to ask about the horse's well-being and ended up buying him for two hundred dollars! That little horse changed her life forever.

A few years later, Susan met her future husband, a fellow police officer, and they quickly realized they both had a deep love for horses. They married, and soon, horses became a huge part of their life together. They began breeding horses for fun and after they both retired, they increased their herd of broodmares, and Susan found herself in a new world—the world of horse racing. The more she was around the racetrack, the more she saw a need that touched her to the core. She witnessed firsthand the hard work and life of the jockeys, grooms, hot walkers, and trainers, and she had this deep desire to help these people and their families. Many of them had very little, and even things like clothing and blankets could help them. She also wanted to share the love of Jesus with these hardworking people. She got involved with the church located at the racetrack, and God has been using her there ever since.

It's heartwarming to think that one woman's passion for horses would take her down a new path and into a ministry for the people who work at the racetrack. You just never know how God will use you if you are open to His calling. Praise the Lord!

~June 2~
The First Time

Seek the Lord and his strength; seek his presence continually!
I Chronicles 16:11

Horses are exhilarating and scary, but for most horse-loving women, once you get a taste for the first time, you never want it to end.

You will catch your breath the first time you put a halter on a horse and be overcome with emotion the very first time you lead him out of his stall. You walk softly, listening to every sound he makes and questioning your every move, fearing you might do something wrong. The first time you pick up his hoof to clean it, you feel like you have just climbed a mountain, and for the first time, you realize the massiveness of his body. The first time you brush him all over and comb out his mane and tail will leave your heart fluttering, and you will wonder why you never did this sooner. The first time you put a bit into his mouth, your hands will tremble and you will worry that you are hurting him. And then you realize you need to pay attention to where your fingers are! Then, you will gently make sure everything fits how it is supposed to. The first time you climb the mounting block and hop on, it will leave your heart pumping like never before. Deep inside, you are a little fearful, but you say a prayer under your breath that nothing will happen. Then it happens....you are sitting on top of the world. Your mind is reeling and you're scared to move, but YOU LOVE IT!

Thank you, Jesus, for the chance to ride an animal that makes me feel like I am on top of the world. My prayer is that I will never forget my "first times" with my horse. I know there will be many more to come, and I will cherish each one. Amen!

Until The Very End

Honor her with all that her hands have done,
and let her works bring her praise at the city gate.
Proverbs 31:31

When a colt is born, he has no idea what his life will be like. He could be born out in a field with only his momma by his side or in a box stall filled with straw and many watchful eyes. He might never meet a human until he is older, or he could have loving hands touching him minutes after birth. He might be destined for greatness, winning races, blue ribbons, and trophies, or have the perfect demeanor to be a lesson horse for children. He might be a little girl's first horse or a retired woman's last horse. He might be hitched to a wagon for work or pull a fancy cart in the show ring. He could be a schoolmaster teaching his riders the fine art of Dressage or be the perfect pasture pet for another aging horse.

There is no limit to what the horse will experience throughout his long life, and for most, it will include many new owners, new homes, and new jobs. And yet they adapt. These beautiful animals can live well into their thirties, which is a long time to care for them, but a horse's senior years are just as paramount as the day he is born.

Today, I want to lift up the women who care for senior horses. A huge responsibility comes with taking care of an older horse, and with that can come medical complications and physical issues as they age. It can be costly, time-consuming, and even exhausting at times. But there are many women who will do everything they can to ensure that the horse they love will be comfortable until his last breath. Thank you, Lord, for these remarkable horsewomen who understand the sacrifices of owning an older horse and do it with a willing heart.

~June 4~
When All Else Fails

Let us therefore follow after the things which make for peace,
and things wherewith one may edify another.
Romans 14:19

Okay, so today wasn't the best day. The kids were more rambunctious than usual, and you felt like the house was going to cave in. You couldn't get anything productive done because you were changing diapers, cleaning up spilled milk, and doing all the things mommas do when their children are young. Then your husband tells you that he will be working later than usual.

You love your family more than anything but sometimes it can be too much, and you just need a little "me time" to gather your thoughts, breathe for a minute, and clear your mind. You start dreaming about your four-legged friend at the stable. If you can just sneak away for a few hours and ride, the world will seem better. Every mother with young children has felt like this a few times. Life can get busy and sometimes she needs a quiet place to rejuvenate.

I remember those days when my own daughters were young. When life got too crazy, I would head to the barn (I was lucky, my horses were out my back door!) and spend some time alone with God and the horses. Just being by them made me feel better. The barn was quiet and I could pray to the Lord with nothing but the sound of the horses munching on their hay.

Lord, I pray for the mommas who are trying to raise their young children, be wives, and take care of all the daily chores in their homes. It is a busy time in a young mother's life. Give her strength and profound peace, and let her know that what she does daily is significant and God-honoring. Also, Lord, I humbly ask that she is able to find time to spend with her horse so she can gather her thoughts and refresh. In Jesus' Name, Amen.

~June 5~
Summer Has Begun

While the earth remains, seedtime and harvest, cold and heat,
summer and winter, day and night, shall not cease.
Genesis 8:22

Summer is here, and there is a busyness in the air as the farmers plant the fields and equestrians hit the trails and show circuit. I love this time of year because it feels like we have been given a clean slate to achieve our goals and dreams. I find great comfort in knowing that as summer approaches, the things I am familiar with, like the farmers planting seeds and equestrians getting ready for horse shows, are again happening all around me. I love the predictability of it all, and in some strange way, it comforts me. The horses also sense the new season and are in top form to give it their all for their riders.

As horsewomen, we each have our own personal goals, and we feel like young girls again, anxious to make them happen. The things that need to be done at our homes are put on the back burner as we head to the stable to ride as much as possible and live life to the fullest. We load up the horse trailers and off we go to new destinations, and our hearts are joyful.

You see new life everywhere you turn, and you can't help but think of God's goodness and all He created. Never has a woman looked so beautiful as when you see her doing what she loves with her horse and living her equestrian dreams. Young or old, we are all the same inside, climbing each mountain and passionately reaching for the stars.

Thank you, Lord, for giving me another summer to live out my horse dreams and goals. I pray that I never take it for granted and cherish each day I have the privilege of hanging around such magnificent creatures. Amen.

~June 6~
More Than Good Looks

Having the glory of God, its radiance like a most rare jewel,
like a jasper, clear as crystal.
Revelation 21:11

In some ancient Arab civilizations, men looking for new horses to add to their herds would go to the horse trader in their area to see what he had for sale. At the time, it was customary to cover the horse's head and neck so that all you could see was his body. This forced a man to look at the horses for sale objectively and not be blinded by their beauty.

When I first heard about this "horse shopping" technique, I gasped and then realized how true it is! The funny thing is that women can be worse than men when it comes to buying horses for their beauty. We fall in love easily and are blinded. I am equally guilty of purchasing a drop-dead gorgeous horse that was not kid-friendly and definitely not the best choice for a beginner rider.

What I have learned over the years (it took me a long time!) is that some of the most amazing horses in the world may not win a beauty contest, but you will always have the best ride every time you head out on the trail or in the show ring. I was lucky that my first horse was as safe as they come but I was often teased about his appearance. He was big-boned, roman-nosed, and not your champion show horse, but I could take him in the shallow part of the lake, sit on his back, and he would swim across without hesitation. He could be ridden down the busiest city streets and never be bothered and he always brought me home safely. The longer I owned him, the more beautiful he became in my eyes, and soon, I didn't care what the other kids said. I would take ten horses like him any day, and he taught me what real beauty looks like.

~June 7~
The Last Owner

Do not cast me off in the time of old age;
forsake me not when my strength is spent.
Psalm 71:9

It is amazing how long a horse can live if he stays healthy. The oldest horse ever recorded lived to the ripe old age of 62! I think about the aging horse that has had many different owners throughout his life and the woman who chooses to become his last owner in his old age. She didn't win blue ribbons in the show ring with him or glide over fences when he was younger. She didn't get the chance to trailer him to faraway places and camp out under the stars after a twenty-mile ride or sit on him as he chased cattle across the plains. But she has cared for him as if he were her own since the day he was born. She is okay with short rides and long baths, special grain and his favorite soft mints. She prides herself on making sure he is not too hot in the summer sun and has the best winter blankets money can buy so that he is comfortable when the snow arrives. She loves the quietness about him, and she finds herself spending time in his stall talking to him. She knows he has done a lot in his life before her, but the joy he brings her now is priceless.

You will experience some of the most precious moments with older equines and fall in love with them. And as they age even more and start to slow down, you will do everything you can to ensure they are comfortable and safe. There is something extraordinary about being the first owner of a horse, but the same is true for the owner who takes care of a horse until his last breath. What an honor the Lord has bestowed on the women who take care of these senior horses. You will never regret it, and they will leave sweet memories to cherish forever.

~June 8~
Queen Of The West

For wisdom is better than jewels,
and all that you may desire cannot compare with her.
Proverbs 8:11

She was one hundred percent cowgirl and blazed a trail for many young women who dreamed of riding horses. Her name is Dale Evans. She was born in 1912 and was inducted into the Cowgirl Hall of Fame in 1995. She married Roy Rogers, and together, they made many western movies and she became an icon. She was called "The Queen of the West," which fit her perfectly.

During the golden era of western movies in the 1950s, Dale Evans did all her own riding, and her favorite horse was a beautiful buckskin Quarter Horse named Buttermilk. Buttermilk was rescued as a colt from the slaughterhouse and had been badly abused. A rancher purchased the horse because he saw something special in him, and after years of gentle care and training, the horse was sent to California for Evans to look at. When she first saw the horse she fell in love instantly but Buttermilk was a challenge to ride early on. He was very reactive at first but the actress was up to the task and soon they became a permanent team on and off screen. Buttermilk completely trusted Evans, and she trusted him to keep her safe no matter what the director asked of them. Buttermilk lived to the age of 31 and was given the best life a horse could have.

Faith played a huge part in Dale Evan's life and she never shied away from sharing the love of Christ to those she worked on and off screen. She was known for her positive attitude and a strong advocate for women's rights. She was a true inspiration for so many young equestrians and opened the gates of opportunity for women in the horse industry. She loved the Lord and people, and of course, her horse Buttermilk.

~June 9~
Having Discipline

Many women do noble things but you excel them all.
Proverbs 31:29

The road to becoming a champion equestrian is a long one for most. It takes years of learning, training, and discipline to excel at your chosen riding discipline. But for the women who took the long road and things didn't come easy, the taste of success is that much sweeter. I often think of the young kids who learn to ride at a barn where the horse is already tacked up for them and all they need to do is hop on and ride. They are missing so much when it comes to becoming an excellent equestrian. The girls who learn to muck stalls, sweep up the barn, brush their horses, clean their hooves, and walk their horses after a hard workout grow up to be more appreciative and disciplined horsewomen. They understand that it's not just about jumping on and riding.

The commitment women have for their horses always makes me smile. They are observant and notice immediately if their horse seems off, and the worst summer storm won't stop them from heading to the barn to make sure their horse is okay. I watch the sacrifices they make for their horse, and they understand the importance of spending time with their equine partner. Women can see the big picture and what it takes to achieve their goals with hard work, and they don't shy away from it.

Watching a woman grow from a brand new horse owner to a seasoned horsewoman is truly a wonderful thing, and I have had the privilege to observe this many times throughout the years. The one thing these women all had in common was their sheer determination and discipline to be all that they could be with horses. Thank you, Lord, for showing us that discipline is good for all parts of our lives, including our journey as horsewomen.

A Kind Word

Gracious words are like a honeycomb,
sweetness to the soul and health to the body.
Proverbs 16:24

A kind word of encouragement can go a long way when it comes to horsemanship. This is so important for women because we are emotional beings and it can inspire us to take the next step with our horses. Unfortunately, many boarding stables don't have a positive and reaffirming atmosphere, which can kill a woman's desire to keep trying.

The fear of failure is very real, and when you add horses into the mix, it can become a huge mountain to climb for many women who are just learning. A kind word from other horsewomen who were once new horse owners is all it takes to light a fire and give a woman the "faith over fear" attitude. She needs to know she is not the only person who has ever made mistakes regarding her horse, but she can try again tomorrow and things will be better.

If you are a horsewoman with some experience, I encourage you to share a kind word with the new woman at your stable. Tell her she is doing fine and there is no reason to panic. Tell her there are no dumb questions, and it is far better to ask than to do it wrong. And tell her that she has an incredible support system to pick her up when she falls. Horse ownership can be scary at first, but with reassuring words, it will leave her feeling like she can do it knowing she is not alone.

The Lord asks us to encourage without ceasing and to teach and guide when needed. The older will help the younger, which would also apply to the seasoned horsewoman who can help the new horse owner. What a wonderful gift to be able to encourage and offer help to other women on their journey of horse ownership.

~June 11~
Which Side?

In the beginning was the Word, and the Word was
with God, and the Word was God.
John 1:1

History plays a part in why we lead a horse from their left side. Before motorized vehicles, armies rode horses into battle. Soldiers were trained to always lead from the left side so that they could mount fast if the enemy was approaching without getting their swords tangled with their legs. You see, every man needed to be right-handed, which meant he carried his saber on his left side, which has been passed down for centuries.

Fast forward to the twenty-first century, and we still often lead our horses from the left side. The other day, I was leading a horse out of the paddock through the mud and trying to avoid the deep areas. I decided to move to the right side of the horse to avoid the muddiest part of the path and quickly realized that the horse seemed confused as to why I was leading him on the opposite side and you could feel his resistance. Then I grabbed another horse and did the same thing, and as I switched to the right side, the horse kept going without a pause. This horse was much easier to handle and it didn't matter which side I was on. Both horses acted quite differently as one was nervous and didn't like change, and the horse was more confident and ready to follow regardless of the situation.

I started thinking about my spiritual life and how I am with God. Am I easygoing when He changes directions for my life and wants me to follow, or do I get frazzled inside and resist because of my fear or confusion? It made me realize that I need to be in the Bible daily so that when the Lord asks something new of me, I can handle it much easier and confidently know that He will be right next to me no matter what side He is leading me from.

186

~June 12~
The Odd Discipline

Then Jesus told his disciples, "If anyone would come after me,
let him deny himself and take up his cross and follow me."
Matthew 16:24

I really enjoy the riding disciplines that are different. My daughter is the same way, and when she was young, she wanted to learn to drive Miniature horses. At the time, only a few kids were driving horses, so it was rather unique around our area. We had a young woman at our stable that did mounted shooting, which was so amazing! Her horse kept cool and calm, never missing a beat with the gun's blast going off. We also have a woman who does endurance riding, which is nothing short of impressive. Women who shoot targets with a bow and arrow while on the back of a horse are fun to watch, and the training involved is incredible. In winter, many riders do Skijoring, where they compete on horseback while pulling a skier over jumps at fast speeds across snow-covered roads. It always catches my interest when I see something new involving horses, and the older I get, the more I embrace that being different is great!

Today, women have so many choices when it comes to riding horses. The ones who go off the beaten path and try something different often seem to be having the most fun. There is nothing wrong with following what others are doing, but variety is the spice of life, and trying something new can teach us so much about ourselves.

Following Jesus may seem odd to some but He will take you to places you never dreamed of and will change you from the inside out. You may feel like you are off the beaten path, but that is okay, because your life will open up to the most amazing things. Embrace being different and enjoy the ride the Lord has planned for you.

~June 13~
City Girl

You have turned for me my mourning into dancing;
you have loosed my sackcloth and clothed me with gladness.
Psalm 30:11

Have you ever felt like you were born in the wrong place? I sure did when I was growing up. I always felt as if I was supposed to be somewhere other than Southern California. I was a girl with a horse stuck in the city, but my life changed when I moved to Wisconsin.

All these years later, I have grown to really appreciate growing up in the city. It was a different kind of world riding horses on city streets and galloping on every patch of grass between sidewalks and driveways. And when we could find an open field that hadn't been developed yet, it was heaven to run on our horses like we were out in the country. Of course, this was the 1970s, and things were very different then.

It's funny, but after years of running a boarding stable and taking care of horses on our farm, I still think back to when I was young and riding horses in a completely different world where we would cross at stoplights to get to the next open field and tie our horses to a hitching post at the market and go in and buy a soda. I guess you never forget your roots and where you came from, which is a good thing. They teach us so much and leave memories that grow sweeter with each passing year.

Today, my prayer is for all the city girls who love horses and dream of someday living in the country. I pray that your dreams will come true and as you grow older, you will have beautiful memories of both worlds with horses. I thank the Lord that I got to experience both in my lifetime.

~June 14~
Not All Bling

Charm is deceptive, and beauty is fleeting;
but a woman who fears the Lord is to be praised.
Proverbs 31:30

When I was showing horses as a teenager, show attire for both the horse and rider was much more straightforward. You had the silver saddles and bridles, but for the most part, the riding outfits were pretty plain. In fact, I don't remember seeing much bling on outfits back then, nor did I even know what the word "bling" meant. Boy, how things have changed in the show ring! The outfits are now covered with rhinestones in assorted vibrant colors, and the glitz and glamour are on full display. It's fun looking at everyone's outfits as they ride by, admiring how the saddle, bridle, pad, and outfit all match the horse. Bling is everywhere!

I have to say I am glad I grew up when I did in regards to showing horses. It was a simpler time where more emphasis was on the rider and less on the bling. We didn't know what we were missing because most of the kids rode in everyday saddles. Sure, some of the bigger shows had fancy silver-laden tack and saddles, but nothing compared to today. The good news is that the pendulum is starting to swing back and riders are starting to do less bling and get back to the classic western shirts and jeans, along with more natural looking saddles and bridles.

Isn't that how life is with horses? We start out simple, and as the years go by, we make things fancier and more complicated, and our horse adapts. Then, somewhere in all the craziness, our eyes are opened to the beauty of simplicity, and we see how gorgeous our horse is without the adornment of gemstones and silver. And we think to ourselves how blessed we are to ride upon such a majestic animal.

~June 15~
You Are Enough

Know that the Lord, he is God! It is he who made us, and we are his;
we are his people, and the sheep of his pasture.
Psalm 100:3

I was standing by the fence waiting for someone to pull into our farm to buy some of our composted horse manure (By the way, it is fantastic stuff!). It was a gorgeous day, and the sky was blue with a few puffy clouds moving above me. I looked over at the paddock and noticed my horse, Chance, walking over to where I was standing. As he got closer, I could tell he was looking to see if I had a treat in my hand as I held it out. When he got up next to me, he smelled my hand and realized it was empty. Then, he quietly lowered his head so I could rub his forehead and cheek. He moved as close as he could with the fence between us, and he slowly closed his eyes as I continued to rub his entire head. He was in heaven and I realized right there that I was enough for him. He felt safe around me and that made my heart swell. He stood there until I had to leave and I thought to myself how blessed I am to own such a sweet boy.

It also made me think about my relationship with God. God doesn't need us to come to him with our money or our works. He just wants us to come as we are and bring our mess with us. He loves us and we don't have to clean up our act to finally feel like we are good enough to pray and talk to God. You are enough just as you are. God is just waiting for you to reach out to Him anytime, day or night.

I am always so struck by how the horses in my life continually show me the beauty of God's love just by watching them. My heart is always comforted when I am reminded of how great God is and that I am enough just the way He created me.

One Special Cowgirl

For this light momentary affliction is preparing for us an
eternal weight of glory beyond all comparison.
II Corinthians 4:17

As a younger woman, I would hang out at the stable and often hear the older women talk about life and horses. Their stories were funny and, at times, very whimsical but dusted with so much truth and wisdom. And sometimes I was shocked at what was coming out of their tiny mouths! These senior ladies were petite, strong, and had ridden many miles in the saddle. They would talk about their lives and how things used to be compared to the current climate of our world today. They held nothing back when discussing horses, young equestrians of today, or their own personal goals and shortcomings. They were a delight to be around and even though their language was sometimes colorful, they had a deep wisdom for horses that was worth listening to.

One particular woman will always stand out in my mind. She was in her eighties, and although she moved a little slower, she loved being out at the barn and rode a couple of days a week. She was quiet but was always happy to share her knowledge about horses and her life. The one thing I noticed that was different about her was the inner peace and joy she always seemed to have. She was always happy to help the awkward kid learn how to ride or share her wisdom with the person struggling with their horse. She would tell stories of her life with horses throughout the years, and with gentle encouragement and a warm smile, she had a way of making your whole day seem better. She would then share about her love for the Lord and thank Him that she was still riding and doing the things she loved the most. She taught me about horses and the love of Jesus, and I will forever be grateful.

~June 17~
A Spiritual Thing

Let all you do be done in love.
I Corinthians 16:14

There is something about the horse that makes me feel closer to God. It was even truer after I had written my history book on the horse because my eyes were opened to all they have endured for man's ambitions since the beginning of time. And now, when I think of God molding this beast into the most beautiful and versatile creature, it gives me chills.

It is incredible to think that a horse will allow a human on his back, learn the cues we teach him, and then obey with a willing heart. It is something not to take lightly. Their strength and size could easily take us down, yet they readily obey and are even willing to run to their death if asked. How can a person not believe in a Holy God when you see this magnificent animal that can make us cry from its sheer beauty and perfection?

The more I talk to other women, the more I realize that I am not alone with this sensation that comes over me when I see a horse grazing in the field as we drive by. The flutters that come over me when I see a horse pulling a carriage for a wedding make me feel like that wide-eyed little girl who fell in love with the horses at Disneyland. It never goes away.

But above all else, it reminds me of God's goodness and how much He loves us. He created this animal that would be a beast of burden for man's survival, and men and women have been falling in love with horses ever since. Today, we are so blessed to be able to enjoy the horse for pleasure and to help us achieve our dreams. Yes, for me, it is a spiritual thing because seeing the horses at our farm reminds me of God's great love for us.

~June 18~
Brat!

And I will give you a new heart, and a new spirit I will put within you. And I will remove the heart of stone from your flesh and give you a heart of flesh.
Ezekiel 36:26

We love everything about horses and in our minds they are perfect in every way. But some of them are just like kids who pick on each other, push each other around, and do things that make us want to yell at them.

Over the years, I have learned so much about horse behavior, yet it still amazes me how much they act like children when they are together. Horses play hard, get on each other's nerves, and even try to break up friendships with other horses. They will show their jealousy and chase off any horse that comes near "their friend" and then turn around and chase "their friend" off, too! Sometimes, they are fickle and moody, and other times, they are as sweet as possible.

When I am bringing horses back in the barn for the evening, I have one particular gelding that will purposely run up and bite the butt of the horse I am leading through the gate. It has gotten so bad that I have to shoo him away with the lead rope because he startles the horse I am leading every time. He is super sweet with me but he can be a brat with the other horses. That is when I must remember that he is a horse, not a human. Observing horses in their natural element can teach us so much, but at times, it can be hard to watch their behavior with each other. Their world can seem brutal to us, but that is how God perfectly designed them.

As people, we can be very hard on each other and do things to hurt and wound each other. I often wonder if God looks down at me when I am in one of my moods and says, "My child, you are being a brat right now!" What a great reminder for me to straighten up.

~June 19~
Wide Open

For you were called to freedom, brothers. Only do not use your freedom
as an opportunity for the flesh, but through love serve one another.
Galatians 5:13

If you are around horses long enough, there will come a day when someone leaves the paddock gate open. Eventually, one of the horses will realize it is open and walks over to take a look. Then it happens. He walks through and immediately realizes he has no fencing around him. What comes next will cause your heart to skip a beat. He shakes his head, gives a loud snort, and takes off! Soon, he is running all over the place and all you can do is stand there because there is no way you will catch him. He is acting like a wild Mustang, and your heart is pounding, hoping he doesn't run out into the street. The saving grace is that horses are herd animals and usually do not stray too far from the rest of the horses. That is when you get a bucket of grain to bribe him or hope he finds a yummy patch of grass and settles down to eat. It is enough to take your breath away, and even after all these years, it still sends my heart racing. After you have caught him and he is safely back with his herd mates, you start to relax, and then you take a moment to relish in the beauty of what you just witnessed.

Watching a horse in all its glory running around absolutely free is breathtakingly beautiful. You can see the fire in his eyes, and for a few moments, you can see how God created him to be. Without restrictions and fences, he is like a bird in flight. As women, we become so busy in our daily lives and schedules that we often find ourselves boxed in without any room to move. I pray that every now and then, you will live life like someone left the gate open, for those are the moments that rejuvenate and remind us that we are beautiful in the eyes of the Lord.

~June 20~
The Perfect Love

Let us draw near with a true heart in full assurance of faith,
with our hearts sprinkled clean from an evil
conscience and our bodies washed with pure water.
Hebrews 10:22

When it comes to horses, we have this preconceived idea of what the perfect horse is. First, we want a horse that is safe to ride and the perfect size. Our horse needs to be gorgeous, the right color, and, of course, have a long flowing mane and tail. We want a horse that will come when they see us at the gate, and we want to be able to wrap our arms around his neck and hug him like a child. What a perfect world that would be. Unfortunately, this is not how it really works. Horses show their love in many different ways, and our job is to learn how each horse expresses it. Horses are very truthful creatures, and there will be no question about how they feel about you if you are watching closely to what they are saying.

My Paint horse loves people and you can wrap your arms all around him and he will lower his head and nuzzle you. On the other hand, my Thoroughbred is as sweet as can be and will stand close by as long as you don't hug her or touch her face. Both horses show love in their own special way, and just like our own children, we learn and adapt to their individual personalities.

Your horse may not run to you when he sees you or let you hug him, but he will show you he trusts you in his own perfect way, the way God created him to be as an equine. God made this extraordinary animal, and we are the recipients of their willing heart. Your horse may not love you back the way you envisioned, but God loves you more than anything and is waiting for you to reach out to Him with both arms raised. What a perfect love.

~June 21~
Personal Therapy

Oh give thanks to the Lord, for he is good;
for his steadfast love endures forever!
I Chronicles 16:34

There is something soothing and peaceful about a horse stable. It might be the quietness of the countryside or the clip-clop sound of the horses walking down the barn aisle. It could be the smell of the leather in the tack room that leaves the senses reeling or how we feel when we take a soft brush to our horse and watch all the hair fall on the ground to reveal a shimmering summer coat underneath the heavy winter fluff. For some women, just taking their horse outside to graze leaves them feeling good about life, and listening to the horses munch on hay does more for the soul than a paid therapy session. And when we saddle up our horse with great care and look at him to ensure he is comfortable, we feel like a proud mother gazing at our handsome guy. We feel like we are on top of the world as we sit in the saddle, and when our horse starts to move forward, our heart begins to beat faster. We look at his ears and watch how quickly they move around as they pick up the sounds around him. We begin to trot and our heart skips a beat. We quickly get into a rhythm and a new and growing confidence sprouts deep inside us. Then, with a cue from our leg, our horse moves into a canter that sends our heart racing. After we realize that we won't fall off, we settle into the cadence of his lope. And for a few minutes, we feel like a schoolgirl again.

When our ride is over and we unsaddle and brush our horse, we know inside that it was the best day ever. We lead him back outside to his herd and fall in love all over again. Thank you, Lord, for this incredible gift of the horse. My heart will never stop overflowing and I will forever be grateful.

His Timeline

For still the vision awaits its appointed time; it hastens to the end—it will not lie. If it seems slow, wait for it; it will surely come; it will not delay.
Habakkuk 2:3

If we are willing to learn from this incredible animal, the horse will teach us many life lessons. Delayed gratification is one of the hardest things to grasp, regardless of age. We can push and force the horse to do what we want, but the more we hurry things along, the more the horse will often rebel and retreat to somewhere deep inside. At that point, we risk going backward and losing the relationship we have built with him.

Younger riders are still learning life lessons and have not yet gained enough wisdom to see the big picture. But something beautiful happens as we age and start to see things more clearly with horses. We develop a better understanding of how they think and a wiser way of teaching them. We adjust our timeline to fit their needs and understand that we may miss the show season this summer because it is more important to form trust and respect first. We take the time to learn our horse's personality and become more keenly aware of what makes him nervous or fearful. We choose to go slow if our horse needs it because we are in for the long game and not just a few fleeting months each summer.

The life lessons horses teach us are never-ending. And as a horse becomes more confident, so do we. We are a team, and we grow together with each passing day. The horse is willing to give his heart and soul for my dreams and aspirations, and I will forever be indebted to him.

How in the heavens could such a creature be conjured up and designed to perfection? I may never know the answer until I meet God, but I will praise Him for such an amazing beast.

~June 23~
The Baby Beef

For great is your love, higher than the heavens;
your faithfulness reaches to the skies.
Psalm 108:4

God gives us an incredible gift of memories that we can tuck away and pull out years later. Sometimes, they might be mistakes we made when we were young or funny situations we got ourselves into. But the most wonderful memories are created by the adventures we have.

One of my most cherished memories was riding my horse with friends to the Baby Beef restaurant to eat. It was about a two-mile ride from our stable and we would have a blast riding bareback and often barefoot on hot days to get a soda and burger. Once we arrived, there were hitching posts where you could tie your horses up and relax under a tree.

I'll never forget the time my friends and I rode to the Baby Beef to grab a burger. My horse was tied up to a hitching post and something spooked her and she broke her reins. Before I knew it, she took off! She ran full speed back toward the stable. We all jumped up, and I hopped on the back of my friend's horse. We went after her like a posse heading after an outlaw! We never did catch her, but we all ended up back at the stable with tired horses and very relieved that everyone was okay.

I was so upset that day, but now, I just smile when I think about it. That ride back to find my horse is one I will never forget. The Baby Beef restaurant is no longer there, but for those of us who experienced it, we will always have fond memories.

Thank you, Lord, for the precious gift of childhood memories. They leave us with a smile on our face and a heart overflowing.

~June 24~
Hollywood Horses

Your righteousness is like the mighty mountains, your justice like the ocean depths. You care for people and animals alike, O Lord.
Psalm 36:6

Southern California was a great place to grow up in the 1960s and 70s. There were still many small stables in the area and some played a huge role in Hollywood. The studios were centered in one location, and when they were going to shoot a western movie or TV show, they had a few stables that supplied the horses for filming. It was common to see filming all over the valley, and if you rode horses long enough, you would eventually see some of your favorite actors on the back of a horse.

The horses used in these movies and television shows were known as the Hollywood horses. Some of the more famous actors had their favorite horses and would use them for every movie they were in. And, of course, if you watched shows like Bonanza or Little House on the Prairie, you would see those same horses at the local stables in the area. Often, when a scene was being filmed that required horses in the background, the crew would go to a stable and start filming, and you just never knew if your horse would be in the show or not.

My horse was one of those horses chosen for the background in the show The Bionic Woman that aired in the 1970s. It was only for a split second, but it was exciting. The one thing I learned from watching the filming of those shows was that many of the horses had multiple stunt doubles because so many of the scenes required complex maneuvers. Each horse was taught one specific thing so as not to overwhelm the animal. The horse's versatility is unsurpassed, and I can't help but smile when I think about the Hollywood horses of the past and today.

~June 25~
Hard Keepers, Easy Keepers

I take joy in doing your will, my God,
for your instructions are written on my heart.
Psalm 40:8

Managing a horse boarding stable will teach you things a college course could never prepare you for. You are dealing with lots of different breeds and ages, and each horse has his own special needs to keep him healthy. I have to say it was very eye-opening when we first opened our business. The one thing that became obvious quickly was that some horses were easy keepers, and others were hard keepers. Some horses could just look at grass and gain weight, while others were fed everything but the kitchen sink and hardly put on a pound. Some horses seemed to get hurt on everything, and others knew how to stay out of trouble and never have any issues. It has always been one of the more challenging parts of the job, especially since we have so many different horses to care for daily. No two horses are the same and if you want them to flourish and be the best they can be, they need to be cared for according to their specific physical and mental needs. Does it make it hard at times? Yes. Is it worth it to dig deeper? Yes! In a perfect world, we would love to all have easy keepers, but I have learned the most from the hard keepers because they force me to do my homework.

I started to think about my own life and began to wonder if I was a hard keeper or an easy keeper in the eyes of God. I have to admit that there have been many times (too many to count!) that I am sure I was a hard keeper, as God was probably looking down at me and shaking his head at the stupid things I was doing. I am thankful He has always kept me in His sights no matter what phase I was in. Thank you, Lord, for watching over your children.

~June 26~
Permission

To love him with all your heart, with all your understanding
and with all your strength, and to love your neighbor as yourself.
Mark 12:33

When I was young, my friends and I would hop on our horses bareback and go riding. My horse Rusty had a wide back and plenty of cushion and you could easily sit on him without a saddle. He would let me run from behind, push with my hands on his butt and lift my body up as if I was vaulting in gymnastics, and I would land on his back without him flinching. Yes, I was much younger, smaller, and more athletic back then! We would spend hours braiding manes, clipping hair, and shining hooves, and our horses quietly endured our primping and high-pitched voices.

When I really think about the horse and his ability to physically carry a human, pull much more than his own weight, and let little girls do all the things they love to do to their horses, it is nothing short of miraculous! No other animal is as versatile or has such a big heart, and the fact that the horse will do it willingly is even more astonishing since he could easily overpower us anytime he wanted.

The horse's beauty leaves us speechless and he doesn't have to do much but just exist. As grown women, we still love to brush our horses and braid their manes. We clip their bridle paths and legs, and it brings us great satisfaction. That is when we realize how blessed we are to be able to live out our childhood dreams. And occasionally, we get to witness our horse's true power when he is out in his herd playing or fighting, and we are reminded that we are only allowed to do the things we do with our horses because he has given us permission. When I think of it in those terms, it leaves me speechless. We have been so blessed to share in his life and I pray I never take it for granted.

~June 27~
Hoofbeats

But let all who take refuge in you rejoice; let them sing
joyful praises forever. Spread your protection over them,
that all who love your name may be filled with joy.
Psalm 5:11

There is something soothing about the sound of a horse's hooves as he walks. Each methodically timed hoofbeat almost feels like the constant waves rolling in and out from the ocean or the tic-tok of the grandfather clock that never misses a beat. I listen to the sound of each hoof hitting the ground in perfect timing and it sends me back to another time when the world was a simpler place and the mode of transportation was the horse-drawn carriage. It was a time when your milk would have been delivered by horse-drawn milk wagons every morning, and the constant of those morning hoofbeats were a comfort to many families in a world that was changing rapidly.

I have learned so much from the horse as he walks, and if I listen carefully, I can tell if he is nervous because of his hurried pace or calm because of the quiet rhythm. I can tell if he is favoring a leg just by the sound of his hooves hitting the ground, and a loose shoe makes the most unique sound with each step. The hoof is truly an amazing thing created to bear the weight of a horse along with the weight of a man and all his belongings.

The next time you hear the clip-clop of a horse walking by, close your eyes, listen, and think about the days gone by when horses ruled the roadway and their hoofbeats were the heart of every civilization. Thank you, Lord, for the calming sound of the horse as he walks. I pray I never take that sound for granted, and it is a great reminder of the generations before me who relied on those amazing hoofbeats to survive.

~June 28~
The Racetrack

*And my God will supply every need of yours according
to his riches in glory in Christ Jesus.*
Philippians 4:19

One of my favorite memories from childhood was spending Saturday mornings with my father. My parents were divorced and he would come by early in the morning and take me out for breakfast. Then, because he knew I was crazy about horses, we would drive to Santa Anita Race Track and watch the racehorses work out as the sun rose. This was back in the 1960s when you could sit in the bleachers and watch the jockeys put the horses through their paces. Then, you could walk by the barns and watch the grooms as they bathed the horses and gave them their rubdowns. I couldn't think of any other place I would rather be.

It may seem like a strange thing for a father to do with his daughter, but I loved it and remember it like it was yesterday. During those years, I dreamed of riding one of those thoroughbreds down the track and feeling the wind hit my body as I hung on. Of course, that never happened, but it was sure fun to dream about.

I think about the people who work with horses at the racetracks today. It's not glamorous, and the job is hard. Their world is a small community of people who together take care of the horses daily. The jockeys, grooms, and the people who care for the horses, from feeding to mucking stalls, are a family. One cannot do it without the other and they need each other to make it all come together.

Today, I pray for the men and women who work tirelessly at racetracks. Dear Lord, surround them with your angels, keep them safe in a job that can be dangerous at times, and let them know they are loved.

Standing In The Rain

Teach me your ways, O Lord, that I may live according to your truth!
Grant me purity of heart, so that I may honor you.
Psalm 86:11

I have watched horses stand out in the rain even if it is pouring. We watch them and ask ourselves, "Why do they do that?" Some horses don't mind the pitter-patter of the rain on their backs, but for most horses, once the rain increases, they are happy to have a shelter to stand under.

I have come to realize that some horses will refuse to stand in the shelter because they are nervous to be in such close proximity with other horses. This is usually because they are at the bottom of the hierarchy and have been chased a lot. It can be heartbreaking to watch this occur especially when the weather is terrible. Often, the only way to fix the situation is to move the nervous horse to a herd that suits him much better or build another run-in.

When I think about the horse standing out in the rain alone, it makes me think about the times in my life (especially when I was in my twenties) when I felt like I didn't fit in with the people I was hanging out with. Something inside told me I needed to find different friends, but making the change was challenging. I believe the Holy Spirit was looking over me and urging me to stop making bad decisions and find healthier friendships. The Lord needed to hit me upside the head a few times to figure this out. Once I found friends who looked out for me on a deeper level, I felt like the rain stopped and the sun came out.

Lord, I pray for the woman who feels like she is out in the rain alone. Please send positive people into her life who will be by her side, comfort her, and help her grow daily into the beautiful person you created her to be.

~June 30~
Riding My Bicycle

And not only that, but we also glory in tribulations, knowing that tribulation produces perseverance, and perseverance, character, and character, hope.
Romans 5:3-4

When I was young, the only way to see my horse was to hop on my bicycle and ride to the stable. Both my parents worked so I would start peddling down the road after school. It was only about a four-mile ride and I didn't think anything about it at the time. I just did it because it was the only way to get there. This would be my mode of transportation for about six years until I finally got my driver's license. I would ride my bicycle with my boots, jeans, and belt buckle on, and after a long day of riding and doing all the things horse kids do, I would hop back on my bike and ride home. I got a lot of exercise back then even if I didn't want it, but those bike rides strengthened my legs and helped me become a better rider on my horse. When I think about those days of riding a bicycle to the stable, I just smile. I never felt like the odd kid out because I didn't have parents to drive me to the barn. In fact, during that time, many kids rode bicycles everywhere! It taught me to face my challenges and not give up.

We each have our "bicycle" to ride, and if we persevere, we will see our goals come to fruition. You might have to spend many months doing groundwork before ever setting foot in the saddle. It might be coming out after work even when you are tired just so you can spend time with your horse and bond with him. Even the shortest visits with a horse can make all the difference for him when he is learning about you.

Lord, please help me be patient and understand that sometimes I have to take the long road and do things slowly for the betterment of my horse and myself as I grow in my horsemanship.

~July 1~
No Filter

The soothing tongue is a tree of life,
but a perverse tongue crushes the spirit.
Proverbs 15:4

As a teenager, I would listen to the older ladies at the stable and sometimes I would be shocked by the things that came out of their mouths. They would talk about horses, politics, or people, and they didn't care what or how they said it. These horsewomen would laugh and tell any listening ears that their filters were gone. Now that I am in my sixties I completely understand what they mean! I guess you could call me an "older" horsewoman now even though I don't feel old. But the one thing I have noticed is how easy it is for me to speak my mind now.

I've made a tremendous amount of mistakes during the first decade of running our boarding stable and now things are leveling out as I near the end of the second decade. It has been a ride, to say the least. But something inside of me changed during the last twenty years in that I feel much bolder when I speak what's on my heart and I worry less about what others think. I guess you can say the filter has come off, but I pray it's not all the way off!

Lord, my prayer is that I learn to use discernment when talking with other women. If I need to correct someone regarding a situation with their horse, help me to do it with gentle truth. Please forgive me for the times I lost my filter and let words of anger or sarcasm come out of my mouth. I know that, in those times, I hurt the other person deeply. I am a work in progress, and I pray that I will strive to speak words of love and encouragement each day. In Jesus' Name, Amen.

~July 2~
Some Things Never Change

The righteous person may have many troubles,
but the Lord delivers him from them all.
Psalm 34:19

I was sixteen years old and excited to take my new mare in a halter class, after all, I thought she was gorgeous. It was a hot summer day, and I was up early to wash her white mane and tail. Back in the day, we used a product called "Bluing" to help make white manes and tails even whiter. As I began washing her mane and tail, I must have put too much Bluing on because when I went to rinse it out, her mane and tail now had a blue hue! That was the beginning of a terrible show day. As she was drying, I put on my boots, which were too small, and got ready.

The first class was a halter class for mares, and I prayed the judge wouldn't notice my horse's blue mane and tail. Right before the class, another kid approached me and told me I needed to put a stud chain on to ensure I was set up right in the class. I thought it strange, but I did it because I didn't know better. As I walked into the class, blisters were already forming on my heels and it was painful to walk. My horse had a blue mane and tail, but I was still okay. I led her into the class and as we stood in line, the judge approached me and asked me gently why I was using a stud chain on my mare. I told him that I thought I was supposed to. He told me that it was not appropriate for a mare halter class. Needless to say, I didn't place. I was embarrassed and limped out with my head down.

Some of the deepest memories we grow old with are often the most painful ones. But if we can find something to learn from those difficult experiences, they will remind us later down the road to help others in the same situation and to always be kind.

~July 3~
Finally Home

If any of you lacks wisdom, let him ask of God, who gives to all liberally and without reproach, and it will be given to him.
James 1:5

I would consider myself a farm girl but my city roots still run deep within me, and the memories I had with horses back then have helped mold me into who I am today. Life on a horse farm differs significantly from boarding horses in the city. It is a great life, but it can sometimes feel isolating, and getting away for a day or week with so many horses to care for can be challenging at times. But it is also very freeing to be your own boss, set your own hours, and go at your desired pace. The farm has taught me great lessons about horses, life, and God's plans for me.

When I hear a woman say she doesn't feel knowledgeable enough to own a horse, I want to be her biggest cheerleader and tell her she can do anything. You don't need to be born into a horse family. You can start at any point in life and some of the best horsewomen I have ever met started out as city girls who had never even touched a horse when they were young. What made them so good at what they do with horses is that they had a heart willing to learn. These horsewomen were like sponges learning all they could and perfecting their chosen riding disciplines. Their road to success may have started out with a few bumps in the road, but they didn't give up and they learned through their mistakes and kept moving forward.

Many horsewomen were born in the city but have country souls. They have a drive to work hard, glean from others who came before them, and find the place where they feel they are home. God bless the horsewoman who has traveled far but is finally home.

~July 4~
Forward Is Still Forward

God is within her; She will not fail.
Psalm 46:5

We are our own worst critics when it comes to our horsemanship skills, and it can even cripple us to the where we won't ride a horse around other people. Why do we do that to ourselves? I have seen this happen a few times at our stable and it breaks my heart. I have watched as a first-time horse owner will get her horse home and be as excited as a schoolgirl. She will spend hours brushing her horse and taking him out to hand-graze, and after she has signed up for riding lessons she is even more excited. But somewhere along the journey, she makes some mistakes with her horse and it starts to paralyze her. She begins to lose her confidence and feels like she is going backward. She has become fearful to the point that she has stopped taking lessons and barely comes out anymore. The saddest part is she doesn't see how far she has come. She is moving forward even when she makes mistakes but she can't see it. It's like a little voice deep inside her tells her she made a mistake and she will never amount to much when it comes to horses.

Today, I pray for the woman who feels like a failure when it comes to horses. She has made a few mistakes which have shaken her to the core. Lord, please cover her with your love and comfort her. I pray that she will realize that forward is still forward, no matter how small the steps.

Lord, please send other horsewomen around her to encourage her daily and help her get back in the saddle. Above all else, I pray that she will feel the love of Jesus shining down on her and find comfort and peace in that. In Jesus' Name, Amen.

~July 5~
Fantastically Different

O Lord, you have searched me and known me!
Psalm 139:1

Horsewomen are all different, which is why they are such a beautiful group of ladies. Some come from a ranching background and learn to rope and ride at a very young age. Some come from families that have always ridden english, while others come from a long lineage of rodeo riders and barrel racers. I have met great horsewomen who were put on a pony as soon as they could walk and others who didn't put their boots in the stirrups unto they were well into their fifties. I have met women who learned how to incorporate their passion and mission in life with horses and began wonderful therapy stables for young and old. Many of these ladies didn't come from horse families but they knew they were going to leave a path for the next generation.

I have learned that each of the horsewomen who have been a part of my life is uniquely beautiful. They each have their own style of barn clothes and approach to riding and I appreciate them all. They respect each other's horsemanship even if different, and still have fun riding together. Each gives a little and takes a little, but they all learn from each other and go home after a long day at the stable with a little more knowledge. I often think how boring it would be if all these ladies wore the same clothes and boots, owned the same horse breed, and participated in the same riding discipline.

As I have gotten older, I have learned that variety is the spice of life, and that has never been truer than when you get together with a bunch of horsewomen. You cannot help but smile.

Thank you, Lord, for the beautiful ladies you have sent into my life over the years. They have added much color to my world and I will forever be thankful for each of them.

~July 6~
Skip Tennis

Give, and it will be given to you. Good measure, pressed down,
shaken together, running over, will be put into your lap.
For with the measure you use it will be measured back to you.
Luke 6:38

So many friends I know are retiring down in Florida or out west in Arizona. They are leaving the Midwest for warmer temperatures and tennis courts. Many of these people have never been crazy about horses, so moving elsewhere is an easy transition. That is all well and good and I wish my friends the very best.

But for us horse people, our retirement looks much different. Some are diving feet first into horse ownership and hitting the road with their trucks and trailers to experience horseback riding in faraway places. While others are more content taking care of horses at their own place, and for them, a quick weekend getaway is all they need. They say that horses tie you down which is true in so many ways, but they don't realize that horses also give us something to look forward to each day. Non-horsey people don't understand that horses become part of our family and life.

It's true that many of us might not ever become snowbirds and travel to warmer climates in the wintertime to play tennis, but we are happy to sacrifice that for the soft nicker we hear when our horse sees us. There is nothing better to warm your heart on a cold winter day. My husband and I will gladly skip tennis for our life on the farm.

Thank you, Lord, for the opportunity to care for the horses at our stable. I know it can be unbelievably hard during the winter, but when summertime comes, I feel as if we are living the best life possible. I pray, Lord, that I will always do everything to honor you and for your glory. Amen

~July 7~
When They Come Back Home

By wisdom a house is built, and by understanding it is established; by knowledge the rooms are filled with all precious and pleasant riches.
Proverbs 24:3-4

The girls who grow up with horses often have to make hard choices after they graduate high school regarding their beloved equine partners. For some, selling the horse is sad, but life goes on, and they are excited for the next chapter in their lives. It is beyond heartbreaking for others who have grown up with this precious animal. So they do everything in their power to keep their horse and balance young adult life, college, work, and their first love — their horse. Some young women move far away, never to return, but once in a while, after a few years, they find that their roots run deep and they are ready to return home and horses find their way back into their lives.

It is different for every young woman, and for some, it takes decades to finally make it back home. I have watched many girls, including my daughters, grow up on our farm. I have said goodbye with tears and hugs as they head out into the world. But I also have had the pleasure of seeing some of them come back as grown-up women. Their horses are often boarded at our stable throughout all those years, and as they grow up, so do their horses. These once intense young teenagers are now much calmer, wiser, and even funny as their true personalities come alive, and you can see the joy in their eyes as they come home to ride their horses again.

As horsewomen, we watch the younger generation make their way in the world, but it always makes us smile as we see them dust off their old boots and saddles and take a ride for the first time in years. It doesn't get any better than that, and it always reminds me of God's goodness.

212

~July 8~
Stop And Listen

Be not quick in your spirit to become angry,
for anger lodges in the heart of fools.
Ecclesiastes 7:9

One of the hardest things I have witnessed as a barn owner is a young person over disciplining their horse. They are often not mature enough to understand the impact they have on their horse or refuse to take the time to decipher what their horse is trying to tell them. Thank goodness I have only dealt with this two times, and each time, I intervened because I could see the horse was becoming very upset and the young rider was making things much worse with sharp discipline that was not appropriate.

A horse will try to tell you when he is hurting or scared, or he's happy and feels safe. He will tell you when he is nervous or confused and doesn't understand what you are asking him to do. If you take the time to stop and listen without all the noise from interruptions, cell phones, and constant chatter, you will learn a new language from this incredible animal. All you need to do is stop and listen.

When I think of the young people who are quick-tempered and lashing out on their horses, I realize that we all can be like that in life, not only with our animals but also with our families. There is a fine line between becoming irritated because things are not going as planned and exploding to the point where we do things we will regret the next day.

Lord, please help me stop and listen to what each horse is trying to tell me daily when I handle them. Please grant me the wisdom to understand their individual personalities and to ensure that I end in a way that will be positive for them. I pray I never take for granted this animal you have entrusted to us to care for all his days. Amen.

~July 9~
The Generations Before

I remember the days of long ago; I meditate on all your works
and consider what your hands have done.
Psalm 143:5

When I first moved to Wisconsin, David and I lived on his grandfather's farm for a few months until we found jobs and a place to live. I instantly fell in love with the old dairy barn. I had never been inside an actual barn before and there were still beef cattle inside at the time. David's grandfather shared stories with us of when he was a kid and how the draft horses were stalled in the barn. He would talk about how he would ride one of the draft horses up the road to the one-room schoolhouse that he attended.

I have never forgotten the stories, and I would spend time thinking about all the history in that old barn. Decades later, David and I still live on the farm and are caretakers of that same old dairy barn. I have come to appreciate all the hard work and how things were done generations ago. The labor was done with horses, and the days were long for both the horses and men who worked the fields. I am sometimes amazed and ask myself, "How did they do it all?"

We have come full circle with that old dairy barn and now it houses horses again. This time for pleasure, and if the truth be told, very little work. But every time I walk into that old barn, I still feel a sense of reverence for the horses and people of the past.

My prayer today is for the next generation of horsewomen. Lord, please send people into their lives to glean from and gain wisdom from as these young women grow up. I have learned that the generations before me still continue to teach us daily even though they are no longer here, and I pray that my life will positively impact future generations of horsewomen. Amen.

~July 10~
The Future

And he answered, "You shall love the Lord your God with all your
heart and with all your soul and with all your strength and
with all your mind, and your neighbor as yourself."
Luke 10:27

Horses are making a comeback in many parts of the world for a new and positive reason. More and more documentaries are coming out about returning to our roots, simplifying our lives, and rejuvenating the land all by way of horsepower—real horsepower.

I am starting to see wonderful things taking shape all around me as small businesses are again, after many decades, using horses as part of the workforce. There are a growing number of professional vineyards incorporating genuine horsepower for many different jobs in the vineyard fields. Many farmers are now using horses again to work the land, plant the seed, and harvest. And small logging companies are returning to using horses to drag the logs out of wooded areas and in the clean-up after the work is done. The one thing many of these people have in common is their love for the horses they own. The cool thing is that women are just as involved in driving the teams and working the land as the men, and this opportunity would not have been possible for most women at the turn of the twentieth century. These horsewomen work alongside their families to feed the horses, brush and tack them up, and hook them up to the wagon. And that is all before the work starts. It is also a lifestyle they love and are passionate about.

The more I learn about the future of horses the more I see the future of incredible horsewomen coming up and changing the world one field at a time. God bless the women who work endlessly to help their family businesses. They are a blessing to all who know them.

215

~July 11~
The Barn

Do not be conformed to this world, but be transformed by the renewal of your mind, that by testing you may discern what is the will of God, what is good and acceptable and perfect.
Romans 12:2

One of my favorite things on our farm is our old dairy barn. It was built in the late 1800s, and the craftsmanship of the massive wood beams inside is truly stunning. Wooden pegs hold each oak beam firmly together and I often gaze at the workmanship of it all.

Our barn has gone through many transformations during the last 130 years. It has been used to house beef cattle and horses and as a parlor for dairy cows. At some point, chickens and pigs also took up residence for a time. Then, when my husband and I bought the farm, we decided to get some ponies for our daughters, and that meant the cow stanchions had to come out and horse stalls were put in. Over the years, many barn dances have been held in the loft with twinkle lights hanging from rafters and the old oak floor transformed into a dance floor with boots shuffling across. It makes me think about the future and what this old barn will be used for generations after me.

As young women, we can be impetuous and sometimes selfish. We feel as if we have all the time in the world. As we age, we become mommas and professionals trying to do it all. We slow down a bit and start to appreciate our friendships a little more. Somewhere in all of that, we begin asking the big question, "What is the meaning of life?" When the Holy Spirit tugs on our heart and we give our life to Jesus Christ, we begin a new transformation that will take us to our heavenly home one day. I love our old dairy barn and the stories it has to tell, but that is nothing compared to the new body I will have when the Lord calls me home.

~July 12~
All Kinds Of Talent

Having gifts that differ according to the grace given to us,
let us use them: if prophecy, in proportion to our faith.
Romans 12:6

When I was young, my world was consumed by horses. Riding horses and dreaming of one day becoming an equine veterinarian or horse trainer is common for many young equestrians, and it was for me too. I didn't realize as a teenager that there was a whole world out there of other equine professions.

I have had the pleasure of meeting many women working in the horse industry in unique jobs. I have always been a little envious of the women who make a living with equine photography. The stunning images they create through the camera lens often leave me breathless, and it is one of the most beautiful art forms we have today. I know a woman who specializes in equine website design, and what she creates on the computer will leave you mesmerized. I drool at the beautiful horse sculptures and paintings created by some of the most talented women in the world, and if I had the means, I would surround myself with equine paintings and sculptures from all around the world.

The world of horses goes way beyond borders, languages, age, or abilities. Horses draw us into their world and our minds begin to dream and create as we immerse our senses in the beauty unfolding right before our eyes. Some of these talented ladies may not ride horses or ever own one, but their love is undeniable, as shown by the fruits they produce with their hands and minds.

Thank you, Lord, for the talented women who see the horse in a way that many cannot and are able to unleash the beauty of these majestic animals in ways that make our hearts go weak. What a treasure these ladies are to all who love horses.

~July 13~
For A Lifetime

Know well the condition of your flocks, and give attention to your herds.
Proverbs 27:23

The horse is ever-changing inside and out. When he is young, his mind is also very young and immature. You can almost see the child in him as he tries to test the waters daily with other horses and the humans around him. But as he grows and matures, he begins to think about things, especially when he is learning something new, and when he licks his lips, you can tell he is catching on. His body is gangly at first, and then as he grows, puts on muscle, and fills out, you begin to see a beautiful, full-grown horse stand where a wiry and often clumsy baby stood just a short time ago.

They say that the teenage years of a horse are some of the best years because he has lived life for a while, he is fully mature both mentally and in physical strength, and has learned a lot. If he has been treated kindly throughout his early years, then his mind will be strong and he will be very trusting. If he has been treated poorly, then he will have many layers to peel before he is willing to give you his heart. As the horse enters his senior years he begins to change again. His body might not be as muscular as it once was and his movements are slower, but he is still ready to give his all. The horse's life is long, and for some, it is very hard. But for the horse that is owned and loved by the same woman his entire life, there is nothing more special.

Today, I want to express my deepest gratitude to the women who have cared for their horses for a lifetime. They understood the sacrifices and challenges and never departed even when it was hard. Thank you for caring so diligently for one of the Lord's most precious creatures. The heavens are smiling down at you today.

~July 14~
The Price Tag

Jesus said to him, "I am the way, and the truth, and the life.
No one comes to the Father except through me.
John 14:6

A well-bred Thoroughbred racehorse could cost you hundreds of thousands of dollars, and yes, a horse with excellent breeding will indeed fetch a lot of money in a sport requiring much money to participate. But I have always been more excited for the underdog. The horse that was extremely cheap and overlooked as rubbish and came back to become a grand champion. Million-dollar horses are beautiful, but when I hear about the horse that no one bid on at the auction and was put on the kill pen truck only to be purchased at the last minute for eighty dollars, my heart starts to race at how the story ends. Often, those last-chance horses are the ones that prove to the world that they are true champions.

The one thing we can do is to share these rags-to-riches stories with the next generation. Our young people are at a point in life where they want the best and it doesn't matter what it cost. Often, they don't want to muck stalls, do the cool down after a hard ride, or do anything that might simulate hard work. I know this is not every young person, but things have definitely changed. I want to gently encourage the horse moms to consider "less the price tag and more the heart" of a horse. Some of the most incredible horses came from humble beginnings and all they needed was time, patience, and love. What valuable lessons to teach the next generation of equestrians.

Lord, I pray for the moms out there who are trying to teach their young children what is truly important when it comes to horses and life. Please give them strength, wisdom, and courage to blaze a new trail for their children.

~July 15~
This Amazing Thing

This God—his way is perfect; the word of the Lord proves true;
he is a shield for all those who take refuge in him.
Psalm 18:30

What is it about the horse that consumes us? We adore every square inch of their body and become mesmerized when we look into their eyes. Horses have this unique ability to just exist, making us feel better inside. I can't think of another animal except our dogs that have this effect on us.

I was reminded recently that how we treat our horses will stay embedded with them for a lifetime. If we choose kindness, our horses will feel secure and safe, but if we decide cruelty, the bond we could have had with them will be broken forever because they will never forget. They may listen to you and do as you ask without hesitation, but you might miss out on the most beautiful thing about them—their God-given ability to show us what perfection looks like. Their gentleness and giving spirit give us a glimpse into what heaven looks like here on earth. Their eyes look at us with trusting faith that we will always be good to them, and just being near them makes us feel complete. Only when we see horses as God created them to be, will we fully see how amazing they are.

What a gift to grow older with horses. I look at them so much differently than I did as a child, and I am thankful for that. I see them on a much deeper level with this sense that I need to protect them from the world around us. I give thanks to all the women who, even later in life, are still taking care of their horses and making sure they are happy. It is a way of life for the horsewoman, and she is a blessing beyond comparison because God has entrusted her with one of his dearest creatures.

~July 16~
Anxious

I am leaving you with a gift—peace of mind and heart. And the peace I give is a gift the world cannot give. So don't be troubled or afraid.
John 14:27

The anxious horse is a very special type of equine. They may have been born with a personality that is naturally a bit high-strung or had a rough beginning to their existence and have since become a nervous nelly. God bless the woman who understands the anxious horse. She has incredible insight on many levels for such a complex animal. She knows she will need to go slow and she understands the flight risk but always approaches with gentleness. She has enough knowledge to know what she is getting herself into with this horse, but she is making it her mission to help him and watch him transform from anxious and unpredictable to calm and confident. She is in no hurry. The anxious horse may not be suitable for the young rider or the woman looking for her first horse, but for one exceptional horsewoman, he is perfect.

I often think about God and how he handles each of us differently according to our quirks and personalities. He already knows our past and is walking beside us in our present. He only gives us what we can handle at the time, and His words are always calming like the ocean, yet set in honest truth, and that is what we need.

Thank you, Lord, for the horsewoman who has a heart for the anxious and even difficult-to-handle horse. She has the incredible ability to look deeper as she works with him, and as the layers come off, she is able to bring out the true beauty that comes from within. Lord, you have entrusted her to care for this special horse with unique needs, and she is up to the task. God bless the horsewoman who is called to care for the anxious horse.

221

Their Funny Quirks

But God showed his great love for us by sending Christ to
die for us while we were still sinners.
Romans 5:8

Horses can be some of the most peculiar animals ever. They are beautiful in every way possible but when you start to really get to know them, you learn fast that most of them have funny quirks. Some horses will turn their head away as you try to put the halter on, and if you stand quietly, they will bring their head back to you. It is as if they are deciding if you are a friend or foe even though you have done this for years. Some horses poop in their water bucket every night, and the next day, you find a bucket full of YUK that needs to be dumped and cleaned out! Some horses will poop in one area in their stall while others poop everywhere and then grind it into the bedding until you no longer can tell what is poop and what are shavings! If allowed, some horses will get into a habit of not peeing outside, BUT instead, wait until you have them in the crosstie area and then let it flow! Have you heard the expression, "peeing like a racehorse?" Well, that is what it looks like! Some horses will spook at the same corner of the arena every day without ceasing, even though they have walked by it thousands of times. Each horse has their own way of walking when being led. Some will walk as close to you as possible, almost knocking you over, while others walk far away from you as if you have the plague. Some horses will snort every morning while walking them outside, and they always leave a small token as a gift on my jacket and even my face if I dare to look close enough.

With all the funny quirks horses have, the one true thing is that they are wonderfully made. Thank you God for this intelligent, funny, and often, quirky animal you created for us to enjoy.

~July 18~
The Rope Halter

Show me your ways, Lord, teach me your paths.
Psalm 25:4

I was in my forties when I first heard the words "Natural Horsemanship." I grew up learning to ride horses in the 1970s, but I don't recall anyone ever using that expression. In fact, many of the training methods I witnessed seemed cruel by today's standards.

When I first saw someone use a rope halter instead of your standard nylon or leather halter, it caught my interest. I had never seen anything like it used on a horse, and when I asked the person why they used it and its purpose, she told me about Natural Horsemanship. It stopped me dead in my tracks. Soon I was reading as much as possible about it and even buying videos to learn more. The concept of soft pressure to help a horse learn and be successful was new, and I fell in love with it. I learned quickly that a rope halter could help teach a horse not to pull when being led much easier than a thick nylon halter. It was made with thin, soft rope, but it made a positive difference when handling some of the most challenging horses.

The rope halter taught me that less is often better and to keep it simple with horses. I learned that I could have a much closer relationship with my horses if I just learned to think like them and look at the world as they do when I am around them. That simple rope halter was a game-changer.

It made me think about my life and how God uses simple things to correct us and show us a better way to live. He knows we can be difficult and rebellious at times, but if we have a heart to learn and do better, we often find ourselves in a place where we are so much more content and happy. Thank you, Lord, for teaching me a simpler way to live.

223

~July 19~
Not A Good Fit

He changes times and seasons; he removes kings and sets up kings;
he gives wisdom to the wise and knowledge to those who have understanding;
he reveals deep and hidden things; he knows what is in the darkness,
and the light dwells with him.
Daniel 2:21-22

Selling a horse is not an easy thing to do, and the reasons are different for every person. Sometimes, it is because the horse has too many issues or turns out not to be as good of a competition horse as you had hoped. It could be that the horse was a nervous nelly and you didn't feel comfortable having your young children ride him, or has some terrible vices that were never disclosed. The reasons why a horse might not be a good fit are endless, and it is heartbreaking to sell a horse that you were once so excited about. It is especially difficult as we get older and we become aware of what could go wrong.

As women, we worry about our horse's life after we sell him, and we become sick to our stomachs at the thought of the horse falling into the wrong hands and being abused. Selling a horse is very emotional, and we find ourselves screening each person who comes to look at him to ensure they will give him a good home.

I pray for the woman who has made the heart-wrenching decision to sell her horse. Finding the perfect person to become the new owner is not easy, and sometimes, our heart tells us to say, "Sorry, but the horse is no longer for sale."

Dear Lord, I ask for your guidance as I interview people as potential buyers of my horse. I humbly ask that you please send the right person or family to love and care for my horse all his days. I know he is not the right horse for me at this time, but I know in my heart he will be the perfect horse for someone else.

My Heart Is Full

A joyful heart makes a cheerful face,
but when the heart is sad, the spirit is broken.
Proverbs 15:13

I can remember riding my bike home from the stable where my horse was boarded and I had such a feeling of happiness inside. It didn't matter that I was at the barn all day long and was tired. I felt like I could keep going and my heart was full. Decades later, I still get that same feeling about horses. I don't ride anymore, but I handle them daily, muck stalls, and take care of their nutritional needs, and I still get that feeling of joy because I know I am where God wants me to be.

When I watch the women at our stable come out daily in all types of weather to ride or just check on their horses, you can see in their eyes that they have a heart overflowing with love and are doing what they were born to do. It might sound a little dramatic, especially if you are not a horse person, but it is a language that all horse-loving women understand. It is a feeling we all share that never seems to fade, regardless of age. My heart is full when I think about the wonderful horsewomen God has sent into my life over the years. Many have mentored me, and I have had the privilege of mentoring some of them. We talk about horses, life, and our goals and dreams, but more importantly, we are there for each other.

Today, Lord, I pray for the horsewoman who is living out her dreams and making new goals. I pray she will be surrounded by women who will mentor and help her through the tough days. And I hope that one day, she will pay it forward and help someone that is new to horses and needs some encouragement. Thank you, Jesus, for the sisterhood of horsewomen.

~July 21~
Leader

Let us then approach God's throne of grace with confidence, so that we may receive mercy and find grace to help us in our time of need.
Hebrews 4:16

As I have studied horses throughout the years, I find it amazing how the dynamics change each time a new horse is introduced into a herd. They start all over again, figuring out who the boss is, and I have often thought that the mares are much harder on each other when it comes to introductions than the geldings.

If you spend time on social media, you will eventually see a funny meme of the "mare stare" with her ears pierced back and a witty caption above. Most horse people understand the "mare stare" and have experienced it a time or two. The gelding memes on the other hand are usually light and silly! I laugh because the memes tend to be pretty accurate for many horses. The communication between horses when they flex their muscles and show each other how tough they can be is amazing to observe, and when one finally backs down, life returns to normal fairly quickly. It is quite the world they live in but they understand each other perfectly.

As women, we do things similar to each other without realizing it. We size each other up, and in a much more civilized way, we silently determine the leaders and followers. Some of us prefer to be followers and feel comfortable in that position while some women are natural-born leaders.

Today, I pray for the horsewomen who have been called to be leaders in the industry. It can be a heavy burden and the pressure is more intense at times, but when you put your trust in God, He will use you for incredible things. God bless the horsewomen who are willing to jump into the fire and keep going without looking back. They are changing the horse industry in so many wonderful ways.

~July 22~
Always Teaching

Train up a child in the way he should go;
even when he is old he will not depart from it.
Proverbs 22:6

One of the stables I boarded at as a teenager happened to be across the street from an extensive training barn. I often sat on the fence and watched the Charros (Skilled horsemen from Mexico) work their horses outside. The maneuvers they could get their horses to do were remarkable. These horses were stunning, with sleek coats and long manes and tails. I was equally impressed with the treatment of the horses afterward. It was often hot in Southern California and these horses were soaked with sweat after their training, but the men would hose off each horse and rub them down. I would watch the horses play with the water hose while being bathed and then yawn with contentment as each one would be massaged. It was like a personal spa day after a hard workout.

As I think about it all these years later, I realize now what an impression those cowboys and the care they gave their horses left on me. People and horses are always teaching us no matter our age as long as we are willing to have eyes to see and a heart to learn. Whether the good stuff or sometimes painful lessons, both have great value and are worth gleaning from.

Today, my prayer is that you will keep learning and never stop. It is not always about riding. Often, it is about what happens before and after the ride that shows the depth of respect the horse and his owner have for each other. And always remember that one day you might notice a young girl sitting on a fence watching everything you do with your horse. What she sees will stay with her for a lifetime. You might be molding the hearts and minds of the next generation of horsewomen. What an awesome responsibility to have.

~July 23~
The Inheritance

So that being justified by his grace we might become heirs
according to the hope of eternal life.
Titus 3:7

Before we built our stable and indoor riding arena and opened our business, we boarded a couple of horses in our old dairy barn. One of the horses belonged to a gentleman who knew my husband through his love of airplanes. They both liked to fly, and he also owned a mare named Lou. Sadly, the man was killed in an auto accident and his wife had to decide who was going to take care of the horse since she was not a horse person. After much thought, she asked my husband if we would keep the mare and care for her for the rest of her life. We gladly did and Lou became a part of our family. She was your old-fashioned cowhorse and you could do anything with her. She was as bombproof as they come. My younger daughter grew up riding Lou and the years went by fast. Twenty years later, we knew it was time to say goodbye to this wonderful mare we had grown to love. She was Thirty-eight years old.

Making arrangements for your horse if something should happen is not an easy thing to think about. Often the inheritance is made known beforehand, but sometimes, it is not. Occasionally, the person inheriting the horse can't afford to take care of the animal and has to rehome him, and other times, funds have been allocated for care.

Lord, I ask for wisdom for the woman making plans for her horses if something happens unexpectedly. It is so important because their lives will be changed forever. Only you know what the future holds, Lord, and I ask that you will bring the right person into each of our lives to care for our animals if we are called home.

A Piece Of Heaven

But Jesus said, "Let the little children come to me and do not hinder them, for to such belongs the kingdom of heaven."
Matthew 19:14

The women in the 1700s might not have been accomplished equestrians like the women of today, but that was only because, in most cases, society placed restrictions on them and wouldn't allow it. But horses were still a huge part of their everyday life. There were women, even during the Renaissance period, who didn't want to be confined to cooking, cleaning, and doing wifely duties. They would sneak off anytime they could to ride one of their favorite horses. These women often took great chances with riding horses. Either it was looked down on by nobility, or it was dangerous because they were forced to ride in a sidesaddle with tack and equipment that often hurt the horse's back. And this often led to unforeseen dismounts at any given time. But it didn't stop these women because when they were on the back of a horse riding across the countryside, they were set free from the confines of society for a short time. It is difficult to imagine how these women felt and the restrictions that were placed on them. But for the few women who could sneak away and find peace and joy while riding through the meadow, it was as if they were school girls again experiencing a piece of heaven for a few fleeting hours.

Oh Lord, help me never to take for granted the gift of the horse and what this incredible animal has meant to so many women, past and present. The women that came before us were tough, often no-nonsense equestrians because they had to be. I am so thankful for the opportunities we have today in the world of horses, and I see now how important it is to share our blessings with others. God bless the equestrian woman and all that she has endured.

~July 25~
Darkness

I have come into the world as light, so that whoever
believes in me may not remain in darkness.
John 12:46

What has always amazed me is how dark the sky is when I step outside and head to the barn for morning chores. The stars and moon are shining brightly against the black sky, and for a few moments, it is breathtaking. I have always heard it is darkest right before dawn, and it feels like it. The horses are just waking up, and some are still lying down in their stalls as I turn on the lights. It is a special time of day when all is good in the world.

As women, we can feel heavy-hearted when something is wrong with our horse. We worry, the world seems dark all around us, and it can easily consume us. Sometimes, the situation doesn't improve and is beyond our control. But other times, we are blessed to be able to witness a miracle happen that we can't believe we are seeing.

I have witnessed several miracles at our barn throughout the years and some still give me goosebumps. I have watched a horse that was near death fully recover when all hope was lost. And I have felt the heaviness of darkness cover our stable when chaos broke out, feelings were hurt, and hearts deeply broken. But even during our darkest hours, the Lord was faithful and soon the sun was rising, and we survived. During those times of despair I got on my knees and asked for God's protection.

I still love to get up early and admire the dark sky with the stars dancing above me. Thank you, Lord, for showing me that even in total darkness, you shine your light for us to follow.

~July 26~
Gaining Confidence

And walk in love, as Christ loved us and gave himself up for us,
a fragrant offering and sacrifice to God.
Ephesians 5:2

Some of us are much more confident on the ground with horses, while others feel more comfortable in the saddle. But for all of us, it is a journey we embrace as we grow. One is not more important than the other when it comes to horses. What is important is knowing what you feel comfortable with and starting from there.

Gaining confidence does not just come from a one-day horse clinic or weekly lessons, even though those are important. It comes from putting one boot in front of the other and taking small steps forward. It comes from doing things over and over until it feels like second nature for you and your horse. Finding your confidence never comes with giant leaps but instead many small steps.

For the woman who loves horses but feels like she has a huge roadblock in front of her that she can't seem to move past – she is not alone. We are all with her, cheering her on as others have cheered us on. Confidence comes in small things that are not noticed by most people. It could be the graduation from riding minutes in the saddle with someone by our side to riding alone and even trotting the rails. It could be learning how to get your horse out of the paddock with several other horses crowding you. It could be learning to pick up a hoof with confidence. The small things are just as important as the big things and we need to remember that.

Today, I want to pray for the woman who has lost confidence and feels like she is moving backward with her horse. Lord, I know you are by her side, and I pray she feels your presence and the peace that only comes from you. In Jesus's Name, Amen.

~July 27~
Anger Management

Be angry and do not sin; do not let the sun go down on your anger,
and give no opportunity to the devil.
Ephesians 4:26-27

Some horses really need anger management classes! Not really, but it sure feels like it at times when dealing with a horse that looks like he has a permanent scowl on his face and his ears are pinned constantly. Luckily, I haven't had to deal with an angry horse in years, but I do have a couple of older horses that I think act like grumpy old men! Why a horse is angry or fearful has so much to do with his past and what he has endured in his lifetime. Unfortunately, many horses have had very hard lives. Some horses have lived under a harsh hand and now don't trust humans, while others have been starved to near death and are now food-aggressive. Most of the time, we will never know a horse's history, but if you watch him closely, he is trying to tell you by his actions.

We had a horse in our barn years ago that was not given enough food when he was young. When he came to our place, you couldn't clean his stall while he was eating his hay. He had become very food-aggressive, even towards humans, and he needed to be pulled out and cross-tied when mucking out his stall. It took years and plenty of food to get him to the point where he felt comfortable.

I truly don't believe horses are born angry but what we do to them can play a huge part in their negative behavior. The next time you see a horse that looks and acts angry, I encourage you to dig a little deeper. You might find a horse that just needs some love and gentleness.

Today, I pray for the horse that is learning to trust again. I pray that he will find himself in the hands of a horsewoman who will go slow, give him lots of love, and give him time to heal inside. Amen.

~July 28~
The Home Tack Room

Do not neglect to do good and to share what you have,
for such sacrifices are pleasing to God.
Hebrews 13:16

Our new horse has just stepped off the trailer and we are ecstatic. Quickly, we are the owner of a tack box, brand new brushes, and a shiny hoof pick, but it doesn't stop there. We are busting at the seams to find the perfect bridle and saddle to start riding as soon as possible. We know deep inside that we are only allotted so much space in the tack room, but we say to ourselves, "No problem, there is plenty of room." But we are fooling ourselves! We are like kids in a candy store every time we go to the tack store, and soon, that space in the tack room overflows into the next person's area. Oops, we are in trouble now. So we quickly decide to bring home the extra saddle and bridle and a few odds and ends until we can find more room at the stable. Quietly, we tip-toe into the house and find the perfect place to hang the bridle. Then we see the wooden blanket rack in the living room and realize it will make a great saddle rack! And the fun begins.

When my girls showed horses in high school, bridles and saddles were often in the living room while we cleaned them and my husband was always good-natured about it. I have talked to a few women who have turned their basements into tack rooms and even their spare bedrooms. The saddle soon becomes part of the home decor and we love how it makes our house smell!

I guess that is all part of being a horse-crazy woman and I wouldn't change anything. Thank you, Lord, for the husbands who understand our love for our horses and smile when they come in and see bridles and saddles in the living room. God bless the man who supports his wife's horse habits!

~July 29~
If They Could Talk

Let your conversation be always full of grace, seasoned with salt,
so that you may know how to answer everyone.
Colossians 4:6

Have you ever wondered what your horse says about you when you are not around? It's a silly question, but as women, we joke about this often, especially when we do stupid things with our horses. I am just as guilty of it as the next woman and I have done things with my horse that I will never forget because it was that idiotic. Thank goodness my horse wasn't hurt. Usually, it is because we are in a hurry and do things too quickly and our horse is just trying to process it all in his mind. Then we quietly take the walk of shame back out to the pasture, take off his halter, and watch as our horse runs to catch up with his herd buddies. At that point, we are just praying he forgets what transpired earlier. Thank goodness they don't sit there and tell each other about their day with their human!

As women, we tend to do the opposite. We love to talk about everything, even the mistakes we make with our horses. We break it down step by step, hoping our friends can analyze it and give us some tips so we don't repeat the same blunder. It is all part of learning. Praise the Lord that the horse is so forgiving of our shortcomings and is willing to let us try again the next day without a second thought. What an incredible animal the Lord put on this earth.

Thank you, Jesus, for this strong, sensitive animal willing to give us a second chance when we mess up. Lord, help me learn to go slow and take my time, especially when we are learning something new together. And most importantly, always end on a positive note. Amen.

~July 30~
Always A Horse Gal

She is clothed in strength and dignity.
Proverbs 31:25

As horsewomen, we are constantly changing as we age gracefully, or at least we try our best to. For some of us, the bravery we had just a few short years earlier is slowly disappearing, and it's not fun to experience. We envision ourselves riding across the field without a care in the world, but when we hop on our horse, the reality comes back in full force, and we freeze. We make excuses why we can't ride instead of being honest with our fellow barn friends so they can help us work through it.

It takes a brave woman to admit that she has recently become fearful of riding. We put so much pressure on ourselves when it comes to what we should be doing with our horses. We have this idea of horsemanship, and for some reason, we feel we need to be riding a horse to be legitimate horsewomen. That is not true at all. I know this because I have struggled with these feelings as I got older. I didn't know what was wrong with me, but when I got in the saddle, I became nervous, which, at times, kept me from cantering my horse. But I had complete confidence in handling any horse on the ground, no matter how naughty they were.

I have worked through my crazy idea of what makes someone a horsewoman or not. We are all horsewomen, no matter if we ride or just watch from the stand, and each of us brings something unique and beautiful to share with those around us.

Lord, please comfort the woman struggling inside because she is dealing with unexpected new fears. Help her work through those new feelings, and no matter what she chooses to do with horses, I pray she will see her value and, most importantly, that she is loved. In Jesus' Name, Amen.

~July 31~
At The Right Time

You have made known to me the paths of life;
you will make me full of gladness with your presence.
Acts 2:28

It's funny how the perfect horse pops into our life at just the right time. I have owned a few horses throughout the years, and it was as if God knew how much I could handle and what my skill level was at the time.

My first horse was a bomb-proof gelding that I could do absolutely anything on, and nothing ever bothered him. It was like feeding milk to a baby, and I was as green as they come at ten years old. Then, as my horsemanship improved, I yearned for a horse that could teach me more and increase my skill level. That is when I got my second horse – a two-year-old Quarter Horse that wasn't even broke to ride yet. Talk about the learning curve going up! She was the perfect horse for me at the time and I learned so much from her because she made me work for it. The same is true as I watch women purchase horses when they are in their senior years. Everything they want in a horse has changed, and if they are patient and take their time, they will find their perfect horse to ride in their golden years.

I always think about God and how His timing is always perfect. The Lord always knows how much we can handle before we know it. He knows when we are ready to learn more and take on the world and when it's time to slow down. As women, we don't see our lives slowing down when it comes to horses. What we do with them may change throughout the years but we still want to be around them as much as possible. What is so beautiful are the perfect transitions we experience throughout the years and the wonderful horses that will come into our lives at the right time.

~August 1~
Gratitude

This is the day that the Lord has made;
let us rejoice and be glad in it.
Psalm 118:24

Some of the most extraordinary women I have had the pleasure of knowing in the horse world grew up in a less-than-optimal home environment. Some grew up in financially unstable situations where they didn't know if there would be enough food to eat. Some grew up in a volatile family and they quickly learned to stay out of harm's way. But the one thing these women all had in common was that they loved horses. And even though many of them couldn't afford a horse as a child, they never stopped dreaming.

When I talk to some of these horsewomen who had a less-than-stellar upbringing, they have something deep inside of them that is missing from much of society. They have incredible gratitude for life. They may have horses now and ride every day but they never take it for granted, and are often the first to help others in need because they remember what it was like to go without.

I love the word gratitude because, by definition, it means: *The state of being grateful, kindness awakened by a favor, thankfulness.* A woman will light up when she is filled with the spirit of gratitude. She is thankful beyond belief for her horse. She is thankful for the smell of fresh hay and newly cleaned leather tack. She doesn't waste a minute but takes it all in daily as if it is her first day at the barn. She is a ray of sunshine to all who know her, and her horse is always relaxed with one leg cocked and eyes half closed because he knows he can rest in her. The horsewoman with a heart of gratitude is more beautiful than a thousand sunsets. She knows what she has is precious and she has a thankful heart.

237

~August 2~
Failures

When pride comes, then comes disgrace,
but with the humble is wisdom.
Proverbs 11:2

The day started out completely normal with my early coffee and quiet time before I headed out with my husband to begin morning chores. I was listening to one of my favorite podcasts and thinking to myself that it was going to be a great day. Then, as the day went on, issues began to arise. First, a horse came in with a new injury that needed attending, and then a misunderstanding between two boarders escalated into much more. I began to feel exhausted and even annoyed by the chaos that had replaced the peace I felt earlier that day. During that time, I forgot to pray to God and ask for strength and discernment with the issues I was dealing with. Instead I tried to fix them all on my own, and my pride and stubbornness led the way. Before long, I was making epic failures that would have consequences, and I found myself wanting to run away from the situation and go back to bed.

I know I am not alone in saying that I have had many days on our horse farm where things did not go as planned and went downhill quickly, and all I could think about was starting over the next day. This was especially true when our business was young and I was still learning how to manage it all. I made many mistakes with my clients and even the horses at times and didn't handle things very well.

Lord, please forgive me for seeking you last when I should be seeking you first in all things. As I face the giants before me, I know, Lord, you are the one fighting my battles. Thank you for always being there for me in everything, and I will trust you. In Jesus's Name, Amen.

~August 3~
Will He Remember Me?

We prove ourselves by our purity, our understanding, our patience, our kindness, by the Holy Spirit within us, and by our sincere love.
II Corinthians 6:6

The horse's memory is amazing. He can remember herd mates from years earlier and pick up just like they were best buddies without skipping a beat. A horse also remembers the gentle hands that rubbed his neck and face or the friendly person who always has a carrot in their pocket for him. They remember the cues taught to them for both groundwork and in the saddle and if you change things up, they will let you know they have not done this before.

Horses have a great understanding of their owners and some even recognize their vehicles as they drive up to the barn. The horse will also remember the harsh hands that caused him pain or the bit that was excruciating when in his mouth. He will listen to your voice and instantly know what kind of mood you are in and turn away if he feels it is unsafe. He wants to please so he tries his best under the worst circumstances.

Over the years, many ladies have asked me if their horse will remember them when they are gone on vacation. Without a doubt, my answer is always yes! He will play with his herd mates and do what horses do when they are together. And when you get back from vacation, his ears will perk straight forward when he sees you and he will be waiting for you to walk over by him—for he remembers your kindness, gentle hands, and loving spirit.

Dear Lord, help me to be mindful of my actions around the horses in my care. How I treat them today will last a lifetime. When I think about the horse and his incredible mind, I am overtaken with love and forever grateful to be woven into their lives.

~August 4~
Power Of The Pace

The Lord will fulfill his purpose for me; your steadfast love, O Lord,
endures forever. Do not forsake the work of your hands.
Psalm 138:8

As women, we are always doing several things at a time to complete all the tasks in front of us. But sometimes, we add too much onto our plate with the belief that we can do it all. I am guilty of this, and when I was younger, it felt as if the more I added to my schedule, the more I got done. But as the years started to creep up on me I couldn't do it all, and instead, I would shut down and not do any of it. Things overwhelmed me when my schedule got too loaded down and I would retreat to the couch to watch a feel-good chick flick.

I have gained a little wisdom and learned the power of the pace, which has changed my life. Learning to pace myself and not try to do it all at once has helped me be more patient with my husband and kids, and I am able to keep a clearer mind when dealing with issues at our stable. I learned to say no when I needed to, and when I started to read the Bible more, God began to unveil things I couldn't see when I was younger and in a hurry.

Pacing ourselves is good for our mind and body and it is great for our horses. Our horses need time to process otherwise they can become overloaded and stressed easily. When too much is put on them in a short amount of time, it can easily overwhelm them, and sometimes they will retreat or rebel. Neither is good or healthy for the relationship we are trying to achieve with them.

Today, Lord, I ask for wisdom and patience regarding my life. You have entrusted these amazing equines to me, and I pray that I will gain understanding when choosing what is important for my life, my family, and the horses I have the privilege of caring for.

240

~August 5~
God's Perfect Timing

The Lord your God is in your midst, a mighty one who will save;
he will rejoice over you with gladness; he will quiet you by his love;
he will exult over you with loud singing.
Zephaniah 3:17

God's timing is always perfect. I learned this first-hand several years ago when, on the outside, things looked like they were falling apart with our horse business. We were having major issues with a trainer and some clients, and amid all the chaos that was going on, I was also in the process of being approved to be a living kidney donor to a friend and fellow horsewoman. The problems we were having in my barn were very stressful for me and my husband. At the same time, I was going through extensive testing to see if I could donate my kidney. I was crying all the time because of all the stress from the business, and at one point, I didn't think I could take it anymore. I wondered how we would financially make it especially after seventeen boarders moved their horses to follow the trainer.

What I didn't realize was that while everything felt like it was falling apart, it was actually falling into place. At the same exact moment that all my clients gave their notice to move, I was also approved to become a living kidney donor and it turned out to be a blessing in disguise. I went forward with the surgery and it was a complete success. The best part was that our barn only had half the horses, which meant my husband could handle most of it himself while I rested and recuperated, which took longer than expected. We decided to keep all those stalls empty for three months and God took care of us financially. I witnessed two miracles that summer and I realized how perfect God's timing is in all things.

You Can't Make Them Drink

But whoever drinks of the water that I will give him
will never be thirsty again. The water that I will give him will
become in him a spring of water welling up to eternal life.
John 14:14

My daughter had a Miniature Horse named Dusty Roads, who could make even the grumpiest people smile just by looking at him. Dusty lived to a grand old age, but when he was younger, she showed him often in driving classes. He was a steady horse and rarely got stressed out except for fair week. That was when the 4H kids brought their horses to the fair and showed them. It was a long week of people and noise, and you could easily tell that the animals were not thrilled to be there. One summer during the fair, we noticed Dusty wasn't drinking any water, which was not good. We did everything we could to get the little guy to drink and we became concerned that he would colic. Finally, someone suggested putting flavored Gatorade in the water. We did, and to our relief, he started drinking.

That situation with our Dusty reminded me of the old saying, "You can bring a horse to water but you can't make him drink." What a true and wise old saying and it reminded me of my journey with the Lord. Before I put my trust and faith in Jesus, I was selfish, and even though He was teaching me how to live a life that was good for both my body and soul, I often refused. Each time I declined, the outcome was never pretty and I was just hurting myself. I finally got tired of struggling and realized that I needed God more than anything. At that point, I started drinking the Living Water that He was offering me and He breathed new life into me. Thank you, Lord, for giving us Living Water that we may never thirst again.

~August 7~
Yield To Pressure

Who saved us and called us to a holy calling, not because of
our works but because of his own purpose and grace,
which he gave us in Christ Jesus before the ages began.
II Timothy 1:9

It is a beautiful thing to watch the transformation of a young green horse into a well-trained, mature horse that looks like he is enjoying his job. You can see it on his face, and his ears are always listening and anticipating his next commands. The one thing this horse has learned well is to yield to pressure. He can feel even the slightest pressure given from his rider's legs or reins and is ready to do his job. He has no desire to fight the pressure but instead wants to please, and he is a joy to ride.

Recognizing a horse that easily yields to pressure is unmistakable because the rider doesn't have to do anything. His hands and legs are quiet and the horse is calm and happy. A horse with a stubborn streak will sometimes fight the pressure being given from a rider's legs. It also could be that he doesn't understand or is confused about what is being asked of him. A wise rider will be patient and consistent with her horse and wait for that one moment when she sees that he is ready to listen and praise him for his willingness.

I started thinking about my relationship with God and wondered if I was like the horse that listened and yielded to pressure or was I the opposite? I have to admit I have had many times in my life (especially when I was young) when I felt God talking to me and I refused to listen and looked the other way. But I am so thankful that He didn't give up on me and kept nudging me with pressure until I gave in to what He was asking me. Those were the times in my life I learned the most and realized how much He truly loves us and wants what is best for us.

243

~August 8~
Confused

Guard your heart above all else,
for it determines the course of your life.
Proverbs 4:23

Every once in a while, this odd feeling comes over me when I am walking the client's horses and my own horses stare at me. I feel as if they are asking, "What are you doing with that other horse?" Now, I know they do not think like humans, but I have often wondered what they actually think.

Horses are such amazing and funny animals with personalities that shine brightly. If you watch long enough, you see their individual traits come out, and they will act silly just like kids when they are playing. If one horse wants to play and another doesn't, they will go to the next horse, and so on, until they find a partner who will play with them. You can easily tell when a horse is down or even depressed and wants to be alone. If one of the horses is not feeling well, you bet the other horses know what is happening. The one thing for sure is that there is no confusion when the horses are together. They communicate loud and clear and they understand each other very well. They don't play games, are very genuine in their feelings, and get over their squabbles quickly.

As women, we tend to make things out to be more than what they are (I am guilty of this, too!) and spend so much time feeling confused about our relationships. I know I have hung on to the littlest of things that bothered me for far too long, and when I released it, I finally felt a weight lifted off of me.

Today, I pray that you will find a peace that only comes from the Lord and that it will consume your whole being and spread to those who know you. Thank you, Lord, for helping me to see things clearly each and every day.

~August 9~
So Many Colors

Consider the lilies, how they grow: they neither toil nor spin, yet I tell you,
even Solomon in all his glory was not arrayed like one of these.
Luke 12:27

As women, we love color in everything. As horsewomen, we are crazy about all the colors and unique markings that horses come in, and we would love to have one of each if our pocketbook would allow it! They say you should never buy a horse because of its color, but for every woman who has owned horses for some time, I can tell you that many of us have done that a time or two. I am first to tell you that I have been blinded by the color of a horse, and my brain went out the window as I was handing the money over to the person selling the horse. I fell in love with the horse and his white body with loud black spots all over, and I just had to have him. That one purchase taught me a lot about using wise discernment when looking at horses. I often think of that loud-colored Appaloosa pony and his magnificent coat. I still think he was one of the most beautiful horses I have ever owned, but now I know you must look deeper than the surface.

When I look at all the horses at our farm, I am still amazed at how they are uniquely marked in the most beautiful ways, from the stars and snips on their heads to the black or white stockings on their legs. Every shade of brown, black, grey, and white makes for a sea of color that I never tire of.

I can't help but think about the Creator and the gift He has given us. The Lord gave us the horse to use for work and pleasure and combined an array of colors to light up our eyes and emotions. Thank you, God, for the gift of the horse in all its splendor. I will never tire of looking at them.

~August 10~
Newer Isn't Better

Wealth gained hastily will dwindle,
but whoever gathers little by little will increase it.
Proverbs 13:11

Like most kids, I wanted my horse tack to be brand new. In my young and very naïve mind, I believed that to win in the show ring, you needed the best equipment and show clothes, and, of course, that was expensive. My tack wasn't new most of the time, and my saddle was definitely used, but those tough lessons of my youth taught me what was really important in life, even though they were painful at the time.

Fast-forward a few years and I am so glad I wasn't given everything I wanted as a child. I am especially thankful that I learned to make do with used tack and saddles. The times I went into the show ring with clothes that I was embarrassed about and a western saddle without a lick of silver on it taught me not to rely on the outward appearance but to dig deep inside because the real gems are within the heart of a person and their horse.

Today, I love looking for bargains and if I can find something for my horses at a tack consignment store or a 4H tack sale, I am excited! Buying new is now my last resort, and now I enjoy the thrill of the hunt when looking for gently used horse stuff. The funny thing is, I am even more proud that I spent less than what it cost new.

The Lord teaches us so much when we are young, but we often don't realize how important those lessons are until we are much older. The Lord, along with the horses on our farm, continue to teach me daily about life. What a blessing.

~August 11~
My Horse Seems Off

But I have prayed for you that your faith may not fail.
And when you have turned again, strengthen your brothers.
Luke 22:32

Every horsewoman dreads the day she goes to the stable and sees that her horse is off. If you are a new horse owner, wait because it will happen eventually. It's one of those times when you look at your horse, and you can feel in your heart that something isn't right, but you can't pinpoint exactly what it is. You look deep into his eyes, hoping he will reveal why he is unusually quiet or seems amped up more than normal. You will observe how he walks to see if you notice him favoring a foot or if he seems abnormally stiff. You watch how he eats his food and drinks his water, and slowly, you put the clues together in hopes that you can deduce what is going on and if you need the vet to come out.

The answers you are looking for are not always clear, and for some, the silence of not knowing is deafening. The one thing I have learned over the years is that the support of like-minded horsewomen is so important. I watch how they encourage each other in our barn, and when a horse is off his game, they discuss it together and try to whittle down the possible reasons. More importantly, they hold each other up when the stress level is high due to an injury or sickness with a horse. It is truly a beautiful thing to observe.

Today, I pray for the horsewoman who is dealing with an injury or illness with her horse and feels alone. Please, Lord, send other women into her life to help her deal with the situation and give her guidance and support when needed. Thank you, Lord, for the sisterhood of horsewomen and for always being there for us. Amen.

~August 12~
Heart And Mind

You will look for me and find me,
when you look for me with all your heart.
Jeremiah 29:13

Finding the courage to live out your dreams with horses is not for the faint of heart. Horses force us to dig deep inside and come to terms with what is real. You cannot wing it with these very intelligent animals and they will know instantly when you are a fraud. But how do we gather our thoughts and transfer all of this into a relationship with our horse built on trust and respect?

For women who are just getting into horses later in life, it is about learning. Getting real with horses and how they communicate and react to good and bad situations takes time to digest. For some of us, it may take longer than others because our emotions get in the way and stop us from seeing the truth about these animals. But once we understand the horse, our relationship with him will grow more profound than ever imagined.

As I have gotten older, my eyes have opened to just how magnificent the horse is. I have also been keenly made aware that how I behave around my horse will last with him for his entire lifetime. He needs to know that he is safe around me all the times, but equally important is that he knows his boundaries

When my heart and mind are in balance and I have a clear understanding of my role in my horse's life and his role in mine, everything else falls into place. My courage increases and my relationship with my equine partner is strengthened, with respect as the center of it all.

If you are struggling, I encourage you to pray and ask the Lord to guide you in all you do with horses, and watch how your faith and horsemanship come together. It will truly change your life.

~August 13~
Choose Wisely

For the Lord gives wisdom; from his mouth
come knowledge and understanding.
Proverbs 2:6

"Choose wisely, for it could be your last" was a line from a Cinderella movie my daughters and I loved watching when they were younger. To be honest, we still do! That one line alone has always grabbed me deep down, especially when choosing the right horse.

Safety was at the top of the list of importance when I was looking for horses for my girls to ride. Needless to say, sometimes I did not choose wisely, and one time, we had to sell a pony that wasn't safe enough for my youngest daughter to ride. I have watched the same scenario play out with others and it can become an emotional roller-coaster of ups and downs with horse shopping. Between your budget, safety, and paying for pre-purchase vet exams to ensure the horse has no lameness issues, it is a long process and can take months to find the perfect horse.

Over the years, I have watched women jump fast and buy horses only to regret it because the horse was either greener than they were led to believe or had some other problem. I have also watched a few women take their time (and I mean a long time), think it through, ride the horse several times and understand that they needed to choose wisely, which may mean going slower than their heart wants them to go. It means thinking with your head and not your emotions.

Today, I pray that you will seek God first in all your decisions regarding your life and your future equine partner. He is a God of clarity, not confusion. Praise God for that!

~August 14~
Getting To Know You

The wise of heart is called discerning,
and sweetness of speech increases persuasiveness.
Proverbs 16:21

A woman once told me, "Buy a horse and learn things deep inside yourself you never knew existed." Wow, was she right! I have never forgotten what she said, and it still applies to my own life with horses daily. Just when you think you have figured out your horse, they surprise you with a new behavior you never saw coming, and you will find yourself driving home from the stable to spend hours googling what you just experienced.

As horse moms, we hover, become overprotective, and our mama bear claws come out fast if anyone says something negative about our horse. We quickly find out how highly sensitive we are to anything regarding these animals we love like our own children. As equestrian ladies, we dig deep and find the courage to do things that make us nervous, and we do it because we know it is the only way to improve our riding and horsemanship.

The horse will take you to places in your mind and heart you never knew existed. But each time you go down that "trail," you are growing as a horsewoman and human being because the horse has shown you all that you can be on the inside, and that is a beautiful thing. I often hear women at the barn talking about their accomplishments with horses and it's never about the ribbons or trophies. Instead, it's about the strength they mustered up to finish what they started with their horse and finding the courage to cross the finish line when exhausted. It always gives me goosebumps, and I love watching these ladies grow from new homeowners to courageous equestrians. That is the good stuff inside you just waiting to come out. You got this!

250

~August 15~
Hindsight

Behold, I stand at the door and knock. If anyone hears my voice and opens the door, I will come in to him and eat with him, and he with me.
Revelation 3:20

Sometimes, we can be the hardest on ourselves, especially when it comes to our horses. I remember one particular lady who went horse camping and somehow her horse's front legs got all tangled up in the tie-line that was attached to the horse trailer. The horse panicked and the rope tightened up more. When she found her horse, he was all sweated up and his leg was injured. She panicked when she saw the pain in his eyes but managed to get him untangled and to a vet clinic as quickly as possible. This poor woman was torn up inside and blamed herself for months after the accident even though her horse had healed completely with no signs of permanent trauma from the incident. She kept wondering if she could have done anything differently. She realized she may have been in a hurry while tying up the horse at the campsite and didn't check it for safety. But the hardest part was that she couldn't forgive herself for her lack of awareness.

Hindsight is always 20/20, and it teaches us so much, but we need to be willing to forgive ourselves, learn from it, and then let it go. It's as hard for me as it is for most women and we can sometimes replay it in our minds for far too long. That is why it is so important to surround ourselves with others who will hug us, encourage us, and help us move forward.

Today, I pray for the woman struggling to move forward because she is stuck in the past with her mistakes. It happens to all of us, and I pray that she will find other women to walk her through this valley and that she will feel the love of Jesus every step of the way.

251

~August 16~
For Such A Time As This

Search me, God, and know my heart; test me and know my anxious thoughts.
See if there is any offensive way in me, and lead me in the way everlasting.
Psalm 139:23-24

Your first horse will always hold a special place in your heart, not only because you were in love for the first time but because that is where you learned the most. As a brand new horse owner, you will quickly realize how much you will doubt yourself with every decision you make for him, and you will sometimes feel exhausted as you are learning. There will be uncertainty as you hold the lead rope, and you will ask yourself if it is too loose or too tight. The first time you pick up a hoof to clean, you will be a ball of nerves, but you will get through it. You will second guess what brushes to use and worry that you are hurting him as you try to get all the mud off his body. You will start to panic that you rode him too hard because he was sweaty after your ride, and you will constantly wonder if he is comfortable with his new saddle and begin to question your choice of tack. You will wonder if he likes the grain and supplements you bought, and at that point, you start to wonder when it will get easier.

The doubts you have will creep in daily but then something amazing happens over the course of the first year. Slowly, you will gain confidence with each new situation and begin to think back to the earlier months and realize how much you have learned and that your horse is still alive! Your doubts will become fewer over the coming years, and then one day, you will go out to the barn and see a woman with her first horse, and you will smile and introduce yourself. And God will smile down on you as you help her through the first year and all the doubts she will wrestle with. God has made you for such a time as this.

~August 17~
Delayed Gratification

You also, be patient. Establish your hearts,
for the coming of the Lord is at hand.
James 5:8

Delayed gratification is extremely challenging when you are bitten by the horse love bug! As women, we are ravenous when we walk into a tack store and the smell of leather consumes us. Our hearts start to palpitate fast, and the endorphins kick in, and soon we are grabbing everything in sight! I have been there a few times in my life when I walked into a tack store for one specific thing and came out with many items, most of which I didn't need or will never use.

Now, in all seriousness, there is nothing wrong with going crazy every now and then when you have the cash to back it up, but if you are struggling, you will have to do some soul-searching to make sure you don't get in over your head. I have made that mistake, and that is when buyer's remorse sets in on the drive home.

We live in the days of instant gratification and it is so easy to buy horse things on credit. Learning self-control is not easy at any age, but the more opportunities we have to practice it, the more at peace we feel when we finally buy that saddle we have wanted for a long time. It's as if the leather smells better and we can enjoy it more. It may have taken longer but it was well worth the wait.

Lord, I am asking for your intervention when I feel weak and want to spend money I do not have. Lord, help me see the big picture and realize that patience and self-discipline are beautiful virtues. Today, I turn my finances over to you and ask you to guide me daily. In Jesus' Name, Amen.

The Golden Years

She does him good, and not harm, all the days of her life.
Proverbs 31:12

There is a beautiful strength that surrounds the older woman. She has gained a little gray hair over the years but no longer has the need to cover it with hair dye. She has lived long enough to know what fashions were hip and which were awful, and she laughs at herself when she thinks about the style of clothing she wore in her youth. She was known as the girl who loved horses more than boys when she was young, but she married her high school sweetheart, and horses became second.

She is now in her golden years and is still madly in love with the same boy who became her husband decades earlier. These days, her husband is seeing a new light in her eyes. She is trading in her trendy city clothes for riding boots, jeans, and western shirts. There is an excitement about her that most of her friends do not understand but they love how happy she looks. She spends hours looking at horse tack and reading the latest articles about horse care. She thanks the Lord for having such a supportive family and she knows her home will never be the same. Her dining room table now has tack sitting on top of it and she has a special area for her barn clothes so that she doesn't smell up the house, even though she loves the smell! Vacations will look different and fewer at times, but she is happy to adjust her lifestyle because of her new love.

She has a horse now to care for and he will be part of the family. He will be in family photos and her husband will learn more about horses than he ever dreamed. She is forever grateful for this wonderful gift she is now experiencing for the first time in her life. Thank you, Lord, for the women who are enjoying horses to the fullest in their golden years.

~August 19~
The Call

Be watchful, stand firm in the faith.
I Corinthians 16:13

As women, we would do anything to keep our horses happy and healthy. We continually watch to make sure they are moving easily and their body weight is where it should be. We make sure we have a first-aid kit and any extras we need just for an emergency, and we find great satisfaction and comfort in knowing we are prepared for any situation. We know we can be obsessive, but we love it and don't plan on changing, even if others think we are a little strange.

Having horses means there will be many times when you must decide if you need to call the equine vet or if your horse will be okay on his own. It means you will sometimes lose sleep wondering if you made the right decision, and you will be on the phone talking with your horse friends and asking them what they would do. At the end of the day, it doesn't matter what it costs and you have them come out because you will never forgive yourself if it is something serious.

Any woman who has ever owned a horse has had this scenario play out in her mind a few times, but the good news is it gets easier. As you experience the ups and downs of horse ownership, you will start to learn what needs to be addressed quickly and what can wait. You will gain confidence in making decisions regarding your horse's health and well-being and you will grow inside as a horsewoman.

Today Lord, I pray for the horsewoman who will need to make a decision on whether to call her vet or wait it out. She may be stressed and not know if the wound or lameness is serious or not. Please send others to guide her through this and give her good advice because it is a heaviness that is hard to go through alone. Amen.

~August 20~
A Reason To Live

So we are always of good courage. We know that while we are at home in the body we are away from the Lord, for we walk by faith, not by sight.
II Corinthians 5:6-7

The little girl climbed up on the red rocking horse and pretended to be galloping across a large field. That is where she first fell in love with horses.

When Cheryl was a child, she would walk to the park to ride the ponies. Her father donated his excess sawdust and the owner let Cheryl ride as much as she wanted. It was the perfect arrangement for a horse-crazy little girl. Soon, her mother was driving her to a local stable to ride the bigger horses. After graduation, she moved to Chicago and the horses became a wonderful memory.

Years later, Cheryl found out she had breast cancer, and as she recovered from surgery, she kept thinking about horses and longed for the day when she would own one. Then, in her early fifties, she got news that both her kidneys were failing. She knew that sometime in the distant future she would need a kidney transplant, so she decided to buy a horse. She wasn't going to let an illness stop her from riding. Over the next few years she rode as much as possible, and even though her health was declining, she would drive out to the barn every day to see her horse. But Cheryl had one more thing on her bucket list. She had always wanted to raise a colt and help train him, and that is when she found a beautiful four-month-old appaloosa colt that she brought home.

Cheryl had a successful kidney transplant and was back in the saddle eight months later. She has always said that God and horses got her through her many illnesses, and the only time she felt good during those difficult times was when she was at the barn with her horses. They gave her a reason to live.

~August 21~
Pray For Recovery

But let him ask in faith, with no doubting, for the one who doubts
is like a wave of the sea that is driven and tossed by the wind.
James 1:6

I got up early and had my morning coffee. The weatherman said it would be a gorgeous day, and I knew I could soon look across the farm fields and see the sunrise on the other end. As I began putting on halters and leading horses outside for the day, I noticed one of the horses was acting a little off when I opened her stall door. She wasn't eating her grain and she stood quietly with her head facing the back of the stall, which wasn't at all normal for her. As I walked closer, I could see that her breathing was labored and she was definitely not feeling good. Then she started pawing at the ground and I knew there was a more serious problem. She was colicking. From that moment on the morning was a blur. I was on the phone with the owner, and soon, the on-call vet and owner were on their way. As the morning progressed, things took a turn for the worse, and by the afternoon, we were just waiting to see if she would pull through. It would be a long night of checking on her often and praying she would recover.

Having a sick horse is every person's nightmare, especially when it could potentially be fatal. The woman who has experienced this often feels helpless, and nothing her husband or friends can say will make her feel better or take away the fear gripping her. When something like this happens it can bring me to my knees, and that is where I should be. The Lord wants us to ask for His help and pray without ceasing. He is always there to comfort us in the darkness. Things may not turn out how we would like them, but true peace comes from the Lord and only Him.

Young And Brave

Put on the whole armor of God, that you may be able
to stand against the schemes of the devil.
Ephesians 6:11

Sometimes, you come across a story about incredible female perseverance and it motivates you to do better. But when you hear about a young girl who helped in the war effort, it is nothing short of inspirational.

Paul Revere may have ridden all night to warn the townspeople that the British were coming in 1776, but a young 16-year-old girl and her horse also road all night and twice as far to get the same message out to anyone who would listen. Her name was Sybil Ludington, and on the back of her horse, Star, she rode 40 miles through bad weather and off the main roads to warn as many people as possible of the impending danger that was coming.

Sybil had watched her father train the militia, and she was very familiar with where each man lived. She and her horse were accustomed to the backcountry and rough terrain, and she knew how to reach people without being seen on the main roads. The evening of her famous ride, she set out at 9 p.m., and the weather was rainy and cold, but it didn't deter her. She knew her horse Star was strong and fit and he could make the journey.

Sybil and her horse proved just as invaluable as the men spreading the word. Despite her tender age of sixteen at the time, her legacy lives on forever as the young equestrian who did her part on a long all-night ride for American Independence.

Lord, my heart swells with admiration when I think about this girl who achieved a remarkable feat from the back of her horse. She will be remembered in history as a truly enduring horsewoman who did not falter, even when the ride became arduous.

~August 23~
The Ranch Woman

As with cattle going down into a peaceful valley,
the Spirit of the Lord gave them rest.
Isaiah 63:14

She rides the plains alongside her family as they move cattle from one place to another. She has chosen the life of a ranch woman and feels blessed to be living her dream. She is tough when she needs to be but can soothe a crying child with her softness. Her hands are weathered and her boots are worn, but she lovingly directs her horse as they go another mile. At the end of the day, she is exhausted and dirty but her heart is full. She knows she needs to tend to her tired horse, for he was a good cowpony today and deserves the best care she can give him. She gazes into his tired eyes and feels this sense of peace as she watches him eat his food. She wonders how she got so lucky to find such a gem of a horse, and she prays silently that he will stay healthy and strong for many years. She knows that the life of a cowpony is hard at times, but her horse embraces it with the willingness of ten horses, and she knows that he will sleep well tonight. It is time to give him his last brushing and rubdown and head to her tent to sleep, for tomorrow brings another day of moving cattle and living the good life. She looks around and sees nothing but open land and the sky above, and she counts her blessings to be right where the Lord has placed her.

I pray for the ranch women who work tirelessly in all types of weather and often spend more time in the saddle than most. These women are wives and mommas and they know their job is never done. Yet they feel blessed to be doing what they do day in and day out. God bless the modern-day ranch woman who still rides her horse for work each day. She is truly a blessing to all who know her.

~August 24~
The Copycat

The Lord will hold you in his hand for all to see
a splendid crown in the hand of God.
Isaiah 62:3

As a young girl, I was a copycat at times. I was very insecure and it seemed easier to copy what the other girls were wearing or doing. Thank goodness I started to mature and create my own style, and I didn't feel the need to be a copycat and follow the crowd anymore. It is definitely a part of growing up. The same is true for the horse world. Fads come, and fads go, but when they are brand new, equestrians jump on them like bees to honey. It doesn't matter if your style is Wrangler jeans or breeches. We are on top of it and want to look good even when riding horses.

I figured out later in life that the jeans I wear are not that important, and I can't even tell you what women wear these days for riding attire. But I have come to embrace the horsewoman who dresses in her own unique style with colors and patterns that will make you take a second look. She boldly wears what she wants, and I must say I am a little envious of her because she has a gift of putting things together that make you feel good when you see her. The truth is I am a pretty bland dresser when working in the barn and prefer my worn-out jeans and tank top. However, if I wanted to walk on the wild side, I know exactly who I would go to.

In a world full of copycats, be the woman who has fun with what she wears when she is riding. Be true to yourself and to who God created you to be. The woman who dares to live on the edge with fashion when riding her horse is a breath of fresh air.

Thank you, Lord, for making us unique, each with our own personality and dreams, and for giving us each our own sense of style in the saddle and out of it.

~August 25~
Too Many Changes

Set your minds on things that are above,
not on things that are on earth.
Colossians 3:2

I love when things stay the same and are constant in my life. Like most women, we need to feel in control as things change around us. It is no different in the horse world. When we first opened our horse boarding stable, I was like a kid at Christmas. We had worked hard building it and setting everything up, and I thought I knew exactly how things would go. After all, it looked good on paper. I quickly realized I needed to make many changes and my new boarders would not be happy.

Those early changes in our business were painful not only for us but equally for our boarders. Nobody likes change, and when it comes to our horses, it can be stressful for them as well. Now, looking back, the changes we made at our stable came with a huge learning curve, which in the end, taught me so much. It wasn't always easy but it forced me to let go of the control and give it to God. The times I tried to control a situation, my emotions took over and things did not always go as planned. But when I got on my knees and asked the Lord to take the wheel and let me be the passenger, things went much better, and I found out that I could handle the ups and downs much easier.

Today, I pray for the horsewoman who will endure many changes throughout her life. She will experience personal changes in herself, and her horse business will evolve as she grows. I pray she will lean on the Lord and let Him guide her through each situation. Please comfort her as she enters unknown territory with decisions regarding the horses and clients at her stable.

~August 26~
Messed Up Priorities

Whoever pursues righteousness and kindness
will find life, righteousness, and honor.
Proverbs 21:21

Every devotional book I read always has one page that stings because it reflects something less-than-stellar in my life. As I wrote today's devotion, I realized this was "that one" for me.

When we opened our stable, I was ecstatic and felt like we were living our dream. Overnight, we went from four horses to forty and my life changed forever. I was busier than I ever imagined and my days started early and ended late. Over the next couple of years my life revolved around the business, horses, and the people, and soon I stopped going to church most of the time because I was just too tired. Like a slow fade, God became less important and the horses became everything. I was losing myself in all of it and struggling. This would be my life for about seven years until God woke me up and showed me that nothing on this earth is worth having unless I have Him as my Lord and Savior first.

When I realized that I needed the Lord in my life first and family second, the business came in third and my life started to change in amazing ways. I now had a purpose bigger than myself and everything with the horses became easier. All these years later, I see God in everything on our farm including the horses, and I am forever thankful that He helped me get my messed-up priorities straight again. It's easy to be consumed in the daily grind with animals and it can pull you far away. I pray you will feel the Lord's presence daily and grow closer to Him.

Thank you, Lord, for always being right there for me and helping me find a healthy balance in life with family and horses and for showing me daily what is really important in this world.

How Old Is Too Old?

In peace I will lie down and sleep,
for you alone, O Lord, will keep me safe.
Psalm 4:8

It is incredible how many of the most famous horses throughout the centuries were ridden up until their late twenties, and even longer in some cases. Before motorized vehicles and steam engine trains, horses were considered work livestock and they were used to help man survive, conquer countries, and build empires. Even looking at old photos of horses being ridden or pulling carriages from the 19th century shows horses that are often frail and worn. Praise God for the men and women who showed kindness to these hard-working equines and helped educate others on a better way to care for them.

For the women who love their horses and have made them part of the family, we know deep down inside that our horses are spoiled rotten but we love pampering them and wouldn't change a thing. We are also keenly aware of how fast time goes by as we watch our horse slow down and acquire some grey hair on his face. We keep thinking that we are seeing things and dismiss them because, in our minds, he is still a youngster.

So, one day, we will ask ourselves, "How old is too old?" as tears stream down our face. When we get our answer, we will know it is time to let him retire with dignity and live out his days in comfort. And we will make sure we are right by his side.

Thank you, Lord, for giving me the honor of caring for my horse into his senior years. I realize now what a gift it is to just watch him eat and brush him gently as he enjoys his life to the fullest.

~August 28~
Books In Her Saddlebag

She extends a helping hand to the poor and opens her arms to the needy.
She has no fear of winter for her household, for everyone has warm clothes.
Proverbs 31:20-21

Sometimes, you come across an inspiring story that makes you realize the large impact horsewomen have had on our world. One such group of women were known as the Packhorse Librarians.

In the 1930s, America fell into a depression, and the state of Kentucky was hit hard. Thousands of families living in the Appalachian Mountains were cut off from the outside world, and many children and adults could not read. The women who worked as librarians during that time witnessed the severity of what was happening to these families and understood the importance of reading as a way for these families to better their lives. That is when the Packhorse Library Project was established to bring books and magazines to these people.

During this time in history, librarians were always women. They would gather books and newspapers, load their saddle bags, and head out to deliver the reading materials. They would each travel in a different direction, which meant these women often rode alone through all types of weather and terrain, and they would ride 50 to 80 miles a week to the remote residences and schools in the mountains. Sometimes, the trails were so steep that the women would have to get off and walk alongside their horses. These women were often with their horses more than their families because they knew how important reading was.

When I think about the courageous women of the past, I will forever think of the Packhorse Librarians. Thank you, Lord, for the brave horsewomen who paved the way for a better life for so many and did it all from the back of a horse.

Underneath The Mud

He lifted me out of the pit of despair, out of the mud and the mire.
He set my feet on solid ground and steadied me as I walked along.
Psalm 40:2

Some horses love the mud, and anytime it rains, they will roll and roll until you can't see the color of their coat. You can tell they are in all their glory and having a blast, pawing and splashing first and then plunging their entire body into the mud like a child. Some horses even manage to get mud all over their faces and the mud on their mane and tail quickly turns to dreadlocks in the warm sunshine.

Every woman who owns a mud puppy knows what it is like to pull into the stable and see their horse looking at them covered in mud and standing proud as a child who just got an A on his spelling test. You can't help but smile even though you know you won't be riding anytime soon because you will be trying to clean him up.

We all know it is part of owning a horse, and even though it can be frustrating at the moment, we secretly smile on the inside because we know he is content and happy. It's amazing how the white horses always seem to get the muddiest, and from a distance, you wouldn't be able to tell they were your horse. We have four white horses at our stable and they all love the mud with a passion. When their owners come out and hose them off, they clean them up just like they were ready for the show ring.

Today, we celebrate the horsewoman who owns a horse that loves the mud and rolls in it every chance he gets. She has her work cut out for her but she is up to the challenge and knows her horse is special among the rest. Underneath all that mud is one of God's most beautiful creations, just waiting to shine.

~August 30~
This Incredible Animal

But, as it is written, "What no eye has seen, nor ear heard, nor the heart of man imagined, what God has prepared for those who love him"
I Corinthians 2:9

We get it wrong when we think that we can overpower a horse because we are smarter and use special devices to make him yield to what we are asking. His power will come out in full force if he is scared or defending himself and he will not stop even if he gets hurt. The one thing I have learned over the decades is that if we ask a horse and he responds positively then he is giving us permission to go to the next level. A horse will allow us to approach him in the field, place a halter over his head, and lead him to the barn. He knows he can pull away anytime but listens quietly and follows. A horse gives us permission by allowing us to climb in the saddle and ride him wherever we want to go. What is absolutely astonishing about the equine is that if he trusts us, he will give us permission to do anything that involves him. He has faith that you will not hurt him and his willing heart leads the way.

I often think of God when I am around the horses because they show me through their power and willingness that only He could have created such an incredible animal. Their mind is sharp and they are always sizing up their surroundings, and as you approach them, they have already decided whether you are friend or foe. The gift is even sweeter when a horse of such power wants to be near you. That is when the bond deepens and the magic happens.

Lord, help me never to take for granted the uniqueness of the horse. He is massive with power yet gentle and willing to listen even when he may not want to. I am in awe of the depth and love that is wrapped up in this remarkable animal. I am forever thankful for the horse.

~August 31~
Broken To Whole

He heals the brokenhearted and binds up their wounds.
Psalm 147:3

The first time she saw the horse, he was worn out and you could easily see that the last few years had been hard on him. The woman tried talking to him but he wouldn't make eye contact. It was as if he wasn't there and just a hollow shell of what once was a stunning show horse stood motionless in the stall. She learned he had been tossed around, and with each new home the trainer was more aggressive than the last, trying to get him to perform and win ribbons. All she could see was this poor broken animal.

The woman made an offer and purchased the horse but had no intention of showing him. She knew she had to have him the first time she saw him standing with his head down in the corner. She thought he was beautiful but saw the deep hurt in his eyes and her heart broke. He quietly walked on her trailer and she drove him to his new home. She had a clean stall, bedding, fresh hay and water, and even some carrots waiting for him. Over the next few weeks, she would lead him outside every day and spend time brushing him in the sunshine. He hadn't been with another herd buddy in many years so she put him with a horse that she knew would be kind to him. Over the months, she began to see a remarkable change in him. He started to play outside and his ears perked up every time he saw the woman. Soon he was following her everywhere. She began riding him on quiet trail rides and you could see that he loved it. He was alert and he had a light in his eyes again. It was easy to see that what was once broken was becoming whole again.

Thank you, Lord, for the incredible women who can see through the brokenness and heal the whole horse. They are a blessing beyond compare.

~September 1~
Riding With My Dad

See what great love the Father has lavished on us,
that we should be called children of God!
I John 3:1

I was one of those kids whose parents were divorced, which was very unusual in the 1960s. But I knew my father loved me more than anything. I would spend my weekends with him and it was my favorite part of the week. My earliest memories of riding horses were at Big Ben's Petting Zoo and later riding horses at Griffith Park Stables. My father knew absolutely nothing about horses, but when we started riding rental horses at Griffith Park stables, he was all in.

It's funny because I actually thought I knew how to ride a horse and that he was along just for the company. Then, one Saturday, we went riding, and this time things went much differently. He was following me on his horse and we came to a long bridge that we needed to ride across. I stopped my horse and watched as other riders crossed back and forth without a problem. For some reason the bridge scared me and I couldn't go a step further. I looked back at my father and he smiled at me and knew what I was thinking. He urged his horse ahead of me and took the lead and I slowly followed him across the bridge. I remember feeling safe as long as he was in the lead and I was following.

That day with my father is one of my favorite memories and always reminds me of my Heavenly Father, who constantly watches over me as an adult. When I try to take the lead and feel unsure, the Lord is always there to guide me and a sense of peace replaces my fear, just like when I was a little girl with my father. Thank you, Jesus, for taking the lead when we are scared to cross the bridge.

~September 2~
Miles

But grow in the grace and knowledge of our Lord and Savior Jesus Christ.
To him be the glory both now and to the day of eternity. Amen.
II Peter 3:18

If you have been around horses for a while, the expression, "That young horse just needs some miles on him," might sound familiar. When you spend a lot of time in the saddle with a young horse, he settles into his new job and usually becomes a nice riding horse. He is more confident and has learned to take things in stride. Those types of horses have been taught by someone who understands that success comes from miles, encouragement, and love.

As horsewomen, we should take some of that wise advice to heart. We get excited about our first horse and jump right in, then wonder how deep it is. I was the same way when I was younger, and now, many years later, I have watched many women jump right in with a new horse and some have become so disillusioned that they sell the horse, never to ride again. Then, you have others who quickly realize that they need some help navigating the road bumps and understand that getting out of the saddle is not an option. Those women are the ones who don't give up but instead keep learning and keep riding. They are willing to go the distance to achieve their dreams and it is a beautiful thing to watch them grow.

Lord, I pray for the woman who has purchased a new horse. She knows she is new to this whole horse thing but she loves every minute of it and quitting is not an option. I pray that she will be surrounded by encouraging people who will guide her and give her great advice. She is a horsewoman in progress and she is well on her way to becoming an exceptional equestrian. Amen!

~September 3~
Beacon Of Light

In the same way, let your light shine before others, that
they may see your good deeds and glorify your Father in heaven.
Matthew 5:16

When you think about the people who really changed the world of equestrian competition, one woman comes to mind. Her name is Lis Hartel, and she was born in Denmark in 1921. As a child, Lis loved horses and began riding at a young age, and by the time she was a teenager she was competing in show jumping. She married at 20 years old and shortly after was tragically struck with Polio. She was almost paralyzed completely, but with the help of her mother and husband, she learned to use her arms, then crawl, and eventually use crutches. Then, to further her therapy, her husband would help her get on her horse and she would ride every day to help improve her muscle control.

Lis had always dreamed of competing in the Olympics, even though women were not allowed to do so at the time. With unparalleled perseverance, she learned to ride using very minimal cues on her horse and soon was competing in Dressage and placing higher than many of the male riders. Her scores were high enough to qualify her for the Olympic Equestrian team but there was one problem. Women were not allowed to compete in the Olympics in 1948. Lis would have to wait four more years until 1952, when the rules were changed and women could now compete.

Lis went to the Olympics with her horse Jubilee and earned a silver medal and she did it completely paralyzed from the knees down. She showed the world that anything is possible if you don't give up. God bless the incredible horsewomen in history who persevered under incredible circumstances and became a beacon of light for others.

Cleaning Stalls

I have told you these things so that you will be filled
with my joy. Yes, your joy will overflow!
John 15:11

Horsewomen are a crazy bunch of ladies. Most of us (including myself) would rather be in the barn cleaning horse stalls than cleaning our homes. There is something so satisfying about mucking out a horse stall and adding fresh bedding that makes you feel good about things. It's clean, feels perfect, and is ready for your horse. I have been mucking out stalls for twenty years now and I still feel great satisfaction when they are clean and ready to go. Then the horses come back in from being outside all day and it is amazing how quickly they mess it up! The truth is most horse stalls look like they were hit by a tornado and you wonder what they did all night to make the stall look so terrible. Many horses will grind everything into the shavings until you don't know what is manure and what is bedding. Only horse-crazy people would endure this every day and love it years later.

There is also something to be said for manual labor like cleaning stalls. The conversations are always great, and we laugh at the stories we share and cry with each other when things are not so good. We talk about everything, and you leave feeling like you have learned something new. It has been said that many of the world's problems could be solved if more people cleaned stalls. I am not sure if that is completely accurate but it sure sounds good. The best part about mucking stalls with other people is that you really get to know them on a deeper level. There is just something peaceful about cleaning horse stalls with other women who share the same passions. It never gets old. Thank you, Lord, for the women who love mucking out stalls. They are a true joy!

~September 5~
Crying Again

Those who sow in tears shall reap with shouts of joy!
Psalm 126:5

As I have gotten older (especially after menopause), I find myself crying at everything. I tear up at movies and can barely make it through a horse movie without Kleenex. I find myself fast-forwarding through the sad parts because I know what is going to happen to the horse. The crazy thing is, I know it is a movie and no horses were hurt in the making of it, but I can't help myself. It conjures up images in my mind that I can't let it go of even into the next day.

I know older ladies can relate to what I am saying about being emotional wrecks with our horses or the movies we watch. We love our horses with this deep passion, and all they need to do is come trotting toward us when they see us at the gate and it sends shivers down our body as we beam with joy. We are like brand new parents taking videos of our horse playing with another horse, and soon, we are showing everyone. But we can quickly become distraught when our horse comes in with a new wound or isn't feeling well, and we have a hard time holding back the tears. Owning a horse will make you feel like you are on an emotional roller coaster, and as we get older, it gets more intense.

What a beautiful thing it is to be able to cry and show our emotions. Some women do this more readily than others, but we all feel the same thing inside, even if we show it in different ways. It's something that bonds us together, and what a beautiful gift it is. Thank you, Lord, for the gift of tears and how they make us feel when they start to flow. Our horses may never understand why we cry when we look at them but they will know they are loved.

~September 6~
The First Fear

I sought the LORD, and he answered me;
He delivered me from all my fears.
Psalm 34:4

Facing your first fear when it comes to horses will be much different for every woman. For some women, the fear of falling off and breaking something began as a child and it has taken them a long time to get over it. For other women, the fear of riding never crept into their thoughts until they reached their golden years and became more aware of how easily things break. The first fear that pops into your head will be a shock, especially if you have never been fearful of horses anytime you can recall. No matter when those fears creep in, it is a journey to work through them and land at a place where you replace your fear with courage and peace.

I didn't have my first fear of riding until I was well into my forties. But suddenly, I became very aware that I didn't want to fall off my horse. It was such a strange new feeling for me because, as a kid, I rode every day and fell off more times than I could count, but I would laugh about it and hop back on without thinking twice.

No matter where you are in your journey as an equestrian, it is okay to feel fearful and take it slow. It might mean gaining your confidence on a quieter horse that moves slower or getting back to the basics and doing groundwork instead. Whichever way you choose will have wonderful benefits and it doesn't matter what everyone else is doing. You need to do what is best for you.

Some fears last a long time, while others are just temporary. The best thing we can do as women is support and encourage each other. We may not always understand what the other is feeling, but loving each other and helping each other grow as equestrians is a beautiful way to show the love of Jesus.

~September 7~
The Other Horsewomen

You made all the delicate, inner parts of my body and knit me together in my mother's womb. Thank you for making me so wonderfully complex! Your workmanship is marvelous—how well I know it.
Psalm 139:13-14

They were considered the "other" horsewomen. Circus horsewomen, to be exact. These young female equestrians grew up in France at the turn of the nineteenth century and loved horses just like any other young girl. They came from different walks of life, but their stunning riding skills brought them together. These horsewomen became famous during that period, all because of the circus. They excelled at dressage riding, did acrobatics on the back of horses, and jumped everything possible. Some of these women would ride in the strangest positions as if they had eight legs and arms and did this while wearing the confining riding attire required at the time. Nevertheless, nothing would stop these women from showing the world their exceptional equestrian skills.

These horsewomen broke through many cultural barriers and worked while married and having children. For many, it was a great life, but a hard road for others. What drove each of these women was their love for horses, and of course, the crowds loved it.

In the echelons of high society, affluent women rarely rode a horse but instead took a fancy carriage even if it was only across town. But these female circus equestrians were the "cowgirls" of the nineteenth century and they changed the stereotype of how a woman was supposed to act in public. These horsewomen endured a lot during a time when women had very few rights.

Once in a while, God calls us to do something entirely out of the ordinary, and it is awesome when He chooses a horse to partner with us on that journey.

274

~September 8~
Later In Life

May the Lord direct your hearts to the love of God
and to the steadfastness of Christ.
II Thessalonians 3:5

Today, I want to encourage the woman who is worried that she has missed her chance to do the horsey things she has always wanted to do. Take the riding lessons, you will never regret it. If you want to take a step further, lease the horse. You are never too old to try something new, and some of the smartest cowgirls are the ladies who have thrown a few ropes and kicked off a few dirt clods in their lives. Those women will be the first to encourage you to enjoy every minute of it. They will tell you to never stop learning and to remember that life with horses is an incredible gift that is not just for the young but also for the young at heart.

Owning your first horse later in life has some wonderful advantages. You are more open to new ways of thinking regarding horsemanship and horse care, but you are smart enough to use discernment that many young girls have yet to acquire. You are old enough to remember the fads and trends of your youth and wise enough to stay away from things that lack substance for a good life. For many women, life with horses just gets better and better, especially when we can truly appreciate them in a deeper way.

I am deeply grateful, Lord, for the opportunity to share my life with such remarkable horsewomen of all ages and experiences. When I start to feel like I am lagging behind in my horsemanship, I need to stop and realize that I am right where you want me to be and it's all in your perfect timing. Praise your Holy Name!

275

~September 9~
The Soft Eye

A soft answer turns away wrath, but a harsh word stirs up anger.
Proverbs 15:1

If the light catches them just right they look like beautiful hand-blown glass balls. Each pair is wonderfully designed with a vast array of colors and shades, and each pair is uniquely different in shape. But there is something even more special about the horse's eye. If you look closer, you will see his personality reflected back at you and he will tell you everything through his eyes.

Over the years, I have had the privilege of taking care of many different horses. Some were old and some were just a few months in age. Some were Thoroughbreds and some were ponies. It didn't matter the breed or age; you could see the life each horse had lived just by looking into his eyes. Some horses had a very tired look in their eyes, and some showed fear that was deep and penetrating. Some had a stubborn or hard look about them, while others looked indifferent to their surroundings. But when you came across a horse with soft eyes, you knew it instantly. His eyes showed his gentle nature and his willingness to be near you. He had this wonderful playfulness that seemed to dance in his eyes and he seemed excited about the day's adventures.

The soft eyes of a horse tell me that he trusts me and has a willing heart to follow where I lead him. He doesn't overreact and takes everything in stride. His eyes will mirror my heart and keep me honest.

I want to pray for the horse that once long ago had soft eyes. Hands have been unkind to him and the twinkle that once lit up his whole being has faded away. Lord, please send a patient, loving woman who will help bring back the softness he once had, for he deserves nothing less.

~September 10~
He Tolerates Me

For it is by grace you have been saved, through faith,
and this is not from yourselves, it is the gift of God.
Ephesians 2:8

The horse looks at us and his expression speaks a thousand words. Sometimes it is an expression of contentment, and other times, it is as if he is screaming, "What the heck are you doing to me!?"

The horse has learned to tolerate the long baths throughout the summer and hours of grooming on any given day. He has learned to stand very still as his mane is being braided for a horse show or when he is getting new shoes put on. Patience has become his virtue as he watches his owner fumble with the new halter or bridle that she repeatedly tries on to make sure it looks nice and fits well. Then he stands a little more as she takes selfies with him and his new duds. He has learned to tolerate when family visits and want to ride, and he knows he needs to stay calm with little feet running around him.

Horses have learned much from the horse-crazy women in their lives, but the one thing they tolerate the most is the constant hugs and, of course, the horse kisses lavished on them every chance we can. Oh, and don't forget the carrots! The horse may tolerate the little girl or the senior woman in his life, but he will never be loved by anyone more.

Women have been in love with horses forever, but only in the last hundred years have they been able to enjoy them for pleasure. Thank you, Lord, for such an exceptional animal who will tolerate us even when we just want to take endless selfies.

~September 11~
The Abundant Life

Now all glory to God, who is able, through his mighty power at work within us,
to accomplish infinitely more than we might ask or think.
Ephesians 3:20

A life with horses is filled with early morning chores and late evening water checks. It's a life where your schedule is pre-arranged according to the horses in your care but can change at any given time. You may think you have plenty of time to nap or do a little shopping after chores, but then one of the horses surprises you with a considerable cut, requiring an urgent vet call. A life with horses means long, lazy summer afternoons when it is too hot to ride, but you end up stacking hay instead. It's a life where your vacation money is now a three-horse goose-neck trailer you will be sleeping in on many road trips. It is laughter with other ladies as you discuss the fine art of learning how to get out of making dinner so that you have more time at the barn. It's a life of trips to the tack store and sometimes to the emergency room when things don't go as planned while riding. It is comforting each other when we need to say goodbye to our horse forever and acting like school girls when we head down the road to look for a new horse to buy. A life with horses means there will be many highs and many lows, but you will grow and learn from all of them. It is an abundant life like no other and we wouldn't change a thing.

God bless the woman who falls in love with horses and is willing to sacrifice and do what she needs to so that her horses are cared for to the fullest. She understands that there will be good days and bad days, but she will trust in the Lord to get her through whatever comes her way. Amen.

~September 12~
Teaching

Let the wise listen and add to their learning,
and let the discerning get guidance.
Proverbs 1:5

Taking horseback riding lessons looked much different when I was young. Often, lessons included hopping on a horse, hanging on no matter what, and waiting for the horse to settle down. I don't remember my instructors talking about natural horsemanship or the unique personality each horse was born with. Because of that, I thought of each horse as the same and without uniqueness, except for their breeding and size. It was a "one size fits all" standard way of teaching new kids to ride back then.

We have come a long way in learning about the horse's individual needs, personality, and physical attributes. Thanks to so many incredible horsemen and women who are teaching that horses have many layers, and in order to form a bond in and out of the saddle, you need to peel back those layers. And most importantly, no two horses are the same. It is a movement that has dramatically improved the horse industry and the relationship between man and horse on all levels. These equine teachers are showing the world that the horse never forgets, and if he trusts you, he will follow you anywhere and give his complete heart to you. The young equestrians of today are learning things I never dreamed of.

Praise God for the incredible instructors willing to teach the "whole horse." They are showing us what is important, and if we are willing to slow down and learn new ways of doing things, our relationship with our horse will be truly extraordinary.

Thank you, Lord, for the knowledge and wisdom that is now being taught by so horse trainers. They are the voices of wisdom for the next generation of equestrians. Praise God!

~September 13~
Falling From Grace

For God so loved the world, that he gave his only Son,
that whoever believes in him should not perish but have eternal life.
John 3:16

Years ago, a story broke in the horse community that made it all the way to the evening news. It was about a woman working as a finance controller in a small town. It turned out that she had embezzled large amounts of money from the city to fund her horse business for decades. She was finally caught and all her very expensive horses (hundreds of horses!) were sold off at auction to help recoup some of the money for the city. Later, a documentary came out about the woman, and one of the investigators talked about how horses were just as much an addiction to this woman as drugs are to a drug addict. It was a very sad story but it made me realize that any of us could easily get lost in the madness of our addiction, leading us to do things we never thought we were capable of.

Every once in a while I think about that woman and her life. Her story made me think of my life and the times I spent too much money on horse tack or something horse-related that I had to have. I knew we didn't have the money but I did it anyway. As women, we will never embezzle millions of dollars but we might hide that we bought another saddle pad or new bridle. We all fall from grace now and then, but we have the most awesome God who forgives us if we ask and loves us unconditionally.

As fellow horsewomen who love the Lord, He has called us to be in constant prayer for each other and to be a beacon of truth in love to all who know us. For we all sin and fall short of the Glory of God, but through His grace and mercy we can be forgiven! Praise the Lord!

~September 14~
What About Him?

Likewise the Spirit helps us in our weakness. For we do not know what to pray for as we ought, but the Spirit himself intercedes for us with groanings too deep for words.
Romans 8:26

When major changes happen in our lives, they affect our horses. We move, change jobs, find love for the first time, or decide to have a baby. Sickness comes and death happens unexpectedly, and these life events often force us to decide what we are going to do with our beloved horse who has been with us forever. We find ourselves asking, "What about him?"

It is a hard decision to make when you decide to rehome a horse. But there are things we can do to ensure that the life change he is about to experience will be as easy as possible. Since you know your horse (his eating habits, personality, love language) better than anybody, you can control who will become his new owner and make sure that his new life is just as good as what you gave him.

Horses are remarkably resilient creatures and they often handle change pretty well. But, occasionally, I come across a horse that is not adjusting to his new surroundings easily, and it breaks my heart. When I see a new horse struggling at my barn, he becomes my top priority to make sure he finds a herd body as soon as possible. The truth is that horses bond tightly with each other, and it takes adjustment when they are pulled away from one another for life.

The Lord has given us the gift of the horse. He has entrusted us with caring for him and delivering him into hands that will also love him while ensuring his well-being. It is not something to take lightly and it is a responsibility bestowed upon us as their owners.

~September 15~
Keep It Simple

The one who gets wisdom loves life;
the one who cherishes understanding will soon prosper.
Proverbs 19:8

Have you ever had a day where you knew you didn't give it your all deep inside? We deal with this in all areas of our life, but when it comes to horses, the bar is raised because the horse knows. Horses are such intelligent animals (even though they lose their brains now and then!), and their watchful eyes can quickly tell what kind of mood we are in. That is why it is humorous when a well-trained horse doesn't act the same for a novice rider as he does for his owner. He can sense that the new rider doesn't know what he is doing. They begin to size up quickly if they are going to be pushed through the paces hard or if it will be an easy day and they can slack off a little.

The same is true for our own horsemanship journey. We know when we start to slack on what we should be doing to improve our skills and knowledge, and sometimes we just want to go out to the barn and hand-graze our horse instead. And you know what? It is okay to rest and just enjoy your horse! We need to remember that it's not a race. It is a marathon that lasts a lifetime. Sometimes, we forget that it doesn't always need to be about learning and working harder. If you are having a not-so-good day today, keep it simple and enjoy the view all around you. Tomorrow, you will hop back in the saddle and work a little more towards your goals.

Lord, please fill me with wisdom to know when to keep going and when to rest. Help me maintain a healthy balance for me and this amazing horse you have entrusted to my care. I am asking for discernment in my daily decisions for myself and my equine partner. In Jesus's Name, Amen.

~September 16~
The Mountain

Wait patiently for the Lord. Be brave and courageous.
Yes, wait patiently for the Lord.
Psalm 27:14

I have the joy of watching horse owners grow in their horsemanship skills. It always makes me smile deep inside when I watch them do things with their horse that they couldn't do a few months earlier.

God has built into each of us this incredible bravery when we are young, and we jump into many things without realizing how hard it will be. Only after we succeed or fail do we think about how we want to proceed the next time. This is unbelievably true for the equestrian. When young girls learn to ride horses, they are very resilient and push through even on the worst day of riding. They could be bucked off, knocked over, or stepped on, but they keep going without thinking about it. That is the beauty of youth. But for us older women, we tend to analyze everything, and sometimes what looks like a little hill to a young girl will look like Mt. Everest to an older person and it can be overwhelming.

If you ever feel like you're "climbing a mountain" in your horsemanship journey, I want to remind you to take your time and savor the ride. It's okay if you only learn one small thing today. Each small lesson you learn will quickly add up, and before you know it, your mountain will start to look more like a small hill and you will be amazed at how far you've come with your horse.

Lord, life up the woman trying to learn as much as she can about horses and riding. When she starts to feel overwhelmed, please show her that the small hills of life hold valuable lessons, and when she is ready, you will guide her up the highest mountain and be right by her side. Amen.

283

~September 17~
The Real Deal

But from there you will seek the Lord your God and you will find him,
if you search after him with all your heart and with all your soul.
Deuteronomy 4:29

When I was in my early twenties, I had sold my horses and was struggling to know where I fit in. I loved to go out dancing (when dancing was cool), but the guys I was dating were really not my type. Deep down, I wanted to date a cowboy and live out on the range somewhere. I envisioned riding horses, baking bread, and living a simple life. The movie Urban Cowboy had just come out and it seemed that cowboy fever had hit big time. Suddenly, every guy wanted to be a cowboy and every girl wanted to date one. But so many of the guys seemed like "wannabe cowboys," and I wanted the real deal. I wasn't impressed by a fancy cowboy hat or lizard-skin boots. I wanted a down-to-earth guy who wanted to live in the country and liked horses enough to own a couple of them.

I finally met the perfect guy who shared my dreams and we moved back to his hometown in Wisconsin. Decades later, I still live on a horse farm and am living my childhood dream. David never wore a cowboy hat and doesn't ride horses, but he is the real deal, and the Lord knew just what He was doing.

I pray for the young woman trying to find her Mr. Right. Lord, it can be very discouraging for her as she searches for someone to share her dreams with, especially as the dating world seems more complicated each day. I pray that she finds direction, peace, and clarity while waiting for her cowboy to come into her life. And Lord, he doesn't need to know how to ride a horse. She can teach him that. Amen!

~September 18~
Crazy Barn Lady

*And I tell you, ask, and it will be given to you; seek,
and you will find; knock, and it will be opened to you.*
Luke 1:9

We all know that one crazy barn lady who walks to a different beat but has a heart of gold. I have known a few crazy barn ladies, and I am sure there have been times in my life when I was that crazy barn lady! If you are around horses long enough, you will eventually meet that one lady who makes you smile and laugh out loud at times but is always there for you when you need help. And if you are around horses even longer, you might just become that crazy barn lady that the younger generation chuckles at BUT who they also go to first when they are in trouble with their horse.

Being different is a good thing. After all, how boring it would be if we all followed the same trail and rode in the same saddle just because we were scared to branch out and try something new. They say the horsewomen who made the most significant difference in the equine world are the women who, on the outside, may have looked like a crazy barn lady, but deep inside, they knew exactly what they were doing. They were not following the crowd but instead forged ahead with new ideas and dreams.

If you feel like the Lord is leading you to do something out of the ordinary when it comes to horses, pray and ask Him to guide you in the direction you should go. You might look like a crazy barn lady to those on the outside, but years down the road, they might look back and see the accomplishments and positive impact you made in the horse world and to those around you. If someone calls you a crazy barn lady, take it as a compliment and keep blazing a trail. God has your back and will be right beside you as you enter uncharted territory.

~September 19~
The Transition

My lips will shout for joy, when I sing praises to you;
my soul also, which you have redeemed.
Psalm 71:23

If you have been in love with horses your entire life then you no doubt have gone through many changes when it comes to your own personal style, athletic ability, and physical appearance. When I was in my teens and twenties, everything was about being sexy. Times haven't changed much for young girls and women from the 1970s to the present. There is this intense pressure to fit in and look good at any cost, which was the same in the horse world. We would wear our pants too tight and our shirts too small, and it was less about our horse and more about how we looked at all times. I am so glad those days are long behind me!

The transition that happens as we age gracefully from our sassy and sexy youth to a new timeless beauty with strands of grey hair looks different for every woman. But oh, what a new freedom it is. It is a wonderful feeling now to put on my loose and very comfortable jeans and work boots and feel like I am home and where I am supposed to be. I love being around the horses every day and I feel I am much better with them because I am less worried about my physical appearance and more attentive to their needs.

Some of the most beautiful women I have known have grey hair and their own unique style. They are more confident now with horses than they ever were when they were young and you can't help but want to be around them. Thank you, Lord, for the gift of growing older. The transition might be painful while it is happening, but once we embrace the new us, our world opens up to so much more. What a gift to be around horses later in life. Praise God!

~September 20~
Competing As A Senior

Therefore, my dear brothers and sisters, stand firm. Let nothing move you. Always give yourselves fully to the work of the Lord, because you know that your labor in the Lord is not in vain.
I Corinthians 15:58

When my daughters competed at high school horse shows, one of the classes was called the "Jack Benny Class." It was for riders usually forty years and older. It was a fun class to watch because some of the competitors were moms riding their kid's horses and you could tell that they didn't have much time in the saddle and were riding just for fun. But watch out because there were quite a few women in their senior years competing all day long in classes with the much young riders and killing it in show pen! These horsewomen were polished and they knew their stuff. They had been riding for a long time and even though age might have crept up on them, it didn't slow them down.

The wonderful thing about competing as a senior is that some of the pressure is gone regarding how we look in the saddle. We are at a refreshing time in our life when we can often laugh at ourselves when we make a mistake and we have learned not to sweat the small stuff. We don't take life so seriously and the ribbon doesn't define us. We are just happy to be riding, and if we want to show horses, we jump in and figure it out as we go.

Today, we celebrate the senior women who compete in the horse world. These older ladies have style and have nothing to prove to anyone. They are just enjoying the ride to the fullest. God bless the senior woman who enters the show pen with a smile on her face and a heart full of life. That is what timeless beauty looks like.

~September 21~
Stronger After The Break

He said, "The Lord is my rock and my fortress and my deliverer;
My God, my rock, in whom I take refuge, My shield
and the horn of my salvation, my stronghold and my refuge.
II Samuel 22:2-3

My daughter fell off a horse and broke her arm years ago. After the surgery, the doctor told me her arm would be stronger than before the break. I have often thought of that doctor's words when I think of what some horses have endured in life.

For many horses, their spirit has been broken through harsh treatment or painfully demanding labor. But for some that have been shattered both mentally and physically, there are incredible women gifted at working with these troubled animals and bringing them back stronger than ever. These horses were once filled with anxiety and anger, but with much patience, love, and gentleness, a deep trust formed between these women and the horses they worked with, and the fear they carried with them for years slowly disappeared.

The bond runs deep between these horses and the women who care for them, and together, they are showing the world that every horse is worth saving. Interestingly, some women working these horses have endured much pain and suffering in their own lives. They know what it's like to be on the losing end of a situation, and they can empathize with these horses to some degree and connect with them in ways others cannot.

God bless the women who work with these broken horses. They understand what they are up against, but they believe love conquers all and that keeps them going. These horsewomen are an inspiration to all of us and have shown the world that when something is broken, it can come back stronger than ever with time and love.

~September 22~
Gain Trust First

You will keep in perfect peace all who trust in you, all whose thoughts are fixed on you! Trust in the Lord always, for the Lord God is the eternal Rock.
Isaiah 26:3-4

We live in a world where everyone wants everything fast and with as little work as possible. With horses, that idea just doesn't work. We might be speeding along the road of life, but horses haven't changed for thousands of years. The horse is just how God created them from the beginning. They are a "flight" animal that will react and flee quickly at the first sign of danger. That is why it is hard on them when we ask them to do something new without giving them time to process it and trust us.

I have watched many young girls ride horses and compete, and the girls who do the best understand that their horse needs to take it all in and learn new things step by step. They have awakened to the idea that if they gain their horse's trust, they will go much further and have a happier, more confident horse. Does it take longer? Absolutely! Does it mean you might not win that first year? Yes! But the bond and trust you gain from your horse will take you further than you ever imagined.

Wouldn't it be awesome if our greatest accomplishment as a horsewoman was to have a relationship with our horse where trust is cemented tight and the bond is unbreakable? That is when great things are achieved. The horse is a complex animal in so many ways, yet such a simple beast that only needs a few things to feel safe and secure. And we miss it so easily.

Lord, I ask for guidance and prayer for the horsewoman. I pray that her eyes will be opened to what her horse needs daily to be successful and content when riding for pleasure or in competition. Only then will she be ready to take on the world!

~September 23~
Strength

For the sake of Christ, then, I am content with weaknesses, insults, hardships, persecutions, and calamities. For when I am weak, then I am strong.
II Corinthians 12:10

When a horse is born, he is a small wobbly knee foal that depends solely on his mama to survive. He stays close to her, gets his nourishment from her, and sleeps a lot during those first few weeks. But each day is a miracle as he grows and becomes more curious about things around him. He soon is running circles around his mother and slowly venturing further and further away from her as she keeps a close eye on him. Soon that little foal is a big and strong horse that has gained muscle and incredible strength. He no longer needs his mother to survive and is quite capable of taking care of himself. He still might have the mind of a youngster when he does things that are not the smartest, but each day, he learns more and his strength increases.

It is amazing to me just how powerful the horse is. If they chose, they could hurt us in a second, but they don't. Instead, they submit to what we ask with a willing heart and trust that we will get them through it without hurting them. They are such gentle animals and they are asked daily to do things that are not natural for them, yet they concede because they trust us. When I think about the strength of a horse and how easily he could refuse me with his power, it sends shivers down my spine. The world of the horse and the world of man are vastly different, but when they come together in harmony, it is a thing of beauty.

Thank you, Lord, for the strength of the horse. I can't recall a more amazing animal that will allow me to ride on his back and deliver me to my whims. When I look at the horse, I see how incredibly magnificent God is and am reminded of His love for me.

~September 24~
Love Language

*The aim of our charge is love that issues from a pure
heart and a good conscience and a sincere faith.*
I Timothy 1:5

Every horse has his own love language that he understands and
gives him a sense of safety and comfort. We know that a horse's
primary love language is, of course, having enough to eat and drink,
feeling safe, and sheltered from the elements. But they also respond
to things we do to them daily.

Some horses are timid, while others are bold and confident.
Some are scared of their own shadow, while nothing fazes another.
Some horses love to be rubbed on their face and under their jaw,
while others don't want to be touched at all. Some horses love to be
around people, whereas others stay as far away as possible. Finding
your horse's love language is something that should excite us
because we are driven to make things better. We love to be around
our horses and we will do anything we can to connect with them
and get them to respond to us positively. More than anything, we
want them to want to be around us. That is the cherry on top!

Learning your horse's love language takes time, and as you
mature in your horsemanship, you will begin to see how different
each horse is. They each come with a unique personality and once
you unlock the door to what your horse responds to, you will fall in
love even more.

Lord, help me be wise and patient when learning my horse's
personality. I know it is so important to reach him on his terms and
make him feel safe in all situations. Just like you created me with my
own love language, help me learn his so that I can better understand
him. Thank you, Lord, for this incredible gift that brings me such
joy.

~September 25~
One Last Ride

So also you have sorrow now, but I will see you again,
and your hearts will rejoice, and no one will take your joy from you.
John 16:22

I was scrolling through social media a few years ago when I came across a post from one of the horse groups. The image on the post was of a cowboy on a bucking bronco coming out of the shoot, and the title was "One Last Ride." The cowboy in the image went home after that ride and took his own life. It was the last picture taken of him doing what he loved. He had left a note that said he couldn't do it anymore. He couldn't live up to the demands and pressure that he had put on himself and he just wanted to go home. The people who knew this cowboy said he was quiet but always had a smile and was nice to everyone he met. As I continued to read the post, I felt the need to stop and pray for this young man's family. I can't imagine what they were going through. And then I wondered how someone gets to the point where they call it quits and are done with life.

Today, I want to pray for the women who work in all parts of the horse industry. It is a difficult business to be in and the pressure to succeed can be overwhelming at times. Lord, please lift up the horsewoman who is hurting and comes to the barn to find solitude and peace. We don't always know what someone is feeling on the inside, but please comfort them and let these women know they are loved more than anything. Let them know they are enough and are fearfully and wonderfully made in Your image. Surround these women with compassionate people who will help them work through the hard situations they are going through, and above all else, please give them hope and show them that nothing is too big for you, Heavenly Father. In Jesus' Name, Amen.

~September 26~
The Bond

When we get together, I want to encourage you in your faith,
but I also want to be encouraged by yours.
Romans 1:12

When two horses bond, they will protect and watch out for each other. I have watched a horse stand close to his herd mate as to protect him when he is sick or down with colic. I observed an older horse protecting a new horse coming into the herd with such fierceness that no other horse dare challenge him. And I have watched a horse whinny with grief when he realizes that his herd mate has died. It is enough to break your heart and you start to get a sense of how devoted equines are to each other.

The bond between a woman and her horse is something to behold. For the horse-loving woman, the bond comes fast and furious. For the horse, it is much different. It takes him a while to trust his new owner and then the bonding gradually begins. For the woman who loves her horse and envisions him running from across the field to greet her, it is a journey that looks different for every horse and human. Some horses are happy to see their owner and come right to the gate and wait patiently. For other horses, it might be more in the realm of being well-behaved no matter what he is asked to do and trusting she will keep him safe. When you get to the place where you know you and your horse have bonded, there is nothing better.

Lord, I ask for patience and understanding as I strive to bond with this incredible animal. I realize it may take longer to connect with him on a deeper level but I am willing to go at his pace. May I always seek to recognize what he is trying to say through his body language and expression and never take for granted his willing heart. Amen.

~September 27~
Change Can Be Hard

I look up to the mountains—does my help come from there? My help comes from the LORD, who made heaven and earth!
Psalm 121:1-2

Sometimes, enjoying the autumn season can be difficult with the impending winter snow knocking on the door. There are heating elements to put in the waterers and electric fences to double-check and winterizing the farm takes time. The ground constantly changes as the temperatures fluctuate from below freezing to balmy and you can feel the winter season looming around the corner.

When you have taken care of horses for a long time you begin to anticipate each new season and all that it brings. I can be overwhelmed with the thoughts of heavy snow and a cold wind that cuts like a knife. And bringing out my fleeced line jeans, long underwear, and my worn-out winter coat can make me feel as if the lightness of the job has become heavy overnight. The change from autumn to winter is probably the hardest to live through but we manage every year, as do many other men and women who take care of horses.

There are also many beautiful things that happen when autumn turns into winter. The farmers are done with the harvest and the horse shows are coming to an end. The barn becomes a little quieter and people head indoors for longer periods of time. We start thinking about making comfort foods to warm the body and it is a time of rest for both horses and humans.

Lord, I life up the women caring for horses daily. I pray for their well-being as the work becomes more challenging. I humbly ask for their safety and these incredible women will escape injury and illness. Thank you, Lord, for watching over your children on farms and ranches everywhere. Amen

~September 28~
Witnessing A Miracle

A man of many companions may come to ruin,
but there is a friend who sticks closer than a brother.
Proverbs 18:24

A few months back, I witnessed how deep the relationship between two horses could be. One of the horses at our stable is a beautiful Cobb pony named Black Jack and he has been at our barn for over a decade. He has a pasture mate, Asher, with whom he has been incredibly close with for years. I knew the two horses got along but didn't realize how close they were until Black Jack began colicking one day. Quickly, the pain increased and the pony was up and down, trying to relieve the discomfort. Then I noticed that Asher would not leave Black Jack's side and stood over him the entire time he was lying down. As things got worse for the pony, I went out there to put a halter on and get him up but he kept going down on me, and Asher never left his side. We finally got him to the gate and Asher quietly laid his head over Black Jack's back and stood as close to him as possible. As I led the pony out and closed the gate, Asher didn't move and watched us walk away. You could tell he was bothered by what was happening to his friend.

Black Jack recovered from his illness and, after a week, was back out with Asher. Their reunion brought tears to my eyes. Black Jack ran around, kicked up his heels, and then ran over to where Asher was standing. Then, they both lowered their heads and ate breakfast together. During that week, I witnessed a miracle and saw the beauty of God's creation in full force. It showed me the love these animals have for each other on a much deeper level and I will never forget it.

Thank you, Lord, for the gift of the horse and all that he teaches us daily if we have eyes to see and a heart to love.

~September 29~
Personal Best

But grace was given to each one of us
according to the measure of Christ's gift.
Ephesians 4:7

When my daughter started showing horses, she gravitated towards the riding discipline of Dressage. Since I grew up riding Western, I knew nothing about Dressage, but I was about to learn.

One of the biggest differences between riding in a Western pleasure class and competing in Dressage is the number of riders in the ring. In a Western pleasure class, you will have a large number of riders competing against each other at the same time. But at a Dressage show, you are alone in the ring and competing against yourself. It was a whole new world for us and we loved it. It felt like the pressure was off, and it was all about doing your personal best. Of course, we all love ribbons, but what seemed to be the highlight was the judge's comments on the sheet that you would receive along with your score. You could see how you did with your horse and what you could improve on. My daughter couldn't wait for her judge's sheet, and after she read the comments, she would create new goals. It was an excellent way to learn and grow.

I know God doesn't score us on how we behave daily towards the animals entrusted to us or the people who come into our lives, but there are consequences for our poor actions. That is why He gave us a manual to guide us so we can set goals to make each day a new personal best. It is not something that happens in one day. It takes a lifetime. It is a journey of learning to be a better person each day and following what God has planned for your life.

Thank you, Lord, for your Holy Scriptures. They keep me grounded and teach me daily.

~September 30~
Not As Planned

Rejoice in hope, be patient in tribulation, be constant in prayer.
Romans 12:12

Women are natural planners and we are always making plans with our horse friends. But as you know, anything can happen with horses and our best-laid plans can come to a screeching halt at a moment's notice. It doesn't mean it is easy while it is happening but it does teach us so much about what is truly important in life.

I have watched tears stream down a young girl's face when she missed her horse show because her horse wouldn't load in the trailer. I have cried with the woman who was planning on riding that day, but her horse suddenly passed away early that morning. And I have hugged the broken-hearted woman who just a few days earlier was gleefully making plans for a long overnight camping trip with her horse, only to be bucked off the day before, ending up with a broken leg.

Life with horses is a series of ups and downs, surprises beyond our wildest dreams, and learning to adapt. Sometimes, when things don't go as planned, they turn out to be a blessing in disguise. When things look like they are falling apart with your horse, they are really coming together as you grow and learn with each new issue that arises. This often forces us to change direction and problem-solve, and the things we learn from each of those experiences are worth their weight in gold.

Today, you might be struggling because all your horse dreams are falling apart. God is saying to you today, never give up on your dreams. Stay in prayer and remain faithful. He will lead you through the valleys and guide you to greener pastures.

~October 1~
Box Of Chocolates

More to be desired are they than gold, even much fine gold;
sweeter also than honey and drippings of the honeycomb.
Psalm 19:10

You will either love the horse with a Roman nose or decide he is not your cup of tea. You might be crazy about the sleekness of a Thoroughbred or find you prefer heavy-coated horses like the Fjord. Some are too tall, while others are too short. Some horses are short-necked, and others look like they could be related to a giraffe. The equestrian who is all about looking good on her steed might be looking for impeccable bloodlines, but the more you are around the different horse breeds, the more you will fall in love with every one of them.

There have been some horses that I thought were okay looking but wasn't what I was attracted to in a horse. But after I got to know them and their sweet personality, I quickly fell in love. Soon, they were so beautiful in my eyes that I became envious of the client who owned such a wonderful animal. There has also been a time or two when a horse came to our stable with the best breeding money could buy. The horse may have been well-trained and won numerous championships, but he was continuously difficult to handle, and his beauty seemed less impressive. The truth is all horses are beautiful creations from heaven above. And sometimes, the horse we fall in love with turns out to be the shaggy coat pony that carries our children on his back around the yard.

You could say horses are like a box of chocolates. You never know what you really have until you spend time with them and see what is on the inside. After all, it is the heart of the horse that makes him beautiful.

~October 2~
The Best Trainers

But the Helper, the Holy Spirit, whom the Father will
send in my name, he will teach you all things and bring
to your remembrance all that I have said to you.
John 14:26

Over the years, I have had the privilege of watching many trainers work with horses. It is amazing how unique each trainer is regarding style and communication. Some of these gifted horsewomen have that special touch and can take a very nervous horse, and within the hour, he is more relaxed, licking his lips, and has become putty in the trainer's hands. It is something that takes my breath away every time. At that moment, you begin to see a more confident horse where once stood a frightened animal.

I have also witnessed some training methods that made me sick inside because of what they did to the horse. Even though harsh training methods are not allowed at my stable, you can find them at any horse show because most people turn a blind eye to what is happening to the animal. Yes, those horses might win everything and their owner might go home with a huge trophy, but was it worth it?

Lord, I pray for the trainers who work with horses daily. It is a dangerous job and what they do is invaluable. My heart aches for the trainer who has lost her way and is willing to compromise the horse. I pray that her eyes will be opened and she will see what is truly important in life. Please show her that it's not just about ribbons at the end of the day. It's about the relationship between the horse and his human. When that is right, there is nothing better. Praise God for all the trainers who understand this and put the horse first, even if it cost them a client. When you honor and value yourself and the horses entrusted to you, you are honoring God.

~October 3~
Not What I Envisioned

The Lord is near to all who call on him,
to all who call on him in truth.
Psalm 145:18

Leasing a horse first is smart if you are new to horses and still learning a lot. It takes some of the pressure off of horse ownership and you still get to enjoy the horse you are leasing. The transition from leasing a horse to horse ownership usually comes with a few bumps in the road, and there is no way around it. It is all part of growing and learning.

Once you are the owner and caretaker of this animal that you have fallen madly in love with, a new kind of pressure and responsibility will start to creep up on you, and that is when you need a good support system to get you through the first few months. During the early days of horse ownership, you will decide what equine vet you want to use, and you will need to choose a farrier. You will decide whether to blanket your horse or not, and choosing which grain and supplements to feed might overwhelm you at first. The decisions will be endless and you may find yourself walking aimlessly down the horse aisle at the feed store in a fog! I remember one woman saying that it was not what she envisioned. It was much harder. I pray for the woman who is a brand new horse owner. For her, it is just like bringing a newborn baby home, but instead, it is a thousand-pound bundle of joy!

Lord, please lift up the woman who is feeling overwhelmed as a brand-new horse owner. It may not be what she envisioned but if she is willing to stick it out, it will be so much better than she ever dreamed. Thank you, Lord, for these courageous women who have chosen to become horse owners and are ready for all that life brings them.

~October 4~
The Spittoon

Many are the plans in the mind of a man,
but it is the purpose of the Lord that will stand.
Proverbs 19:21

When I was young, all I wanted was a cowboy to marry. My girlfriends and I would go to the local rodeos just hoping to catch the eye of a good-looking cowboy. Well, I finally did meet a cowboy and I was crazy about him and the black cowboy hat he wore. He lived about ninety minutes from me, and since we were both in high school we didn't see each other very much. But one Saturday, I was going to drive to his home and spend the day with him. I got up early to make sure I had the perfect jeans on and that my makeup and hair looked good. It was the first time going to his home and meeting his parents. As I drove up to his place I couldn't believe all the cattle in the pastures surrounding his house. He showed me around and told me that I would meet his parents at the cattle auction not too far away. We hopped in his old stick shift truck, and, of course, I sat right next to him.

Now, this cowboy chewed tobacco and it never bothered me, but I noticed that a spittoon was sitting right on the center dashboard when I got in his truck. I forgot about it quickly as we drove off because my head was in the clouds. Here I was with my cowboy in his truck and going to a cattle auction. Life was perfect! Then the unthinkable happened. As he was pulling into a parking spot and shifting downwards, his truck jumped forward and the spittoon fell off the dashboard and onto my lap upside down! The contents of it spilled all over me! My jeans were wet with black spit and I thought I was going to die. As you can imagine, that date didn't go well and ended quickly. I never saw that cowboy again. Sometimes, who we think is perfect for us is not the man God has planned for us.

~October 5~
The Seat Of My Youth

For we are his workmanship, created in Christ Jesus for good works,
which God prepared beforehand, that we should walk in them.
Ephesians 2:10

"The seat of my youth is long gone." I often hear that phrase from older women who were lucky enough to ride a lot when they were young. We know how we are supposed to look in the saddle, but somewhere throughout the years, we've evolved into something a little less tight and firm. And I am not talking about the flabbiness of my butt! What I am trying to say is that our seat and our balance changes as we age when it comes to riding horses!

When you watch a young woman on the back of her horse, it doesn't matter if she is bareback or in the saddle. Her butt is glued to the saddle, just like she is part of the horse's back. That horse could move in any direction and she never loses her balance. But as we age, some of that glue loses its stick and it's never quite the same.

Growing older is not for sissies and it can be hard to acknowledge that things are not quite what they used to be. But if we open our eyes, we will see things with wisdom that our younger self didn't have. We might not look the same in the saddle but we have so much to offer the younger generations coming up as equestrians. We have learned great discernment and because of that, our mistakes are fewer. We can see the world on a much deeper level, and when it comes to horses, I believe many women have a deeper joy when riding than they did when they were young.

Yes, it is true. My seat may not be what it was in my teens and twenties, but that is okay. I am where I am supposed to be. Thank you, Jesus!

~October 6~
Repeat Again

Rejoice always, pray without ceasing, give thanks in all circumstances; for this is the will of God in Christ Jesus for you.
I Thessalonians 5:16-18

You can't be in a hurry when it comes to learning new things with horses. "How hard can it be?" we ask ourselves when we first jump into the world of horses. Then, we find out real quick how much we don't know. Even the simplest thing, like putting a halter on, takes time for everyone in the beginning. It might mean putting a halter on several times a day until it becomes second nature or bridling your horse every day until you feel comfortable. I have noticed a new horse owner putting the saddle on too far forward or too far back, but unless someone helps that person, they will not know if the saddle fits correctly and that they could actually be making their horse uncomfortable. It takes practice tacking up a horse and even more time in the saddle. It is something you need to repeat and then repeat again to get good at it .

As women, sometimes we can easily become frustrated when we don't catch on as quickly as we thought we should. We look around at the other people in the barn saddling and bridling their horses and they make it look so simple. We often forget that they were new at one time and walking the same path you are walking now. You will make mistakes, and that is okay because that is how you learn.

Today, I want to lift up the woman who has lost her confidence and feels like she is racing to catch up with everyone else. She might feel like she isn't getting it and keeps repeating the same mistakes over and over. Lord, please send other women into her life who will give her encouragement, mentor her, and be truthful so that she can grow in her horsemanship. She is a beautiful work in progress.

303

~October 7~
Puddle Of Water

Do nothing from selfishness or empty conceit, but with humility of mind regard one another as more important than yourselves.
Philippians 2:3

There is nothing scarier to some horses than a puddle of water. They will dance around it and snort, throw their head up high and jump, and do everything in their power not to walk through it. It's actually quite comical to watch this huge animal do anything possible to avoid the one-inch puddle of water that is so harmless. But in their mind, it is so much more and the fear is real.

When I am leading horses out to their paddocks and we have had a rainstorm the night before, there are puddles of water everywhere. It is a young child's play yard, but some of our horses will nearly knock me over trying to avoid that "deep wet hole." If I take my time and let them lower their head, they will snort a little and then move around to the furthest point of the lead rope until they are forced to come closer. The funny thing is these same horses will go out in the wettest part of their paddock and play in the mud until their entire body is covered. The sweetest thing is that you can see how happy and proud they are of themselves.

It is truly hard to say what is going on in a horse's mind when he refuses to walk through a puddle of water, but for some horses, it sends them into a tizzy while others walk through it like it doesn't even exist. I guess that is what makes horses so fascinating. They each have their own quirks, vices, strengths, and talents, but each is perfectly and wonderfully made.

You will never be bored if you hang around horses. They will keep you laughing often, and sometimes, the tears will flow, but one thing is certain, you will love them more today than you did yesterday—mud puddles and all.

~October 8~
The Lies

Be sober-minded; be watchful. Your adversary the devil prowls around like a roaring lion, seeking someone to devour.
I Peter 5:8

When it comes to horses and our personal journey, it's all too easy to get caught up in the lies that float around in our heads daily. As women, we can easily talk ourselves out of learning something new with horses, and it happens more often as we age. Thoughts start to creep in, telling us we are not good enough to enter that class at the horse show or have enough experience to tackle an endurance ride. There does need to be some reality to what level of experience we are at when it comes to our horse, but that doesn't mean that we can't begin at a lower level and set goals for the future. Baby steps keep us motivated when we see small achievements that we might miss otherwise. Don't get caught up in the lies floating around in your head, but instead, rise above it and try something new.

Today, I encourage you to share your heart with horsewomen who will be truthful in a loving way so that it doesn't crush you but instead helps you set new goals that are perfect for where you are at. Ride with others who will help you work through the fears that keep you from moving forward. When you feel those lies start to dance around in your mind that is when the Lord is waiting for you to reach out to Him. His presence will keep you grounded and your anxiety will begin to fade away.

Lord, help me seek you first in all I do, including my horse activities. You know my deep love for these animals, yet I struggle to fight off the fear I feel around them at times. I know that through you, all things are possible. Thank you today for allowing me to learn and grow around these amazing equines.

~October 9~
First Job

Teach me your way, O Lord, that I may walk in your truth;
unite my heart to fear your name.
Psalm 86:11

Back in the 1960s and 70s, the San Fernando Valley was covered with orange groves and horses. When I was young, it was a great place to grow up. The weather was awesome and I only had to ride my bike a few miles down the road to find horses. There was a stable that I loved to visit known as Studs Lane because they had a lot of stallions and horse breeding was their business.

One summer, I rode my bicycle to the stable and asked the owner if he had any jobs. He recognized me, knew I came there a lot to see the horses, and told me he would hire me to clean stalls. I thought I had hit the jackpot! I was so excited and ready to work. I rode my bike there the next day and he showed me what to do. I was very young, but that didn't stop me. I started cleaning the first box stall and quickly realized how much work it was! But I kept going. I remember the stalls were dark and heavily bedded with straw, and picking through them was exhausting. After about an hour, my face was flushed red from the day's heat and hard work. I found a hose, drank a bunch of water, and sat down for a bit. The owner came over and sat beside me under a tree. He was a nice man and he gently told me to wait until I was a little bigger and then come back to work there. He had an easiness about him and we talked a lot about horses.

Soon after that, I got a horse of my own and never went back to Studs Lane, but I will always remember working there for that very short time and the kind man who taught me a lot without ever realizing it. Thank you, Lord, for the people you send into our lives to teach us no matter our age. Your timing is always perfect.

~October 10~
Big Milestone

Oh come, let us sing to the Lord; let us make a joyful noise to the rock of our salvation! Let us come into his presence with thanksgiving; let us make a joyful noise to him with songs of praise! For the Lord is a great God.
Psalm 95:1-3

It is your one-year anniversary as a first-time horse owner. Every woman who reaches this first big milestone understands how awesome it is—not because she has owned a horse for a year but because she has made it through the first year and never gave up.

The first year of horse ownership is a time of great highs and some unexpected lows. You learned what kind of horse you really have and realized he has some quirks, but every horse does. You also found his sweet spot where he loves to be scratched and you learned he loves carrots but not mints. You became aware of what makes him nervous and survived when he almost knocked you over! You learned that he is a timid horse as you anxiously watched him meet his new herd mates for the first time and figure out his place in the group. And a flood of relief came over you when he bonded with another horse and started to play. Then came the day when you discovered a few bite marks on his neck, and you were devastated. However you got through it and realized that boys will be boys and they play rough at times. You started taking lessons and your confidence began to grow. You feel like your horse is finally bonding with you and even walks up to the gate when he sees you, and you still get goosebumps every time. You are starting to feel like you are getting this whole horse thing down and you can't believe a year has gone by so fast.

You are an incredible horsewoman and you should be so proud of yourself. The first year is always the hardest, but you did it, and the best is yet to come!

~October 11~
80 Years Young

I will be your God throughout your lifetime— until your hair is white with age.
I made you, and I will care for you. I will carry you along and save you.
Isaiah 46:4

Sometimes, you come across a story that touches every fiber in your body and encourages you in ways you never thought possible. This is that story for me, and I hope it has the same wonderful effect on you, too.

Every year since 1972, Jane Dotchin has packed a few articles of clothing, food, and a tent, and if she has a riding companion, she takes a few dog treats. She makes sure everything correctly fits her horse and heads out yet again for the long journey on horseback. This isn't just your average ride across town. She is riding 600 miles from her home in Hexham, Northumberland to Inverness, Scotland. What makes it even more remarkable is that she is now eighty years old and still making the same trek.

Jane has had many riding partners (horses) throughout the years, but recently, she has been riding Diamond, her trusted pony. Along with her dog, Dinky, who sits in a special pouch right on the saddle, she travels between 10 and 20 miles a day, depending on the weather. Since beginning this long-distance journey over forty years ago, Jane has met many wonderful people who watch for her every year. She has become a true inspiration and has proven many times over that age is only a number. All you need is a good horse that trusts you, and you trust him, and, of course, who can resist an adorable puppy for a riding partner.

Thank you, Lord, for the resilient horsewoman who has chosen not to let age define her. She is an inspiration to so many.

~October 12~
Always On My Mind

The Lord has appeared of old to me, saying, "Yes, I have loved you with an
everlasting love; Therefore with lovingkindness I have drawn you.
Jeremiah 31:3

Something happens to us when we fall in love with horses. Suddenly, they consume our thoughts and we find ourselves spending hours reading all we can about them. We look at horse ads constantly as we scheme and plan to one day own a horse of our own. We work second jobs and sell our most valuable belongings once we realize that our dream is close to becoming a reality, and all that extra cash will be spent on the new love in our life – our horse.

It is a crazy kind of passion that we cannot turn off because these incredible animals are always on our mind. As the days get closer to our new horse stepping off the trailer and into our life, we lose sleep and the house becomes a mess. We are now on a mission to make him as comfortable as possible, giving him the best of everything his little heart could desire. Our husbands wait patiently for the craziness to fade and things to return to normal. But what they don't realize is they never will from here on out.

We overthink everything regarding our horse, which tends to be the norm for most women, including myself. We are consumed and worry too much, but celebrate with joy as we watch our horse eat his hay like it is the first time he has ever eaten hay! Yes, it is crazy love, but we wouldn't change a thing.

My heart is beaming with joy each day as I head out to the barn, and I know this incredible animal waiting for me is a gift sent from Heaven above. Thank you, God, for the gift of the horse. When I look at him, I have a glimpse of what Heaven must be like.

~October 13~
Running Out Of Steam

As far as the east is from the west,
so far does he remove our transgressions from us.
Psalm 103:12

I first heard the phrase "running out of steam" at the racetrack. A man was referring to a racehorse they were watching that clearly had become tired as the other Thoroughbreds flew past him. For some reason, that phrase never left my head, and years later, when I was with my daughters at a horse show, I heard it again. This time, it was regarding a horse that had been shown all day and was completely exhausted. The horse refused to listen, and you could easily see that he was mentally and physically drained. He needed to rest and the young rider didn't understand that.

It was a wake-up call to me about how fragile horses really are. Growing up, I never thought about how tired they could become. Now I see it so clearly and understand how important it is to make sure our horse is trained and in peak condition to handle what we ask of him. Unfortunately, that is often not the case, and it is heartbreaking to see it happen at a horse show. It also makes me realize how selfish we can be when we want something so badly but do not want to put work into it to obtain it. We don't want to train the way we should, and we instead choose to push through it hard on the day of the competition. We forget that we are making decisions for an animal that would give us the world if he could, and when he runs out of steam, we become upset at him.

Lord, forgive me for the times I pushed my horse too hard. He was trying to tell me he couldn't do anymore, and I didn't listen. I humbly pray for wisdom going forward and that I will always put the horse first over ribbons and accolades. Amen.

~October 14~
Passing The Torch

And God is able to make all grace abound to you, so that having all sufficiency in all things at all times, you may abound in every good work.
II Corinthians 9:8

It's a funny thing about growing older. Your mind still feels young but your body tells you otherwise. When we opened our horse boarding facility, I felt strong and nothing seemed to bother me physically. I didn't have a care regarding my body and health and was ready to take on the world as a new barn owner. I have to admit, for the most part, I have been blessed to have had a good run so far with my health and physical stamina, but I can tell you that getting out of bed is a little more challenging these days, especially when I feel and hear creeks with every step across the floor. The one real blessing is that all the physical work of walking horses outside in the morning, cleaning stalls afterward, and then bringing twenty-seven horses back in for the evening has been a workout on my body for almost twenty years and it has helped me tremendously. My body still gets sore and aches occasionally, but the exercise I get from taking care of all the horses has been the best thing for my physical health.

I am thankful that I still feel strong and capable of doing the work as I head out to the barn each morning, but I know there will come a time when I need to pass the torch on to someone younger than me. Every horsewoman will come to that crossroad sometime in her life and it will be emotional for her as she tries to figure out the next chapter.

Today, Lord, I pray for the horsewoman who feels like the clock is ticking, yet she has so much she still wants to accomplish. I ask that she stay strong and healthy and has renewed strength daily in all she does with horses. In Jesus' Name, Amen.

311

~October 15~
Making Arrangements

And I pray that the sharing of your faith may become effective for the full knowledge of every good thing that is in us for the sake of Christ.
Philemon 1:6

There is nothing more heartbreaking than when a person is terminally ill and doesn't have long to live. The agony of leaving her family and friends before she is ready is something we all pray we never experience. But for the woman who owns horses, she feels an added weight and responsibility to ensure that they are well taken care of after she is gone.

I knew a couple of women that were making plans for their horses if they should be taken home unexpectedly. They were not planning on leaving this earth anytime soon, but they also were older and understood that life was precious and only God knows the day and time that He will call us home. The most amazing thing about these ladies is that they had such peace when discussing the care of their horses after they were gone. Their horses were young and if they stayed healthy, could live a long time. These ladies were going to do everything in their power to ensure they never were sold into cruel hands. As women, we are devoted to our horses in a way that only horse lovers would understand.

Today, I lift up the woman who is dealing with a terminal illness. Lord, she already is feeling the stress of being sick and her heart is breaking because she will be saying goodbye to her family until she sees them again in heaven. I pray that she finds peace during this time and that she can rest easy knowing that her horse will be well cared for after she is gone. You have entrusted him into her care for a time and now she is asking for someone who will love her horse like she loved him. In Jesus's Name, Amen.

~October 16~
You Are Needed

Each one must give as he has decided in his heart, not reluctantly
or under compulsion, for God loves a cheerful giver.
II Corinthians 9:7

Every woman, regardless of her horse experience has a unique and valuable gift to give others. But sometimes we feel inadequate about helping someone because we still have so much to learn ourselves. It's not just about horse knowledge; it's about the family of people who take care of each other in all seasons of life.

Don't underestimate your immense value and what you can offer to other people at your stable. We are always students of the horse, and the learning curve goes up with each new equestrian adventure, riding lesson, or simple one-on-one time hanging out with our equine partner. You are needed for the young person struggling to bridle her horse or pick a hoof on a difficult horse. She might be on the verge of tears, but your smile will give her the comfort and the confidence she needs at the right time. You are needed for the older woman who is a brand new horse owner and is feeling overwhelmed. You may have recently been in her shoes but your gentle and encouraging words will let her know she is not alone. You are needed for the barn owner, manager, or employees who might be having a bad day due to the horrible weather and challenging horses. Even seasoned horsewomen have awful days and a hug is all it takes to make someone feel better. You are needed to comfort the person who has just lost her horse. We all have experienced loss sometime in our life and your empathy will help ease the pain.

You have so much to offer at your barn or stable. It is a community of people who love horses and care deeply about each other, and that is when it becomes a barn family.

313

~October 17~
A Good Tired

For I will satisfy the weary soul,
and every languishing soul I will replenish.
Jeremiah 31:25

Horses can make us tired for many different reasons and most of those reasons are good ones. Being the caretaker of horses can be tiring at times. You hear the call of the wild right outside your window and you want to sleep a little longer but know they will become more impatient as the clock ticks. Working on a horse farm can be exhausting now and then, with early morning chores and evening checks to ensure all is well before you close the barn. It is a "good tired" you have when you work hard all day and feel like you accomplished something for the greater good of the horse.

Another type of fatigue is for the horsewoman who has had a long day riding her horse at a horse show, trail ride, or other equine activity. She is exhausted at the end of the day as she loads her horse to go home and has a great sense of accomplishment as she returns to the barn. She knows her horse needs to be taken care of first, and only then can she start to relax. When she gets home, she is more tired than she can remember, but it is a good feeling of tiredness, and she feels like she has made huge strides toward her goals. She soaks in a hot bathtub and has such great contentment and peace. She recounts every moment of the day and thinks to herself how blessed she is to have such a good horse.

Thank you, God, for a good day of hard work and accomplishment. Lord, I want to honor you in all I do with horses daily. Thank you for teaching me what hard work is and that the horse comes before my own personal needs. Help me to always remember that no matter how tired I am, my horse worked even harder and gave his all for my aspirations. In Jesus' Name, Amen.

~October 18~
Soft To Lead

Your word is a lamp to my feet and a light to my path.
Psalm 119:105

Leading a horse that quietly walks beside me makes my job easy. The horse that is soft to lead walks next to me without hesitation and neither pulls ahead or drags behind like a sack of potatoes. You can learn a lot about a horse's personality just by leading him, and walking several horses will give you a great education. The horse that is soft to lead is a pleasure to handle and sometimes it feels like they are few and far between. He is quiet and attentive and listens to directions given through the lead rope. His footfalls are steady and he doesn't walk too closely or far away. You can see he is thinking about what is happening around him, but he doesn't overreact.

It often takes maturity, practice, consistency, and fair correction when teaching a horse to walk with perfect ground manners. It doesn't just happen. And if truth be told, I have watched horses with impeccable ground manners suddenly become naughty on the lead line with someone they don't know. Some horses will revert to their old nature and do things they wouldn't normally do. But the horse with a good mind will walk softly no matter who is leading him.

I think about my walk with God and how, at times, I rush ahead of Him without looking back. That is when I got myself in trouble because I wasn't following His plans. Then, there have been times when the Lord urged me to do something I didn't want to do, and because I was scared, I dragged my feet behind him like a sack of potatoes. But when I walk quietly beside God, life seems to go smoothly and I feel His presence all around me. Thank you, Lord, for guiding me all my days.

315

~October 19~

The Hectic Life

Be still before the Lord and wait patiently for Him.
Psalm 37:7

As women, we put a lot of pressure on ourselves. We worry about how our home looks and how our children act. We create lists and check off boxes because it gives us a sense of accomplishment. We often overwork ourselves and join too many groups and activities because if we are busy, then we don't have to think about our disappointments. It can be a vicious cycle if we don't put things in a healthy perspective, and sometimes we need to scrap it all for a few hours and head to the barn to see our horse!

I have met many women at our stable throughout the years who are professionals in the workplace. They are lawyers, doctors, teachers, etc., and they are trying to do it all in life. They have families, work full time, and have managed to hold on to their horse through all of it. They don't have the time they used to have to come out to see their horse daily, but they do make it a priority to come out a couple times a week. It is their time to breathe and slow down from the busy life they lead, and the sound of hoof beats and nickers is enough to lower their blood pressure.

I love seeing the transformation from businesswoman to horsewoman for a few hours. She comes in her business clothes with an expression that says she had a tough day at work, but once she changes into jeans and boots, she turns into a cowgirl ready to ride and relax with a smile that could light up a room.

I pray, Lord, for the woman who is trying to do it all and is running ragged. The barn should be a safe haven for her to come and unwind, forget about the world's craziness for a while, and let her horse be the calm she needs in her hectic life. Lord, above all else, I pray that she will find refuge and peace in you daily. Amen.

~October 20~
Unstoppable Team

The eyes of the Lord are everywhere,
keeping watch on the wicked and the good.
Proverbs 15:3

Her grandmother told her she could choose any horse from their farm. After looking at all the horses her grandmother owned, her eyes fell upon a gangly but adorable Appaloosa colt. He was only a few months old, but she knew there was something special about him. The two became inseparable, learning everything together, and their bond was undeniable. As she grew into a young woman, they became an unstoppable team in Dressage competition. They trusted each other no matter what they were doing, but little did they know their trust would be tested like never before.

After a few years, the Appaloosa started having problems with his eyes and it was soon discovered that he had Uveitis, also known as Moon Blindness. His eyes would tear up and squint often at first, and quickly became progressively worse. With each flare-up, his eyes became more sensitive and more damage was happening to the horse's vision. He was losing his eyesight. It became extremely painful for the horse and when his right eye ruptured, it had to be removed. Soon after, his other eye became inflamed and ruptured and needed to be removed also. He became totally blind.

This woman, who had grown up with her horse, had to make a difficult decision. She chose to take it slow and he would let her know when he was done. She worked with him daily and got him a companion pony. He settled into his new life and gained back his confidence. Soon, she was riding him and listening to the voice he had known all his life. Once again, they were an unstoppable team. Sometimes, God will teach us the greatest lessons in life through the horse and help us to see what is truly important.

~October 21~
The Good Stuff

I will sing to the Lord as long as I live;
I will sing praise to my God while I have being.
Psalm 104:33

When I was young, all I wanted to do was ride, go to horse shows, and, of course, have fancy bridles and saddles dripping with silver. That is what I called the "good stuff." I never had a fancy bridle or silver-laden western show saddle, but I did have a ton of fun. It wasn't until I was much older that I started to see life and horses in a much deeper way. My eyes were opened to the good stuff again, and it looked much different this time. It was no longer about the silver brides or saddles, the trophies and ribbons, or the registration papers that said your horse had pristine bloodlines. It took me a while to see all the beauty and good stuff right before me, but it changed my life once I did.

I started looking forward to the morning sunrise and loved the sound of the horses nickering when the barn lights came on. The first time you let the horses outside after a huge snowstorm, they run and play like children and it is something to behold. And when you watch a new horse in a herd bond with another horse, it always makes me tear up because I know how hard the adjustment is for them. The good stuff is watching women at my barn accomplish things they never thought possible and how their face lights up with excitement. And nothing can compare to a grandchild riding grandma's horse for the first time and all you hear is precious giggles.

Thank you, Lord, for the good things in our lives. They may change over the decades, but they just keep getting better and better. Thank you for showing me the good stuff here on Earth because it gives me a glimpse of what Heaven will be like.

~October 22~
All Consuming

Remembering before our God and Father your work of faith and labor of love and steadfastness of hope in our Lord Jesus Christ.
I Thessalonians 1:3

We look at the horse and he consumes us daily. We spend our free time figuring out how to save enough money to buy our dream horse, and our emotions get all wrapped up in this animal to the point that it almost seems impossible to control.

It is a crazy kind of obsession that usually starts when we are quite young and it never really goes away. Life gets busy and we never mention the word horse to our family, but it is still there deep inside of us waiting for the right time to leap off our tongues and shout out to the world that we are going to take riding lessons and lease a horse! From there, it only gets better.

Yes, for a horse-obsessed middle-aged woman, it is consuming and we love every minute of it. We become like the young girls taking selfies on our horse every chance we can. We spend a lot of time deciding what colors will look good on him and try to match our outfits to his saddle pad color for the day. No one can possibly understand a human's relationship with a horse except another human who is also in love with these majestic animals. We are designed to love, nurture, and care for our families and animals – including our horses!

Lord, I know we can be consumed by our horses but I need to make sure I find a healthy balance so that my family's needs are not second. I pray that everything I do with this animal you have entrusted to me will be God-honoring and used for your kingdom. Please help me to be consumed for the right reasons.

What a wonderful way to share the good news of Jesus, while riding with friends. What an awesome mission field. Praise God!

~October 23~
Horses, Horses, Horses

Worthy are you, our Lord and God, to receive glory and honor and power, for you created all things, and by your will they existed and were created.
Revelation 4:11

Horses come in all shapes and sizes. Some are short and pudgy, and some are tall and sleek. Some equines are built for power and heavy work, while others are born with lightning speed built into their DNA. Some horses are smaller than dogs, and others are so massive in size that the only words that come to mind are "gentle giants." Some horses are in the middle of the road in size, but their agility is unsurpassed. Some horses are petite but can travel far distances like no other equine.

Throughout history, man has tried to create the perfect equine. So much of the horse's existence was determined by the ruling kings and queens of each century, and kingdoms were built and destroyed from the back of the horse. The size of the horse was often determined by the ruling elite and from one century to the next, horses were bred for that country's ambitions. Some kings wanted massive horses to ride, while others preferred smaller quicker horses for warfare. Women were often courted with the help of a horse. A strong and respectable man always rode a stallion and would never be seen on a mare or gelding, for those were the horses of the lower class. Horses were also the wedding gift of many cultures, and if a man wanted to marry, he needed to have horses of his own to prove he was worthy to her parents.

I often think about God and the creation of this perfect animal that would bring down nations and win countries in battle. He knew this amazing equine would be part of the courtship between men and women and seal the marriage deal in some cultures. What an influence the horse has had on warfare and love.

~October 24~
It's Not Too Late

Love is patient and kind; love does not envy or boast; it is not arrogant or rude.
It does not insist on its own way; it is not irritable or resentful.
I Corinthians 13:4-5

As a teenager, I remember one horsewoman who seemed to have it all. She owned grand champion show horses, was a horse show judge, and was married to a well-known actor who was also a cowboy and loved to ride. She was everything I wanted to be in my young impressionable mind, except for one thing. She wasn't very nice and she had a way of making you feel bad about your horse. I remember her telling me that she thought my horse was dangerous without a reason and it crushed me. My mare was the sweetest horse ever, and you could do anything with her. I often wondered why she said those cruel things. I will never know, but I do think of her occasionally, and this sadness overcomes me because she missed what is truly important in life.

It's never too late to offer simple and kind advice when asked and to remember that your actions will always speak louder than your words. You can make a difference in another woman's equestrian journey just by how you encourage her, or you could be the straw that breaks the camel's back and crushes her dreams.

I pray that we can be a beacon of light to the new horse owners, young and old, and walk beside them as they learn. Above all, never underestimate the power of prayer and a kind word of encouragement.

Lord, please forgive me for the missed opportunities to help another person in their journey as an equestrian. I pray that going forward, I will never miss a chance to encourage someone when needed, and let them know they got this. Amen.

~October 25~
A New Path

Therefore, confess your sins to one another and pray for one another, that you may be healed. The prayer of a righteous person has great power as it is working.
James 5:16

When your child chooses to do something different with horses other than what you are familiar with, it becomes a pathway for the entire family. When a woman who has raised her children and done her wifely duties decides to get her first horse, it will be a new adventure for the entire family. A husband is definitely not off the hook, and his wife of many years will now ask him to come out to the stable and watch her ride, or just brush the horse with her. He might have mucking duty or make runs to pick up grain and other fun things for his wife's new love. It becomes a new experience for everyone, and soon, the grandkids will be visiting in hopes of petting grandma's horse and riding. It is a beautiful season of incredible changes as she becomes a horsewoman, and her family watches as a new person emerges from what they were familiar with. Sometimes, that new path may lead to miles of open road and adventures with camping and trail riding in the steepest mountains. Sometimes, it leads to endurance riding or the show ring. Along her journey, she will make new friends and have many conversations about everything related to horses.

Each woman's journey will be slightly different, but it brings us closer to each other. We are madly in love with horses and can't get enough of them. My prayer is that the new path you are on will parallel with many wonderful horse-crazy women who will make you laugh or hug you when you feel like crying. Above all else, I pray that you will include the Lord in all your adventures and let Him always be your guide.

~October 26~
The Prodigal

Just so, I tell you, there will be more joy in heaven over one sinner who repents than over ninety-nine righteous persons who need no repentance.
Luke 15:7

Years ago, we had a new horse come to our barn that will always hold a special place in my heart. He was young, still growing both mentally and physically, and definitely had a mind of his own. His owner hired a trainer to break him out for western riding but he was very rebellious. He constantly tested what he could get away with and was often extremely hard to handle. At times, he was so naughty that he would pull away and run around the farm like a wild beast! As this young horse matured, he began to calm down and behave much better both under saddle and in-hand.

Ten years later, he is one of the sweetest horses in my barn and definitely one of the best behaved. You could call him the prodigal equine. Chester (his name has been changed to protect the innocent!) reminds me of my own walk with Christ. I often think about my youth and how rebellious I was in school and during my twenties. I knew I shouldn't drink or do drugs but I did them anyway, even though it was destroying my body. I didn't care. It wasn't until I hit bottom and realized that this stuff was going to kill me that I came back to my Father's arms and straightened out my life. I am the prodigal who came back to the Lord seeking forgiveness.

We all have our prodigal moments and the Lord is just waiting with open arms to take us back into the fold. I guess that's why Chester is one of my favorite horses at our barn. I remember when he was a naughty youngster, but he grew into an incredible horse with the biggest heart ever. What a blessing to witness such a beautiful transformation.

~October 27~
Savor The Moment

*The Lord is my strength and my shield; in him my heart trusts, and I am
helped; my heart exults, and with my song I give thanks to him.*
Psalm 28:7

As horsewomen, we sometimes forget that life has its ups and
downs. We might be on top of our game as a teenager because our
parents bought us a well-trained push-button horse that makes us
look good. But if the truth be told, that show horse taught us more
about winning and maybe not enough about how to lose gracefully.
And sometimes, we begin to think we know more about horses
than we actually do. Then we grow up.

Life happens, and we often become horseless for many years as
we do all the things adults do. But the love we have never fades.
Then, one day, we finally decide it is time to find our forever horse,
and all we can go off of are the things we learned back when we
were young and rode every day. It's as if there is a blank space of
time between our teen years and our older mature years. We realize
quickly how things have changed, and this time, we are wise enough
now to know we have a lot of new things to learn.

The day finally comes when your new horse has backed off the
trailer and you are more nervous than you ever imagined. You don't
want to mess up this beautiful animal that is now entrusted to you.
At that moment, you realize it's not about the ribbons you won in
your youth. It's now about the relationship you will nurture and
build slowly with your new equine partner. Your mind is constantly
bouncing back and forth from your youth to the present hoping to
find the answers to all your questions immediately, but they don't
come. It will take time, but that is what makes it even more special.
This time, you will savor every moment and enjoy the ride so much
more the second time around.

324

~October 28~
Learning Something New

I keep my eyes always on the Lord.
With him at my right hand, I will not be shaken.
Psalm 16:8

I am the first to admit that when I feel overwhelmed, I love watching a good movie that doesn't require any thinking. I realized a few years ago that some horses struggle to learn new things and can also become overwhelmed. The result can be one of two outcomes. Either he willingly keeps trying until he gets it, or he shuts down and refuses or worse. I have watched a horse stop and refuse to move one step further no matter how much the rider pressured him, but he was saying loud and clear, "I need a break!" Of course, the horse cannot verbally speak to us, so we need to be wiser, read his body language, and look into his eyes. We also need to understand what is typical for his personality and what is completely out of character. Sometimes, all a horse needs is a day of rest and time to rejuvenate his mind. He has a fantastic memory, and if he has a willing spirit, then trying it the next day can lead to success.

We all struggle from time to time when learning new things. As women, we have the luxury of stopping when we want to, and instead, spend the day shopping or watching movies. But the horse doesn't have that option and he may need a little extra time to process what is being asked of him.

Lord, I ask for discernment when teaching my horse new things that might be hard for him to grasp initially. Teach me to be attentive to how he communicates with me and to recognize when he needs to rest and try again the next day. Let me never take for granted his willing heart, which can be so fragile at times. Amen.

~October 29~
Find Your Passion

But I have raised you up for this very purpose, that I might display My power
to you, and that My name might be proclaimed in all the earth.
Exodus 9:16

Find your passion and see where it takes you. If you are head over heels in love with horses, dig deeper and find out what you love about them. If your heart is in helping horses that are sick or injured, then explore the world of equine veterinary. If you are crazy about babies, then learn as much as you can about breeding horses. If you are good at photography and have an eye for taking pictures of horses, go for it! The one thing we all have in common is our passion for horses and the world out there is vast, with more options than ever before. I wish I had known this when I was young. As a teenager, it seemed as if the only two options for careers with horses for women were horse trainer/instructor or equine veterinarian. My eyes were opened to many new possibilities as I got older, and now the opportunities are endless for people who want to work in the horse industry.

I pray for the woman who is confused about what she wants to do with her life. Lord, she may be young with her whole life ahead of her, and she is trying to figure out how to have a career with horses. It can be daunting and seem impossible to achieve at times. Lord if it is your will, please give her the courage to put one step in front of the other and find her calling in life. It can feel isolating at times when trying to figure it all out. Please surround her with people who will mentor her and positively influence her life, especially on those challenging days when things are unclear.

Thank you, Lord, for always being there for us when we call out to you. In Jesus' name, Amen.

~October 30~
Giving Back

Carry each other's burdens, and in
this way you will fulfill the law of Christ.
Galatians 6:2

When I was a younger woman, I must admit I was selfish at times. I struggled to share the things I had been blessed with but instead hung on to them as if they were gold or something silly like that. I have lived a few decades now and have watched many women share their horse tack, show clothes, and even their horses, and they do so with a joyful heart. I have watched a younger woman willingly share all that she has with other young girls who are less fortunate, and it has melted my heart. And I have witnessed the giving spirit of older ladies who share their horse trailers and trucks and happily share their equine partners if needed. These incredible women have taught me so much about what it means to give back.

Nothing is cheap with horses and not everyone can afford to own one. But if you have been blessed with the means to own a horse and you are not riding him, then maybe you have an opportunity to light up someone's life. You never know how God will use you and sometimes it is done in the simplest ways. It might be allowing someone to groom your horse and teaching them about horse care and all that goes with it. It could be that a youngster is in need of a horse to show because their horse is lame and show season has just started.

There are so many ways to give back and the joy you receive will be greater than you can imagine. Lord, teach me to have a giving spirit and to realize that everything I own is yours to begin with. When an opportunity arises to bless someone with my horse, I pray I will follow with obedience and love. Amen.

~October 31~
Couldn't Look Away

And of some have compassion, making a difference.
Jude 1:22

Dorothy Brook was newly married and followed her husband to Cairo, Egypt. It was 1930 and the war had been over for more than a decade and there were business opportunities in Egypt. When Dorothy and her husband got to Cairo, her eyes fell upon the horses working in the streets. She had never seen such sad and sorry animals. Their hips and ribs were protruding as if they would break through the skin at any time, and their legs were permanently bent from years of being forced to carry loads too heavy for their body. All the horses looked extremely old, and Dorothy quickly learned that after the war, thousands of British warhorses were sold to Egypt as workhorses. These once proud warhorses were now forced into hard and abusive labor until their death.

Dorothy couldn't look away and knew she had to do something. Slowly, she started buying as many of these old horses as she could. Soon, the word got out that this woman was paying good money for old broken-down warhorses, and quickly she became overwhelmed with people wanting to sell their animals. She put together a committee called the Old Warhorse Campaign and Rescue, and by 1931, she had rescued many horses. She hired scouts to find as many warhorse veterans as possible. Between 1930-1934 some 5000 army mules and horses were found and identified by their army brand. In 1934, Dorothy opened the Old Warhorse Memorial Hospital in Cairo, which is still a working equine hospital today. Dorothy loved horses and spent her remaining years saving as many horses as possible. She will forever be remembered for her great compassion and willingness to make a difference in thousands of horses' lives.

~November 1~
All The Sweeter

And you will know the truth, and the truth will set you free.
John 8:32

My father used to say, "The truth shall set you free." I have to admit, as a kid it annoyed me, but he was trying to do his best to teach me how to live a good life. I have often thought about that saying throughout the years and even applied it to horse ownership.

When I was a young horse-crazy girl, I fantasized about horses. I didn't have a realistic view of these massive and often unpredictable animals, and it put me in a couple of dangerous situations because I didn't think anything bad could happen. It took a few hard bangers before I realized that I could get seriously hurt or my horse could get injured if I wasn't careful. I needed to always look out for my horse and his safety first, not the other way around.

I have met a few horsewomen over the years who think the way I used to. I love seeing the joy in their eyes and the dreams they are living out, but I am also aware that they don't think anything can ever go wrong when it comes to horses. Then, when it does, they are devastated to the point where they want to get out of horses completely. Sometimes, they sell the horse, never to return. It always breaks my heart when this happens.

The woman who understands the truth and realness of horses grows in her horsemanship by leaps and bounds. She knows her horse is not infallible and things happen, both good and bad. But once she understands this, her connection to her horse will become even stronger. She creates goals and dreams within the realm of what her horse is capable of doing and loves her horse no matter what happens. She has gotten real with horses, which makes it all the sweeter. She will go further than she ever dreamed because the truth has set her free.

~November 2~
The Path Less Traveled

But now, O Lord, you are our Father; we are the clay,
and you are our potter; we are all the work of your hand.
Isaiah 64:8

I have always appreciated the woman who dares to go a different path with horses. She may have grown up riding Western or English, but somewhere in life, she saw something that captured her interest and took off with it. It may not be the most popular equine activity or the easiest, but she is hooked and doesn't look back. These women dare to drive a six-team hitch with all its horsepower, and they do it well. They ride horses at breakneck speed in timed events while shooting targets with sheer precision. These ladies compete in endurance riding and spend more time in the saddle than anywhere else. They are jockeys, calf-ropers, and mountain trail guides. There are female forest rangers whose trusted steed is a surefooted mule and the mounted police officer who walks the beat with her equine partner daily, and the list is endless.

The horsewomen who have changed direction and tried something completely out of the ordinary are the same women who are paving the way for others to follow. It doesn't mean the road they traveled was easy and they may have dealt with some resistance from others, but they kept going and persevered. They are the movers and the shakers who dare to dream outside the box. I admire these types of horsewomen because they see possibilities everywhere. They might be going into unknown territory but they go with hearts full of courage.

I want to pray for the women who dare to follow a path less traveled in the world of horses. Lord, keep them safe as they live out their dreams and experience new adventures, and above all else, please let them know they are loved more than anything. Amen.

~November 3~
Changing Landscape

The grass withers, the flower fades,
but the word of our God will stand forever.
Isaiah 40:8

Each autumn season brings a fantastic sensory overload here on the farm. There is something about the cool crisp days of autumn that rejuvenate a person's soul. I can't explain it, but you can definitely feel it.

New changes are also taking place with each horse on our farm. Their coats are growing thick and their ears are full of fluff. Their once smooth faces are now fuzzy, and many look like teddy bears that you want to hug. The one thing wonderful about a boarding stable is all the different breeds of horses. You can see the changes taking place with each breed, and the differences are remarkable. We have Thoroughbreds that are thin-skinned and barely grow a coat, and soon, they are donning brightly colored blankets. Then, we have draft horses and other heavy-coated breeds that easily handle colder temperatures and fit in perfectly with the snow-covered landscape. The scenery looks amazing with trees bursting with color, and you can tell that colder days will soon be upon us. The hay is increased and the horses are packing on extra calories to get them through the coldest part of winter, and they can sense the changes that are coming fast. The horses are frisky and playful after a long, hot summer and I get the feeling they love this time of year!

Thank you, Lord, for the changing landscape that is taking place right before our eyes. The experienced horsewoman understands the work that lies ahead with the change of seasons. Lord, please walk by her side as she does chores during this time of year. Each day will be unpredictable, but she will see the Glory of God surrounding her daily. Amen.

~November 4~
Quietly Dreaming

Because you are precious in my eyes,
and honored, and I love you.
Isaiah 43:4

There was a woman who had a loving husband and children, excellent health, and a long, prosperous career. But something was missing in her life. She longed for the day when she could own a horse of her own. She was so thankful for how blessed she had been in life and felt guilty of even asking for one more thing, so she never spoke a word of it to her husband.

In the early mornings, she would grab a cup of coffee and sit on her computer. She would read anything related to horses, watch YouTube videos about horses, and quietly dream about horses. Then, one day, as she was rushing out the door to work, her husband happened to go on the computer, and the tab was left open to where the woman had been reading earlier that morning. He became curious and began looking at the previous history, and he was stunned at how many links led to horse-related pages!

When the woman got home from work that evening, she sat down with her husband for dinner and they began to talk about their day. Then he reached under the table and gave his wife a gift in a wrapped box. She had this puzzled look on her face but opened it quickly and stopped as she gazed at the bright red halter and lead rope. Tears started flowing down her face as she looked at this man whom she had been married to for over thirty years. And then he told her it was time she lived out her dream of owning a horse.

God bless the incredible husbands who support their wives and encourage them to live out their horse dreams. Some of these men have no idea what they are getting themselves into, but God will see them through!

~November 5~
Absolute Power

God, the Lord, is my strength; he makes my feet like the deer's;
he makes me tread on my high places.
Habakkuk 3:19

The horses had been inside the barn for a few days due to the terrible weather. It seemed as though Mother Nature had thrown everything at us from rain and sleet to ice and now beautiful snow. The bad weather had passed and it was time to get the horses back outside. As I dressed, I knew it would be a challenging morning because the horses would be overly excited with the fresh snow. I prayed that everything would go smoothly.

As each horse was led to their paddock, many of them started rolling in the new snow and running around. They quickly fed off each other and I knew some of the more difficult horses would be a handful. Well, the morning didn't go as planned, and three horses got away from me and my husband! It quickly reminded me of how small I am and how powerful a horse can be when he wants to be. You don't realize how much power the horse has until you are hanging on to the lead rope of a horse that is getting ready to bolt. With each step you can feel them get bigger and bigger. That is when you pray that you make it to the paddock. It will send your heart pounding every time, and it still does me, even after all these years. The beauty of the horse is that even with his power, he will try his hardest to contain himself and hold it together because you are asking him to. It doesn't mean he is perfect and will do it every time, but in most cases, he will try.

Lord, thank you for showing me the awesomeness of the horse through his strength and power. I am humbled by this incredible animal, who, at times, leaves me speechless. I know today had its frustrating moments, but tomorrow is a new day. Praise God!

~November 6~
Faith Over Fear

When the cares of my heart are many,
your consolations cheer my soul.
Psalm 94:19

Some horses overreact so much that it almost becomes comical. We have had a couple of horses with this personality type in our barn. They spook if anything new is placed in the aisle and look at it as if it were a monster. It could be a jacket on the floor or a new blanket still in the plastic bag. It could be a spot of water where a bucket spilled or a coffee mug! It doesn't matter what it is. If it is different, they notice it immediately and try to walk as far away as possible. The same is true in the indoor riding arena. Some horses notice immediately if something new has been put in the corner where our jump standards and trail course equipment are stored. They look at it and try to take their rider away from it as quickly as possible, and sometimes, the rider ends up on the ground as the horse bolts in a different direction! That is where trust is so important if you are the lucky owner of this type of horse.

Then, there are other horses that pay no attention to the new objects in the aisle, and you could have flags blowing in the arena and they would walk by as if they had seen them a thousand times before. Both types of horses can teach us so much but learning how to deal with a horse that shows fear before faith takes patience and time. He needs time to process what he is seeing, meaning it might take a little longer than a naturally calm horse. He needs time to turn his fear into faith and trust you completely.

God is asking us to trust him completely and have faith over fear. For some, this comes easier than others, but the Lord waits patiently and teaches us to trust him no matter what is in front of us. He will always walk beside us. In that, we have His assurance.

~November 7~
Most Trusted Partner

Beloved, let us love one another, for love is from God,
and whoever loves has been born of God and knows God.
I John 4:7

Her alarm went off like it had done thousands of times before. She slowly made her way to the bathroom and as she looked in the mirror, she saw a few more strands of grey hair and knew she had made the right decision. She put on her neatly ironed uniform, pinned her badge on her shirt, and grabbed a cup of coffee and a couple of apples. It was dark when she got to the barn, and as she looked around the memories began to flood her mind. She quickly pushed back the tears and headed in to see her partner. They had worked together for fifteen years and both were retiring on the same day. She approached her partner's stall and watched him quietly munching on hay. He looked up at her with soft gentle eyes and greeted her with a quiet knicker.

Kelly and her equine partner Charlie had worked on the police force for many years and knew each other inside and out. They both started out as rookies when she was a new mounted police officer and he was a new police horse. Together, they learned how to be a team and to trust each other no matter the situation. Kelly gazed down at Charlie and noticed he also had a few grey hairs, which made her smile. The force had been good to the both of them over the years. Kelly looked into Charlie's eyes and felt this peace and joy come over her because she knew that after her final shift had ended and the long goodbyes and hugs were done, Charlie was coming home with her. She had made plans to adopt her longtime partner and he was coming home to her farm forever. Her most trusted partner would now be her trail riding partner with new adventures ahead for the both of them. Her heart was full.

~November 8~
Don't Stop

For I, the Lord your God, hold your right hand; it is I
who say to you, "Fear not, I am the one who helps you."
Isaiah 41:13

Several years ago, a famous barrel racer gave a clinic at the Midwest Horse Fair. When I was a teenager, she was a fierce competitor on the barrel racing circuit, so I knew she must have been a little older than me. I listened to her teach the students in the clinic, and as I watched her ride, I was impressed with how well she handled her horse. What moved me even more was what she told the students in the clinic. She told them to never stop creating goals no matter how old they were. I knew she must have been in her late sixties, and she talked about the goals she now had at her age and how they refresh her and keep her going. Then she explained that the horses she rides need new goals, too, which keeps their minds working and the boredom far away. Her advice was just as good for the horse as for the rider.

I often think about that clinician and her wise words. Horses are always changing as they age, and mixing things up a bit is good for them. It doesn't need to be anything complicated or hard. It can be simple and fun.

Today, I want to encourage the young-at-heart horsewoman. Keep trying new things and don't be afraid to fail the first time because that is when we learn the most. The Lord has given us this extraordinary mind to use no matter our age. You might not ride horses anymore but there is so much you can do with horses without ever getting in the saddle. Anything you do with horses will make you feel so much better mentally and physically. The sky's the limit! And remember, with the Lord by your side, anything is possible.

~November 9~
It's Okay If You Don't...

Therefore, as God's chosen people, holy and dearly loved, clothe yourselves with compassion, kindness, humility, gentleness and patience.
Colossians 3:12

As a teenager, I would ride my horse to a place where all the kids would meet. It was a field surrounded by small houses and cement sidewalks on all sides. The only reason this field did not have homes built on it was because some of the main powerlines and the structures to hold them up ran right through the middle of each field. It was considered a barren wasteland, but it was where we all hung out on their horses and where I experienced my first bout with peer pressure. This was back in the 1970s when kids would sit on their horses, smoke cigarettes, and talk about their lives. I was one who never liked the smell of cigarettes, and in fact, it gave me a headache, so I always opted out when the other kids pressured me to smoke. All I wanted to do was talk about horses and ride, and I remember feeling out of place many times.

All these years later, I am glad I didn't succumb to peer pressure. I now realize that it is okay not to do what all the other kids or adults are doing, including horse activities and practices. It's okay to say no to harsh bits and training equipment. It is perfectly fine if you just want to hang out with your horse and talk about horse stuff instead of gossiping about the new girl in the barn. And it is okay not to be okay with the gossip you hear.

What a fantastic opportunity as a woman to help create a positive and safe atmosphere at your stable just by how you live. Let them see your love for your horse and others around you, and they will begin to see the love that Jesus has for us. It all starts with you.

~November 10~
The Mountain Horse

*"Do not be afraid of them, for I am with you
to deliver you," declares the Lord.*
Jeremiah 1:8

When I was in my twenties, I had the incredible opportunity to go on a week-long trip deep in the Sierra Mountain Range. We rode in on horseback with pack mules following behind us, carrying all our gear, food, and anything else we needed. It was breathtaking, and I was so happy to be riding a horse instead of walking. At the time, I never really thought about how treacherous and steep the trails were or how surefooted those amazing mountain horses and mules were.

Many years later, a group of women I know went on a week-long horseback riding adventure up in the mountains of Canada. When I saw the pictures I was blown away by the sheer beauty of the mountain ranges and their steepness. It reminded me of my adventure to the Sierras years earlier. I began thinking about these remarkable horses that are surefooted and steady and know the mountain ranges better than the humans riding on their backs. My eyes were opened to how exceptional the mountain horse is and that not every horse is cut out to be good mountain horse. In fact, most horses living on the "flat lands" would be exhausted, nervous, and have a very difficult time walking over rocks and downed trees, through riverways, and on cliffsides. I am the first to admit I would rather be on the steady mountain horse or mule than any other equine in the low country.

Praise God for the incredible horses and mules that live their entire lives in the high mountains. They are the unsung heroes of the equine world. Thank you, Lord, for creating so many kinds of horses, each with special talents, strengths, and natural abilities.

~November 11~
That Lonely Feeling

If the Lord had not been my help, my soul would soon have lived in the land of silence. When I thought, "My foot slips," your steadfast love, O Lord, held me up.
Psalm 94:17-18

I was surrounded by my family and horses and was living the dream, yet this loneliness flowed over me. I worked at home, and even though I loved the job, this strange sensation would overcome me during any holiday. I understood and gladly accepted the life that my husband and I had created together, but no one could have prepared me for the demanding commitment level. I must admit, at times, it overwhelmed and exhausted me, and that is when I would feel this great heaviness that I was alone. The truth is I was never alone. I just needed to change how I did things and not let the business consume me. I wanted a life outside the farm even if it was just for a few hours each week.

Today, my prayer is for the women who work on farms and ranches. They are often isolated, and even though they have the beauty of God's creation all around them, they may be feeling like they are missing something. These hard-working horsewomen raise their children and take care of their family's needs but sometimes they have a strong desire to step out of their life for just a few hours. It is a struggle that I felt early on in my business, and I want them to know they are not alone.

Dear God, I submit my heart, mind, and will to you today. Help me to see clearly your plan for my life when I have lost my vision and feel alone. I pray I will live less by how I feel at the moment and more by what your promises say to me each morning when I open your Holy Word. Thank you, Lord, for always covering me with your love. Amen.

~November 12~
Embarrassed

But earnestly desire the higher gifts.
And I will show you a still more excellent way.
I Corinthians 12:31

When my girls were in their early teenage years, they were at that awkward age where they wanted to fit in with all the other kids at school. Many of the families had huge mega houses but ours was a small farmhouse. I used to tell them that many of their friends would love to come to our home because they could ride horses and have fun outside, but my younger daughter would never invite her friends over.

Years later, she told me that during that period in her young life, she was embarrassed by our small house and tiny television! As a teenager, she didn't realize how blessed she was to own a horse that she could ride anytime, along with all the other fun things you can do on a farm. She is a grown woman now, and even though she no longer lives at home, she loves coming home as much as possible which fills me with joy. She loves the horses and is happy she grew up where she did, and now she loves talking about all the crazy adventures she had as a farm kid. I guess that is a normal part of growing up. We always want what we don't have at the moment, and even though we may have a lot, we sometimes lose sight of our blessings and start to feel like everyone has it better.

Lord, help me never to take all that I have in my life for granted. I am blessed beyond measure, and I never want to forget what a privilege it is to care for such amazing animals. Help me to have an open heart to share what we have here on the farm with others who may not have the same opportunities. Thank you, God, for your unceasing love. Amen.

~November 13~
Realistic Expectations

So we do not lose heart. Though our outer self is wasting away,
our inner self is being renewed day by day.
II Corinthians 4:16

Having realistic expectations with horses doesn't always happen right off the bat. In fact, I would venture to say that it doesn't usually happen until you have been around horses for a couple of years. It doesn't matter if you purchase your first horse or start a horse business. Sooner or later, the life you envisioned with horses may hit a few bumps in the road. I am the first to say those setbacks will make success all the sweeter if you hang in there and trust in the Lord's plan for your life.

When we first opened our new boarding facility, I couldn't fathom that people would leave our barn. After all, we were a brand-new stable with a huge indoor riding arena. Was I wrong! We went through a high turnover of horses and clients in the first two years. My expectations were unrealistic, and it wasn't until I came down to earth and looked at it more sensibly that I began to see what needed to be done to keep our boarding stable viable. When my unrealistic expectations of barn management came crashing down, I needed to lean upon the Lord more than ever. I needed to pray and find out what His plans were for my life and business, and that is when things started to turn around for the better.

I pray for the woman who is struggling because her expectations have been shattered, and she does not know which way to turn. Heavenly Father, please reveal yourself to her so that she will gain peace and understanding. Then, she will see the plans you have for her life. Amen.

~November 14~
Menopause!

Praise the Lord! Oh give thanks to the Lord, for he is good,
for his steadfast love endures forever!
Psalm 106:1

After growing up and having horses in a hot climate, I couldn't believe anyone would want to own horses in this frozen tundra. But here I was in Wisconsin and working at a show barn. The barn was heated but it still took everything I had to drive to work each morning. It didn't matter how many layers I put on because I was always cold. I only lasted about a year and a half at that job and I told myself I would never own horses as long as we lived here. Famous last words!

Years later, I was back into horses with my children and building a barn and indoor riding arena. I slowly settled into the Midwest winter climate and couldn't keep horses out of my life. So what do I do? I jumped in with both feet and opened a horse boarding stable with no heat in the barn! Well, after twenty years, I have to say I survived every cold winter. But the one thing that has helped me tremendously was when I went through menopause! It made the winters much more bearable. I was always hot, and my poor husband was sometimes cold and irritable due to working in the frigid temps. It was a game-changer for me!

It's the little things like menopause that can make our life with horses easier, as crazy as it may sound. And it is the little things like menopause that I can praise God for because I am warm even when it is freezing outside and walking horses through the snow and cleaning stalls in sub-zero temps. It's not the perfect working conditions, but today, I will praise the Lord for the changes my body has undergone because it has helped me tolerate the frozen tundra and the life I have chosen with horses.

She Is A Blessing

He has made everything beautiful in its time. He has also set eternity in the human heart; yet no one can fathom what God has done from beginning to end.
Ecclesiastes 3:11

We are encouragers and caregivers and ready to give advice if asked. Those are wonderful qualities to have with people, but sometimes we miss what our horse is trying to tell us. We may push too hard because we are so passionate about our goals and dreams that we forget to put on the brakes when our horse tells us that he needs to slow down for the moment. I have been guilty of this in my younger years and it is something most women struggle with from time to time as their horsemanship grows and they become excited about everything they are learning.

What I love about the seasoned horsewoman is that she has ridden a few miles in her life, has nothing to prove, and will always have your best interest at heart. She will walk beside you when you need someone and stand back when she sees you are ready to fly on your own. She will speak up when you are pushing your horse too hard and comfort you as you struggle to gain a healthy balance for both you and your horse. She may be gruff and rough around the edges but her heart is pure gold, and she would be there at a moment's notice if you were in trouble.

Lord, I am praying for the horsewoman who needs your divine intervention. She has lost connection with her horse and those around her and has taken a step off the path. She needs a wise friend to come alongside her and guide her back. Please send an encourager into her life to help put her back on solid footing and rebuild her relationships with the people in her life and the horses she loves.

~November 16~
Well-Behaved Moments

I will praise you with an upright heart,
when I learn your righteous rules.
Psalm 119:7

There is something to be said for the well-behaved horse when you are just learning to ride. I was lucky that my first horse was very well-trained. I thought I was a good rider, but in reality, I was as green as they come. I quickly became confident in my riding ability, but as a child, I took all the credit and gave my horse none. It wasn't until I got a new horse when I was fifteen that I realized I wasn't as good as I thought. I was now the owner of an up-and-coming two-year-old mare that was intense at times and had never had anyone on her back. We were going to learn together and I was about to have my eyes opened and my horsemanship skills tested.

This young mare taught me things my first horse could never teach me because she made me work for everything. She wasn't as calm as my first horse and had moments when she would spook at the silliest things. I thought I had a good seat with my first horse but I quickly realized that my seat was lazy, and this mare taught me what it meant to stick to the saddle like glue. She humbled me and took me down a notch, but she was one of the best teachers I could have ever had. She taught me to use my body and be consistent with my leg cues and she wouldn't listen to anything less. I learned to be clear on what I was asking and, above all else, remember that she was young and a work in progress.

I will never forget my well-behaved first horse. But I will always remember my second horse because she taught me to cherish the well-behaved moments she gave me and to love her unconditionally. Praise God for the lessons we learn daily from the horses in our life.

~November 17~
Her Potential

But since we belong to the day, let us be sober, having put on the breastplate of faith and love, and for a helmet the hope of salvation.
I Thessalonians 5:8

So much gratitude is given to the woman who has devoted her life to horses. She has watched as trends have come and gone and fought to keep things the same when she saw destruction looming ahead for the majestic equine. She has worked tirelessly on farms and ranches in the heat of the day and the sub-zero temperatures of the winter without ceasing because she knows that God had put her on this earth to care for these incredible animals. She has put on many different hats in her life, including caretaker, equine veterinarian, midwife, trainer and riding instructor, teacher and mentor, businesswoman, and farm hand, and she has done it all to the best of her ability. She has made mistakes but managed to keep going, and she has had great accomplishments that most people will never know about except her family and a few close friends. She knows her role is important while not taking herself too seriously, and she has learned how to laugh at herself when she has those dumb moments we all experience. She is a horsewoman who loves what she does and she prays that she can create an environment where her horses thrive.

Today, Lord, I pray for the woman who has jumped both feet first into the deep end of the horse industry. She is new at this and will need positive and encouraging mentors to help her get through the first few years. Lord, you know how hard the life she has chosen will be, and sometimes, the world can be cruel to new people trying to make a living with horses. I pray she will see her full potential and understand that her strength comes from the Heaven above. In Jesus's Name, Amen.

~November 18~
Horsewoman Second

So teach us to number our days that we may get a heart of wisdom.
Psalm 90:12

It is so easy to dream big with our horses. Our goals often consume us as we inch forward to make our horse dreams come true. I know this all too well because I have the type of personality that when I decide to do something, everything else takes a back seat.

When we decided to build and open a horse stable, everything about it consumed me. My children were very young and they waited a lot for me (more than they should have) as David and I spent two years trying to start the business. Then, after years of learning how to manage a stable (by making many mistakes!), I wrote some books to help others so they didn't do the same dumb things I did. Those books also consumed me in the early years and my family often came second while I was writing them. During this time of boarding horses and writing books, my daughters were also showing horses a lot. Again, I was consumed as a horse show mom, and God became second in my life as He was with my other distractions.

It took me a few years to see that I had my priorities wrong. I pushed and pushed to make things happen with the business, the books, and the horse shows, and I didn't leave any space for God. During those years, many things went wrong and I didn't seek God first. I just plowed straight ahead without seeking His guidance. Once I realized the most important thing in life was missing, I got on my knees, asked for forgiveness, and made God first. When I became second, my life changed for the better, my marriage and family became stronger, and our business became healthier. Praise God for His enduring patience.

~November 19~
A Glimpse

And above all these put on love, which binds
everything together in perfect harmony.
Colossians 3:14

As a horse learns new things, his mannerisms, facial expressions, and even licking his lips tell us that he is beginning to understand what we are asking him to do. Back in the 1970s, horse training looked very different for most equestrians. Often, the trainer wanted a quick and correct response from the horse, and nothing less would do. I am sure a few people were teaching Natural Horsemanship back in the day, but they were nowhere to be found where I lived. I didn't hear about Natural Horsemanship until I was in my late thirties! It always makes me sad when I think about it because if I had known what to look for, I would surely have had a much better relationship with my horses.

What a blessing that as humans we have come so far in our knowledge of how horses think and how to read their body language. A horse will share glimpses with us every day of how he is feeling and what his mood is like. He shows us by his pace as we lead him outside, and if we watch him interact with his herd mates it is easy to see if he is not himself. He might become stressed and dance around in place if he does not understand what we are asking of him, but once it clicks, his demeanor will settle down to a quiet confidence. He may pin his ears when upset or mad, but he will also be listening to everything you are saying to him from the ground or in the saddle. He wants to please you but he can only show you in his language. Cherish the small glimpses you get from him every day because he is telling you about his world.

~November 20~
Riding Through The Pain

Be of good courage, and He shall strengthen your heart,
all you who hope in the Lord.
Psalm 31:24

Lisa fell in love with horses as a child and often begged her mother to take her to the stable to ride. From that moment on her passion and love for horses only grew deeper. She began taking riding lessons and did as much with horses as possible. Then, in Lisa's late twenties, she started to have some pain every time she rode. She first noticed it one day when a sharp pain shot up through her hip. She continued to ride through the pain until it got so bad she finally went to the doctor. It took ten years for the doctors to figure out what was going on and it was finally discovered that even though she was 39 years old, her hips were that of a 70-year-old and she would need hip surgery. Lisa first had hip resurfacing surgery and was pain-free for three years. During this time, she never stopped riding but then the pain came back in full force. This time, Lisa had total hip replacement surgery but the second surgery caused her femur to crack. Now she had excruciating pain in more places and the recovery would be much longer. Lisa never gave up and her goal was to ride again. Nine months later she was back in the saddle riding her horses! During the surgeries and recovery, it never once crossed Lisa's mind to sell her horses, even though she was nervous the first few times in the saddle. She loved her horses more than anything and they were part of her family.

Lisa rides several times a week now and is pain-free for the first time in decades. She says that her horses are what keep her moving forward and give her a reason to keep going. She needed them as much as they needed her, and through it all, her love for them has grown even deeper.

~November 21~
Forgiveness

And whenever you stand praying, if you have anything against anyone,
forgive him, that your Father in heaven may also forgive you your trespasses.
Mark 11:25

I love watching the interaction between horses when they are together. They play and fight, become obsessive and jealous and sometimes act downright silly. But they are also very loving and nurturing and forgive each other easily. We can learn so much from horses if we take the time and watch them. I always find it fascinating how two horses can pierce their ears straight back at each other and then both spin around with hooves flying, and then a few minutes later, those same two horses are eating out of the same hay pile, playing face tag, or scratching each other's withers. It often reminds me of young boys who are best friends one minute and then swinging at each other the next.

As women, we can be harder on each other than most boys will ever be. We tend to hold grudges and jealousy comes easily, but learning to forgive each other is often difficult. Over the last twenty years, I have had many lessons on learning to forgive people at my barn, and there were times when it was tough. It was as if I was hanging on to some sort of badge that I felt I deserved because someone had hurt me. The only one who it was hurting was me.

The horse stable is not immune from people who make mistakes and even hurt each other at times. But I have learned that the more I reach out to God to help me deal with the pain and hurt, the more He changes me from the inside out. It is a journey of learning how to let go and forgive, but only then did I finally feel true peace.

Watching the horses interact constantly reminds me of the power of forgiveness. Then, I see God's grace in full color. There is nothing more freeing or beautiful to see in action.

~November 22~
One Day You Will Laugh

He will once again fill your mouth with laughter
and your lips with shouts of joy.
Job 8:21

If you have ever been to a horse show with teenage girls then you know all the emotions that spew out all day long. It's like being on an emotional roller coaster and you can bet there will be tears flowing at least once during the day. I have experienced it as a horse show mom of two daughters and I have witnessed countless other mothers dealing with the same things. My husband used to say to me when it was a stressful day showing horses, "Why do you do this to yourself weekend after weekend?" And I would always say, "Because we love it!" I adore my husband but he didn't see all the good things we were experiencing at the time. All he saw was the pouty faces of two girls who looked like they were having a horrible time.

My daughters and I now laugh about those difficult teenage years while showing horses. I have come to realize that even the worst day at a horse show was still a great day, and it taught them so many wonderful lessons that they will have for the rest of their lives. I watch the young mothers now as they help their teenage daughters get their horses tacked up, show clothes on, and put the finishing touches on before they enter the show pen. I am again flooded with memories and that is when I say a prayer for these incredible mommas because they will need it.

God bless the mother who gets up early to make sure the horse is fed and watered and then begins a long day helping her daughter. She may not know it, but only a few short years from now, she and her daughter will laugh about these days and forever be thankful that they got to experience them. It will come, I promise.

~November 23~
The Badge

He will cover you with His feathers; under His wings you will
find refuge; His faithfulness is a shield and rampart.
Psalm 91:4

When I was young, you could ride your horse to the market and you could still find hitching posts at the entrance. You could tie your horse up, get your groceries, and ride home. Now, you're probably thinking I am one hundred years old, but I am not! This was still happening in the very early 1970s in places all over the United States, and I was lucky enough to experience it in the San Fernando Valley, where I lived.

Motorized vehicles had taken over the roadway but the remnants of a past way of life were still holding on and taking their last breath before the modern world completely took over. You could still grocery shop and go to a restaurant to eat by way of the horse, and even though it only lasted for a brief period before it was gone forever, I will never forget those experiences. Back then, horses were still used as working animals for daily necessities, and in some parts of the United States, they still are. Riding horses in the city today is not the same as when I was a kid. It almost seems crazy even to attempt it in most large metropolitan areas today, but a few still do.

Lord, I ask for protection for all the police equestrian units that patrol the streets. They already have a very dangerous job, and then you add in cars and trucks zooming by, and at times, it must feel like a danger zone. The women who ride these incredible police horses are brave beyond compare. They are there to protect the people, but it is equally important to them that their horses are safe at all times. God bless the police equestrian units and the women who wear the badge and ride these horses.

~November 24~
Thankful For...

I will give thanks to the Lord with my whole heart;
I will recount all of your wonderful deeds.
Psalm 9:1

Today, as I was walking the horses in for the evening, I was talking to a friend and we somehow got on the subject of health and getting older. I told her how thankful I was that I could still do what I do every day with the horses. Over the last few years, I have gone through a few surgeries, and, of course, getting older doesn't help. I was feeling good that day and was so thankful that I was pain-free. Then, for a brief moment, my mind flashed back to my youth and how my physical health was the least of my priorities. I guess that is normal for most young people.

I look at horses and my life so much differently now. Today, I am so thankful for my good health and strong bones. The Lord knows I have been banged up a few times over the decades with horses but I have always been able to bounce back stronger, and I am grateful for that. I am thankful every day at the end of the evening chores when all the horses are back inside the barn and no one got hurt, especially when they run around acting crazy with incoming weather. I am thankful for the friendships made at the barn and the great conversations about life, love, and, of course, horses! I never tire of it and it makes my heart happy to sit down in the grass on a summer day with other women and talk about everything under the sun while the horses quietly munch on the grass. It doesn't get any better than that.

Praise you, Lord Jesus, for the gift of health and well-being and the beautiful relationships created because of this incredible animal. I will forever be thankful.

~November 25~
An Honest Horse

And God saw everything that he had made, and behold, it was very good.
And there was evening and there was morning, the sixth day.
Genesis 1:31

A horse will become great when he is in the hands of an honest trainer. A horse will become confident when his well-being comes first over the ribbons. A horse will become bomb-proof when he knows that the person on his back will take care of him no matter what. A horse will become playful when he doesn't need to worry about having enough to eat or drink and feels safe. A horse will become honest and tell the truth about his life when none of these things exist for him. You will see it on his face and his performance will never be at its peak because he has lost his heart to give his all.

Horses are among God's most honest creatures. They'll let you know when they are nervous or scared, and their happiness and contentment shine brightly when they are well cared for. They ask for so little, yet give their all when treated fairly and with respect, even in the face of mistakes.

Many people miss the opportunity to experience what an honest horse feels like to ride because they don't know what to look for or how to obtain it. If they create an environment of great care and the training methods are gentle and fair, then an honest horse will rise to the occasion. It may not happen overnight, but if you are patient, you will begin to see a transformation that will take your breath away. An honest horse will always be a reflection of who we are inside.

~November 26~
Turning In Your Saddle

Now may the Lord of peace himself
give you peace at all times in every way.
II Thessalonians 3:16

There comes a time in every horsewoman's life when she will hang up her saddle for good. For some, it might be when they are young, and for others, like Queen Elizabeth, it might never happen until you are called home to heaven.

When I was a teenager, I had a skewed view of horsemanship. I thought that only "real" equestrians were the ones that rode on the back of a horse. The rest didn't count. Boy, did I have it wrong and it took me a long time to figure it out. All these years later, I have watched women at different times in their lives hang up their saddle for good and learn to do new things with horses. They decided for many reasons that riding was no longer an option, but they still wanted to be involved with horses. Women are embracing many new adventures with horses and having the time of their lives. Some are learning to drive six and eight-hitch teams and competing, while others are driving carriages for weddings and events and having a ball. The things you can teach a horse on the ground are endless and the bond you create will be just as tight.

You don't need to hop in the saddle to be every bit a horsewoman. It is about having a relationship with your horse and sometimes the best relationships involve the warm sunshine and some quality time watching him munch on the grass. And if you feel like hooking up that six-horse team and taking a spin around the arena, go for it! You won't regret it.

Thank you, Lord, for the gift of the horse. This amazing animal's versatility gives us so much to experience without ever getting on his back, and I am thankful for that!

354

~November 27~
Horses In Heaven

Now I saw heaven opened, and behold, a white horse.
And He who sat on him was called Faithful and True.
Revelation 19:11

It is absolutely heartbreaking to say goodbye to a horse we love, and often the question will come up, "Will my horse be in heaven?" I see it on social media from many people who have lost their heart horse. The truth is we don't know for sure if our horse will be in heaven BUT we have proof that horses will be in heaven and we will be riding them one day!

Taking care of horses daily on our farm always reminds me of God's great love for all animals. Horses are talked about a lot throughout the Scriptures, and it is exciting to read that one day we will be riding on the backs of white horses with Jesus Christ! He ensured Noah would preserve every species, male and female, in the Ark before the Great Flood (Genesis 7:8-9). This was so the animals would roam the land again. In the Bible it also talks about how Elijah was taken up to heaven in a chariot pulled by horses! (2 Kings 2:11). In Revelation 6:2-8, it tells us that horses are in heaven. In fact, there are lots of horses, enough for incredible armies of the heavens to ride (Revelation 19:11:2 Kings 6:17). It also tells us that in heaven the lion will lie down with the lamb, which gives me this incredible peace knowing that yes there will be horses in heaven and they will have no predators. What a beautiful vision.

As horse lovers, we would love to know if our favorite equine will be waiting for us in heaven. We may never know the answer until we enter the pearly gates, but we can have peace knowing that God loves us so much that his plans for our lives include horses. It doesn't get any better than that. Praise God!

~November 28~
Working Through It

When you pass through the waters, I will be with you, and the rivers will not overwhelm you. When you walk through the fire, you will not be scorched, and the flame will not burn you.
Isaiah 43:2

When I was young, I was fearless, as were many of my friends who rode horses. We did so many dumb things on the back of our horses and never thought about how hurt we could get if things went wrong. As I got older, that carefree feeling started slipping away and this strange new fear replaced it. I wasn't at all nervous about handling horses on the ground but the thought of cantering in the saddle started to bother me. I often questioned myself and wondered how I went from a little girl who could ride her horse bareback all over town to a mature woman who had a hard time enjoying the ride because I was worried I would fall off and break something. It drove me nuts and I must admit I was disappointed in myself because I had always thought of myself as an experienced rider, but now I wasn't riding at all.

This is a real fear that some women experience when they enter their senior years, and it is something that each woman needs to work through at her own pace. Some feel more comfortable in the saddle, while other women (like me) have more confidence with horses on the ground. We are all working through the hiccups in life together. The most important part of it all is that we surround ourselves with other horsewomen who will encourage us daily.

I want to pray for the woman who has become fearful of riding horses in recent years. She probably never expected to feel this way, but here it is, and she feels heartbroken. Please, Lord, surround her with your love and protection and wise women who will walk beside her as she works through these new feelings.

356

~November 29~
What Success Looks Like

Give thanks to the Lord, for he is good;
His love endures forever
Psalm 118:1

Younger women who ride in competition often put a lot of pressure on themselves as they try to make a name for themselves and their horses. It is something I did when I was young and I often see it with teenage girls still trying to figure out who they are inside. They feel the adrenaline rush when they place high in the show ring, making them feel good about themselves. But the one wonderful thing that comes with age is the ability to ride horses in competition and still have fun. That is what I love about growing older with other horsewomen. Many of us have done the hardcore competition when we were young and have wonderful memories, but there is nothing like being around horses when you are older. As we age gracefully, we laugh more and let the bad rides slide off much easier. We are more forgiving of our horse and can see when he is not at the top of his game and we are okay with it. There is no more pressure to keep up with everyone else, which is freeing.

Success looks much different as you age. When I see seasoned horsewomen competing and still have the ability to enjoy the ride when mistakes are made, I see what success looks like. Their ride might not be perfect, but they glean from their misjudgments and wait for the next class with anticipation to try again. The world of competition really does look different as you age, and in some ways, it is so much better.

Thank you, Lord, for showing me what success looks like with horses. Even the worst day of riding is far better than the best day at work, and I have already won the prize just by being around these incredible animals daily.

Behind The Scenes

She considers a field and buys it; with the fruit of her hands she plants a vineyard. She girds herself with strength, and makes her arms strong.
Proverbs 31:16-17

I want to honor the women who work behind the scenes in all parts of the horse industry. It takes a lot of blood, sweat, and tears to get a rider and his horse to the highest level of competition. It's not just the rider and it's not just the horse. It is a team of grooms, trainers, exercise riders, hay suppliers, farriers, veterinarians, barn owners, stable hands, and more.

These ladies working behind the scenes are incredible horsewomen. They are the glue that holds everything together so that the horse has the best care possible and the rider is ready to ride. They are not noticed very often and don't usually get all the accolades they deserve, but without them, it would be challenging for the competitors and horses to be at their best. It is hard work, and it's not glamorous, but these women do it day in and day out and love what they do. They don't do it to be famous or become rich. They do it because they love the horse and want him to succeed at whatever he is asked to do.

The horse industry was largely considered a man's world a century ago. As things started to change, women took greater chances and their perseverance and natural ability with horses changed the world for today's horsewomen. We owe a debt of gratitude to the brave and talented horsewomen who, throughout history, have paved the way for today's female equestrians. Their courage and determination have made it possible for women to excel in every aspect of the industry. They may work behind the scenes, but their contributions are invaluable and the horse world is richer because of them. They are a true blessing.

~December 1~
Today Was A Good Day

She is a tree of life to those who embrace her,
and those who lay hold of her are blessed.
Proverbs 3:18

One of the gifts of growing older is that you see things more clearly. God has given you the ability to look at the big picture instead of an isolated instance, and it often helps you see that things are not that bad. This is so true when it comes to horses. I have watched many young people become upset at their horse because he wasn't listening. They overreact, lose their temper, and do something they will think about and regret years later. What they can't see are all the positives that transpired and what they can learn from today. And I understand this because I was young once.

The beauty of growing older is that you start to look at life and everything you do with gratitude. You appreciate that you can afford a horse and that he is well cared for. It makes your heart happy to know you can still throw the saddle on his back and pick out his feet without help. You begin to understand the immense value and learning opportunities that arise when your ride is not so good and your horse misbehaves. You may not be happy with him at the moment, but you still love him and understand the importance of leaving on a positive note. You take those bad moments, study them, and learn how to improve them next time. You embrace the good and the bad and understand that today was only a snapshot of the entire picture and tomorrow is a new day.

Thank you, Lord, for the ever-increasing wisdom I am gaining daily. I am grateful for the lessons learned and for the ability to see the big picture when things are not going as planned. Today was a good day and I will forever be thankful.

~December 2~
The Stuntwoman

In the day when I cried out, you answered me,
and made me bold with strength in my soul.
Psalm 138:3

Many little girls fall in love with horses and spend the rest of their lives doing everything they can just to be around them. Then, once in a while, you will find that one little girl who not only loves horses but has been born with a daredevil spirit. Fear is not a part of her vocabulary, and she is the kid at the stable who is standing on the back of a horse while he is galloping in circles. She may fall off but it never deters her. She keeps going, and one day, she grows up to become a Hollywood equine stuntwoman!

These incredible horsewomen hit Hollywood by storm in the 1940s and the movie industry was never the same. Soon, they were jumping off trains and stagecoaches onto the back of a horse, dragged through sand and sagebrush, and performing every other stunt imaginable. They doubled for movie stars like Marilyn Monroe and Julia Roberts when horseback riding was involved, and preferred being a stunt double over being famous. In those early days they didn't make much money and were often asked to do dangerous stunts without safety measures in place. It wasn't about fame because no one ever knew who they were. It was always about their great love of horses and seeing what they could do from the back of a horse.

Today, many of these horsewomen travel the world performing at rodeos and fairs and working on movie sets. These ladies are a true inspiration and you can't help but be a little jealous of what they do for a living. Their trust and connection with their horses is something to behold. And you realize the enormous gift they are sharing with the world—the gift of hope.

~December 3~
Slow Down

In peace I will lie down and sleep,
for you alone, Lord, make me dwell in safety.
Psalm 4:8

What a world we live in. Everything seems to be accelerated, and the days speed by so quickly. The people who come to hang out with their horses make every moment count and truly enjoy the peacefulness of the stable, but that was not how it was just a few short years ago.

When my girls were in high school, our stable was filled with a lot of young people who rode and showed their horses. Life was pretty hectic back then. Some would rush in, grab their horse, and put him through the paces, then head off to the next thing. At times, it was frustrating to watch because I could see many of the horses becoming anxious. These were all great kids, but they were in so many activities and it felt like the horse was just another activity crammed into their busy schedule. Sadly, many of these young people missed the best part about horse ownership. They missed the bonding that happens between a horse and his owner.

Those busy days are gone and most of our clients are a little older now. They enjoy their horses and are not rushing to the next activity. Becoming an older horsewoman is wonderful because we can slow down and not feel like we are missing the next big thing. And often, we don't care if we do miss it! We are content just hanging out at the barn with our friends and the horses and living life a little slower. What a true blessing it is.

Thank you, Lord, for opening my eyes to the realization that I no longer have to rush. It has given me the freedom to enjoy Your creation to the fullest, which is a wonderful feeling. Praise Your Holy Name!

~December 4~
Sweaty Armpits!

For we aim at what is honorable not only in
the Lord's sight, but also in the sight of man.
II Corinthians 8:21

There was a popular deodorant commercial back in the 1980s with the catchphrase, "Never let them see you sweat." That one simple phrase sold millions of dollars of deodorant! I have thought about that phrase many times throughout the years when I was nervous about something. My body would get warm and I could feel the sweat coming.

Horses will do that to us and it happens even more when we decide to start a horse business. At least it did for me. When we opened our stable, I was overjoyed but completely scared. Overnight, my life was on display for new clients who were looking to board their horses. Many of these people were also equine professionals looking for boarding or just checking out our facility. At times, it became overwhelming, and I must admit that I bluffed my way through some of the questions I was asked. It wasn't the smartest thing to do, and I often felt guilty as I was mid-sentence talking with them. I had a lot to learn about being completely honest with my clients.

Thinking back to those early days, I probably needed a lot of deodorant because I was sweating bullets simply because I didn't know how to say, "I'm sorry, but I don't know the answer to your question." I am so glad those days are behind me! I have learned a lot about myself from those early years and I praise God for teaching me how important honesty is. Being honest and not trying to put on a charade is so freeing and it tells people that you live your life with integrity. What a great feeling. And the best part is I no longer have to worry about sweaty armpits. Amen to that!

~December 5~
Trail Of Redemption

*In Him we have redemption through His blood,
the forgiveness of sins, according to the riches of His grace.
Ephesians 1:7*

Horses are such incredibly smart animals, but sometimes, they show us a whole new side of their personality at the least appropriate time. That is when we find ourselves saying, "I hope he can redeem himself today," especially when we are at a horse show.

I have been at a show where my horse was utterly naughty. The first day he acted like he left his brain back at the barn, then decided to be in one of his rebellious moods and I just knew the judge was going to ask us to leave the show pen early because he was causing such a raucous. Then I walked him back to his stall and decided to call it a day, knowing we would try again the second day.

If you have shown horses at any time, then you know exactly what I am talking about. You get a good night's sleep, get up early to feed your horse, and silently pray that he will redeem himself today. You can call it the trail of redemption and horsewomen have experienced this with their horses no matter what they were doing. This amazing animal is unpredictable at times, yet we never give up because we love his spirit and have faith that he will redeem himself.

Our walk with God is no different. We start off doing what is good and faithful and then sin grabs hold of us, and just like the unruly horse, we act unpredictably and even out of control. The good news is that the Lord is always waiting for us to ask forgiveness and try again the next day. The Christian walk leads to a trail of redemption in Jesus Christ, and oh, what a gift that is! Praise God!

~December 6~
New Traditions

My mouth is filled with your praise, and with your glory all the day.
Psalm 71:8

You can feel the excitement when the house decorations, including the Christmas tree, are up in full force. Young families start new traditions with their children, and grandmas and grandpas watch with joy as they see their children carrying on some of the same traditions they began years earlier. The horse world is no different. Wreaths are put on barns and lights are hung on barn doors. There are stockings hung on the stalls that will be filled with carrots and candy canes. Soon, women are taking selfies (and even some professional pictures) with Santa hats on their horses and talking with other women about the Christmas presents they will buy their horses. They talk about how much their horses will love the new bridles and halters, embroidered riding pads, and horse blankets and laugh because they know their horse doesn't care about all that stuff. I smile because I have done the same thing with my horses. But one of the sweetest traditions is the Christmas Day ride and it usually comes at the end of the day when the festivities have slowed down. By mid-afternoon, the cars start pulling in, and soon, the entire family is out to see the horse and go for a Christmas ride. It is a wonderful tradition that will leave memories seared into the hearts of the little ones forever.

Thank you, Lord Jesus, for the Christmas Season. It's a magical time with family and friends and there is nothing sweeter than having our loved ones around us. I pray that the traditions we carry on each year will be a reflection of God's love for us and all that He has given us. Also, thank you for the horses that stand patiently as their owners put the Santa hat on and proceed to take lots of pictures. They deserve extra carrots and mints in their stockings!

~December 7~
Cowgirls Aren't Made

But even before I was born, God chose me
and called me by His marvelous grace. Then it pleased Him.
Galatians 1:15

I have always loved the saying, "Cowgirls aren't made; they're born," and I guess it has always resonated with me because of where I grew up. We lived in many different apartment dwellings (too many to count!) because of my family dynamics, and I was a city girl in every sense of the word. But I was crazy about horses and when I got my first horse, instead of riding in the country, we did a lot of street riding and searching for any open field so that we could run our horses as fast as they would take us. I may not have been born a cowgirl but my heart was all cowgirl growing up.

I have since talked with many women who also grew up in the city. They fell in love with horses at a young age and dreamed of one day moving to the country, raising children, and owning a couple of horses. They came from families that knew nothing about horses but it didn't stop them from following their dreams and waiting on the Lord to send the right man into their life. The one thing many of these women had in common was that they put their trust in God and waited patiently for Him to answer their prayers. It may have looked a little different for each of them but they each had the same passions and dreams.

God knew long before you were born that you would make one heck of a cowgirl one day, and the road to get there would leave you with wisdom and understanding. You may have been born a city girl, but He instilled in you the drive and determination to achieve your dreams. Thank you, Lord Jesus, for knitting the love of horses inside of us while we were still in the womb. Amen

~December 8~
The Barn Family

Oil and perfume make the heart glad, and the
sweetness of a friend comes from his earnest counsel.
Proverbs 27:9

I never tire of watching a woman buy a new horse and witness her excitement as she watches him back off the trailer. The rest of us wait anxiously with her and are just as excited as she is! As the horse slowly backs off the trailer, you can hear a pin drop, and the silence is deafening. But once he is off the trailer and in his full glory, we let out a sigh of relief and swoon over him like a newborn baby. It happens every time without fail.

For the woman who has now become a horse owner, it is a moment she will never forget. She is like a proud momma all over again, and even though she is scared out of her mind about what to do next, she already has a wonderful support system. It is her new barn family and they will hover over her, support her, and give her advice or encouragement when she needs it. They are her cheering section and her biggest fans as she becomes a horsewoman through and through. Her life is about to change in ways she can't imagine; she will grow in her knowledge of horses and do it all with her new barn family by her side.

What a blessing to be surrounded by so many incredible horsewomen who love and support each other. They will do anything to help pave the way for success for the woman who is brand new to horses. They already know that she will have good days and frustrating days but they will walk her through it all until she is ready to fly on her own. Life is good when you make memories with your besties from the barn.

Thank you, Lord, for the beautiful friendships you have blessed us with. God bless the barn family.

~December 9~
Fork In The Road

When I am afraid, I will put my trust and faith in you.
Psalm 56:3

There comes a time in every horsewoman's life when she will stand at the fork in the road and need to decide what is best for her and her horse. She might wonder if she should move her horse to a different stable or find a new trainer. She could think about changing riding disciplines and question whether her horse will easily adjust. She might find herself at a difficult time when she sees her competition horse slowing down and wonders how much longer he can keep going or if she should retire him for good. If she is lucky enough to enjoy her horse well into his senior years, she will eventually come to a time when she must decide what his end of life looks like.

The horsewoman will have many decisions to make regarding these amazing animals, and some will be easy, while others will be gut-wrenching. The beautiful thing about the "forks in the road" that life throws at us is that they help us grow in many ways and make us stronger for the next one that comes our way. Some of our decisions will work out great, and some will result in terrible regrets, but we can't sit in self-pity when we choose poorly. Instead, we learn from our bad choices and move on. After all, as women made in the image of God, we are resilient and will get through it.

Lord, please give each woman wise discernment regarding the horses in her life. Help her see things clearly when the world is screaming at her to go in one direction, but her heart is telling her to go in another. Guide her daily, keep her safe whenever she saddles up for another ride, and let her feel your presence when she feels scared or unsure of the decisions she is faced with regarding her horse.

~December 10~
They Don't Change

Listen to advice and accept instruction,
that you may gain wisdom in the future.
Proverbs 19:20

A wise woman once told me, "The horse has not changed on us, but instead, we have changed and the horse doesn't know how to respond." I remember those words piercing my soul and I have never forgotten them.

Decades later, I think about the horses that have lived on our farm for many years. Except for slowing down a bit as they age, they are the same as they were the first day they got off the trailer. They have their same herd buddies and play the same games with them every day. They move from hay pile to hay pile each morning in the same fashion and the top horses in the herd are still the top horses. They don't wake up each day inventing new ways to do things because they are bored or get tired of the food they eat daily. Instead, they feel content and safe when things are familiar to them. They are comfortable when they know what to expect each day and rest much easier knowing the routine is the same.

On the other hand, we become restless and bored easily. When we jump from one thing to the next our horse doesn't know what to expect, which can lead to confusion and even stress for him. He has a willing heart to change and do what you ask but he needs time to process it. He is just asking us to be patient as he adjusts to his new surroundings, new routine, new herd buddies, or even a new riding discipline. He trusts you to keep him safe and he watches you to see how you respond to everything around him.

I encourage you to consider the quote my wise friend gave me years ago. It will give you a great perspective of the horse and the world around him.

~December 11~
Blazing Her Own Trail

And blessed is she that has believed, for there shall be a
fulfilment of the things spoken to her from the Lord.
Luke 1:45

Every woman has dreams and goals she wants to accomplish with her equine partner. Some women were lucky enough to grow up in a family and have access to horses at a young age. Others grew up in the city, so their horse experience was very limited but it didn't stop them from learning. Some scrimped and saved every penny and sold worldly possessions just to buy their forever horse and were all the better for it.

Horses have given women the drive to quit drinking, get fit, and become healthier. Women have changed careers and simplified lifestyles because they realized they found true happiness around their horses. Many of these ladies finally feel like they are home and blessed beyond measure. It may have taken some of them a few decades to get there, but when they arrived, they knew it was where God wanted them to be.

What makes each woman's journey so unique is that we all come from different backgrounds, upbringings, and religious or non-religious beliefs. But when we get together to ride or just talk about horses, we realize how much we have in common and how wonderfully made we are—all in the image of God.

Thank you, Lord, for the incredible women worldwide who love horses deeply. We may come from different walks of life but we would recognize each other anywhere horses are found. Together, we encourage and cheer each other forward as we each blaze our own trail in the world of horses. Amen.

~December 12~
Praying For Strength

We also pray that you will be strengthened with all His glorious power so you will have all the endurance and patience you need. May you be filled with joy.
Colossians 1:11

Horses are big and powerful animals but also fragile in many ways. When I was young, I watched anything with horses in it, and the horses were always beautiful, strong, and seemed invincible. I didn't understand until I got my first horse how easily they can get injured, become sick, or worse, die.

Now that I am older, I look at the horse through a different lens. If God had created this invincible animal that never broke a leg, got sick, or worse, then there would be no reason to try as hard as we do to ensure that they are healthy and happy. We would become lazy as we tend to do when things are too easy. But because their care is so vital to their existence, it forces us to look at the horse realistically and try harder.

Yes, God created the most perfect animal, but his care still needs to be at the forefront of everything. The horse teaches us to care for something other than ourselves, which is one of the greatest lessons we will ever learn. The woman who has owned horses for any length of time has learned some very difficult lessons from the horses in her life, and if she allows these experiences to help her grow, she will be a much better horsewoman on the inside.

May the Lord deliver you and give you wisdom as you learn some hard truths about the horses you love so much. I pray that through these sometimes difficult experiences, you will grow into a stronger woman who understands that her equine partner is solely dependent on her and never to be taken lightly. Thank you, Lord, for opening my eyes to this remarkable animal and all that he needs to keep him safe, healthy, and happy. Amen.

~December 13~
Tempted

Watch and pray so that you will not fall into temptation.
The spirit is willing, but the flesh is weak.
Matthew 26:41

I am the first to admit that I have been tempted a few times while running my horse business. The temptation to cut corners, make promises that I knew I couldn't keep, or do a sloppy job just to get the job done faster have all been temptations, and for me, they usually happen when I am extremely tired or in a hurry. I have learned that you cannot cut corners with horses. They are intelligent creatures that instantly know when you are doing things differently, and they don't do well if you rush around them constantly. They are very perceptive and wise up quickly when things are not on the up and up.

I have learned that you can't rush the horses outside each morning just to save time because someone will end up getting hurt or they will get amped up and break something. You can't rush a horse onto a horse trailer just because you are in a hurry. His senses will go into overdrive and you will be met with resistance and come to regret it. You might even be tempted to skip picking your horse's feet before you ride because you feel lazy at the moment, but it might be the one time he has a nail stuck in his hoof. The reasons we are tempted are different for all of us, but they all lead down the same path if we listen to that voice of deception inside us.

The beautiful thing about horses is that they teach us to take our time and do things the right way. When we finally understand this and kick temptation out the door, a new inner peace will take over. When God created the horse, He not only created something extraordinary but also taught us daily how to become better people. Praise God!

~December 14~
Fences

I will not leave you as orphans; I will come to you.
John 14:18

Horses need other horses to feel safe and for companionship. They are highly social animals, and many horses become very anxious when they are the last ones left alone in a paddock or even a stall.

We have five large paddocks at our stable, each separated by electric fencing. Every morning, as we walk all the horses to their respective paddocks, they already know which direction we will be going. They are very familiar with the routine and the horses are all very close to each other in their herds. Three strands of electric fencing are the only thing separating all the horses from becoming one massive group. They eat together and play with each other in their separate paddocks and you can see that they feel safe within the fencing parameters as long as they are near their herd mates. But when it is time to bring in all the horses for the evening, something fascinating happens. The last horse left in a paddock will run around and call out as if he is completely alone even though horses are on both sides of him in adjoining paddocks. He can see the other horses and even touch them over the fence but he still feels alone without his tribe. I have often wondered what he is thinking and why he doesn't stand by the fence to be near the other horses.

When we are alone, we can easily overthink things. Sometimes, the craziest thoughts pop into our minds and we begin to feel anxious. You may have four walls around you, but you are never alone. The Lord is waiting for you to reach out to Him. He will calm your heart and mind and give you rest. What an awesome God we have who fills the void in our hearts and comforts us. Amen!

~December 15~
Nurses On Horseback

Blessed is the one who perseveres under trial because,
having stood the test, that person will receive the crown of life
that the Lord has promised to those who love him.
James 1:12

During the turn of the 20th century, a group of courageous women would put on their nurse's uniforms and pack their saddlebags for any kind of medical emergency. These women would get on their horses and head to the most remote areas in the Appalachian Mountains. It was a time of both great poverty and sickness and the doctors struggled to keep up with all their patients, so the nurses began making the long and often dangerous journey on the back of a horse to help the sick. They traveled many miles in all kinds of weather, and often, the terrain was so muddy or steep that they would have to get off and walk their horse.

As the need for nurses grew, the need for strong and healthy horses increased also. Soon, a nursing service was created to ensure that the horses were ready to go at a moment's notice. These women were called "couriers," and their job was to ensure the horses were well-fed and in healthy condition for the long rides day or night. These nurses were now doing everything the doctors were doing and their horses were often the difference between saving a life or not. They were incredible horsewomen who often rode alone and without street lights to guide their way, but they trusted their horse and their horse trusted them, and together, they made a huge impact on many people's lives.

God bless the nurses who traveled on horseback to help others. Not only were these women dedicated to saving lives, but they were amazing horsewomen who understood the importance and value of the incredible equines they rode daily.

373

~December 16~
Ten Times More

This I recall to my mind, therefore I have hope. Through the Lord's mercies
we are not consumed, because His compassions fail not.
They are new every morning; great is Your faithfulness.
Lamentations 3:21-23

For every one thing a horse does to frustrate us and bring us to our knees, there are ten things that will cause us to fall in love with him even more. Every time you have a terrible ride and question whether you should sell your horse, you will have a great ride the next day and decide it's time to buy a horse trailer and hit the trail! Every time you become frustrated because he won't stand still while you are grooming him and picking his feet, the next day, he will follow you around like a puppy dog in the arena and nuzzle you on the shoulder. And you will find yourself running to the feed store to buy the most expensive and yummy horse treats you can find. Every time he gives you attitude and you become fed up, he will be like putty in your hand the next day and you will feel like you have the best horse at your stable! He will step on your foot and stand there as if he doesn't know he is breaking it, yet once you get him off, he looks at you with his big brown eyes and melts your heart all over again. He may have some bad habits that sometimes annoy the heck out of you, but then you have the best ride ever and spew love sonnets all over social media.

This crazy love affair is real and such a blessing because we learn to love the horse unconditionally. That means we will take the good with the not-so-good and learn from it. What an awesome teacher we have in the horse. If we are willing to learn even when it is tough, we will fall in love ten times more.

374

~December 17~
The Milky Way

Look up into the heavens. Who created all the stars? He brings them out like an army, one after another, calling each by its name. Because of his great power and incomparable strength, not a single one is missing.
Isaiah 40:26

If you have horses at home on your own property, you know what happens when you get up, turn on the lights, and start making coffee. If your horses can see you, they will tell you quickly that they are waiting for breakfast! Some horses are much more demanding than others, and if you start to hear pounding on the stalls or wood fencing, it can kick you into high gear fast. Horses have their clock ticking and can sense exactly what time it is, just like we can. That is why it is very helpful if you are a morning person.

My husband and I are out the door very early every morning and there is something magical about feeding horses while it is still dark. It is pitch black outside and the stars are at their brightest before the dawn breaks. I often gaze up into the sky and look for the Milky Way, which always leaves me in awe. For those few moments, I have horses all around me and the stars above me with darkness in between and it is nothing short of miraculous. It is a reminder of how small I am, but I also can sense how big God is, and His closeness surrounds me with peace. Even after all these years of caring for horses, I never tire of looking into the sky to find the Milky Way and see His awesomeness all around me.

Lord, I pray I never take the stars and Milky Way above me and the horses around me for granted. What a gift to be able to care for such amazing animals under a starry sky and to see the glory of God's creation in full force. Praise your Holy Name!

~December 18~
Callused Hands

As water reflects the face, so one's life reflects the heart.
Proverbs 27:19

As a young girl, I remember looking at this woman's hands at the stable where I boarded my horse and thinking to myself how old and rough they looked. I could see calluses on the palms of her hands as she brushed her horse and sometimes I caught myself staring. I always thought she was pretty for being an "old" person, but her hands, for some reason frightened me. I didn't want that to happen to my hands, and then, of course, my young and naïve mind told me that it never would!

Many decades later, I often look at my hands, which are callused and even crooked at the knuckles, and think about that woman who was probably the same age as I am now. My hands are just like hers! The funny thing is I now have a wonderful thankfulness for a life lived to the fullest with horses. It has made me realize that the woman from my youth was probably living her best life. It's not a glamorous life by the world's standards but a full life that I wouldn't trade for anything. Now when I look at my callused hands, I thank the Lord for bringing me this far and still going strong. What a wonderful gift from God.

I often wonder if the young girls who ride at my barn ever look at my hands and have the same reaction I had all those decades ago. I think about it and smile because they don't realize that my callused hands represent a beautiful life filled with a loving husband, children, dogs, and, horses.

Thank you, Lord, for the women who have lived a full life with horses and can smile at their callused hands because they truly understand that their hands have cared for some of God's most precious creatures.

~December 19~
Trust

*"But blessed are those who trust in the Lord
and have made the Lord their hope and confidence.
Jeremiah 17:7*

We often ask so much of the horse without thinking about the fear they may be experiencing. We load them into horse trailers, put them on airplanes, and pray they make it safely to their destination. Horses have been loaded onto ships and forced to live in dark cramped conditions while crossing vast oceans. We have lowered them miles down below the earth's surface into dark holes to a new life as pit ponies, and they learned to ride the rails which proved hazardous for many equines. Horses have been everywhere except the moon, but they have trusted their humans to take care of them. They can't tell us how they are feeling but there is no denying when a horse is nervous or panicking.

The one incredible trait about the horse is his willing heart. If he trusts you, he will do the most unnatural things to please you, and his natural instinct of flight or fight takes a back seat. When I think about it that way it gives me chills, and I start to understand the magnitude of his trust in me. The horse would literally walk to the ends of the earth if we asked.

I started thinking about my relationship with God and if I was as devoted and willing as the horse. I would love to say that I am, but I know there have been many times that I have firmly put both feet on the ground, refusing to go in the direction the Lord was asking because I was scared. That is when I lost faith that He would get me through it safely. Those were the times that I had to pray fervently for God to lead me and help me see the light at the end. And those were the times He proved to me that He would deliver me out of harm's way. His love never fails.

~December 20~
What A Workout

For while bodily training is of some value, godliness is of value in every way,
as it holds promise for the present life and also for the life to come.
I Timothy 4:8

Have you ever stopped to think about how heavy everything is with horses? First of all, horses are big and heavy animals. If you have ever had your foot stepped on by one of these gentle giants, then you know what I am talking about. Hay bales are heavy whether feeding your horse or unloading the wagon into the hay mow. The bags of grain we love to feed our horses are a workout in themselves and it seems like they get heavier as we age! Their water buckets are heavy when topped off, and dragging the hose around to fill the water tanks sometimes feels backbreaking. But nothing can compare to cleaning dirty stalls! These animals we love so much actually keep us strong and fit and I appreciate that now that I am older.

When we first opened our stable, I was much younger and doing chores was no big deal. I could unload grain bags with ease and cleaning stalls was a breeze. During the summer I would help unload hay and I enjoyed it! Well, the days of unloading hay are few and far between, but I still do the rest of the chores daily and love it. And I discovered a hidden blessing. I realized all the manual labor done on our farm has kept me healthy and strong, and when I had knee replacement surgery, it benefited in a much faster healing.

Horses and everything involving them are heavy, but ladies, that is a good thing. We are using muscles that we might not otherwise use, and these animals keep us feeling young and fit! So today when you are heading out to the stable, thank your horse for an excellent workout, and praise the Lord for the physical ability to keep doing it year after year. What an incredible gift!

~December 21~
Chores

My flesh and my heart may fail, but God is
the strength of my heart and my portion forever.
Psalm 73:26

There is something extra special about feeding the horses during the Christmas season that always brings me back to the birth of Christ. The quietness of the horse stable is wondrous and even spiritual at times. But the truth is it can be a lonely time for many women caring for horses.

The world seems to run at even a faster pace with holiday parties and children's Christmas programs, baking cookies and wrapping gifts. Those are all wonderful additions to the season but the chores still need to be done and the sick horses need to be tended to. The water tanks need to be filled and the snow needs to be plowed. That is all part of the horsewoman's life she has chosen and she gladly embraces it, but once in a while, it can feel lonely when you have to leave the holiday party to head home in the dark and do the evening chores. You will never hear her complain and she wouldn't trade it for the world, but it has its setbacks like any other career or lifestyle.

I understand how these women feel because I have had those same emotions many times during the holiday season, especially when my children were young. That is when I got on my knees ask the Lord to remove the heaviness I felt in my heart.

If you are feeling a little overtaxed trying to get everything done for Christmas while still doing the farm chores, I encourage you to pray and ask the Lord for strength, emotional peace, and comfort. Taking care of horses is a dream come true for so many, but it does have a price tag attached. I pray you will find the peace you seek, which only comes from Jesus Christ.

~December 22~
Two Different Worlds

Trust in the Lord, and do good; dwell in the land and befriend faithfulness.
Delight yourself in the Lord, and he will give you the desires of your heart.
Commit your way to the Lord; trust in him, and he will act.
Psalm 37:3-5

Back in the 1960s and 70s, the smog was horrible in Southern California. You could literally feel your lungs hurting by mid-afternoon on hot summer days if you were outside a lot. The cloud of smog you would see across the San Fernando Valley was something that we all just got used to back then. Thank goodness the air quality has improved over the decades for both humans and animals. When I moved to Wisconsin in 1990, one of the first things I noticed was how clean and fresh the air was. It was as if my nostrils came alive! I couldn't smell the fumes from the vehicles that drove by, but I could smell the newly cut grass on the farm and I loved it. I had never seen so much open land, trees, cows, or horses. It was as if I had died and gone to heaven.

I was given the incredible gift of being able to experience two completely different worlds with horses, and both were wonderful and taught me so much. I learned two completely different ways of taking care of horses because of the extreme differences in climate, and it has helped me become much more rounded as a horsewoman and human being. You can travel from one part of the country to another and you will feel like you are learning many things for the first time, and your knowledge will expand and that is a good thing.

We should never stop learning and the more we experience the differences in the world with horses, the more we become whole as a horsewoman. I hope you have the chance to experience horses in many different places throughout your life. It is truly a gift.

More Leg!

Seek the Lord and his strength; seek his presence continually!
I Chronicles 16:11

"More leg!" yelled the riding instructor to her student as she trotted by on her horse. Those were the two words she dreaded hearing the most at each lesson, but she also knew her horse needed a little extra leg to motivate him. The consistent pressure around his belly urged him forward without confusion and you could read the calmness in his body language as she increased her leg pressure.

The horse is a magnificent creature and if we are willing to study his personality and what makes him tick, we will better understand him and our bond will grow even closer. It is so interesting that many riding instructors can see instantly if a horse needs a more consistent leg on their sides or if they will respond better to short bursts of pressure. It has been said that a "hot" horse usually does better with steady pressure when using leg cues and that helps keep him at an even pace, while a more laid-back horse often reacts more positively to sudden bursts of leg pressure.

I started thinking about my relationship with God and wondered how attentive I was to His requests? Does God need to keep poking at me to get me moving because I am lazy or tune him out? Or does He already know how easily I become anxious and instead gives me a long steady nudge that builds my confidence and sends me forward without hesitation? The beautiful thing about God is that He knows us inside and out, which is such a comfort.

The next time your instructor yells, "More leg!" from across the arena, you can smile and think about this incredible God who loves you so much and is always there for you. He just might have to nudge you a little now and then to get you moving forward.

~December 24~
The Gift

So now I am giving you a new commandment: Love each other. Just as I have loved you, you should love each other. Your love for one another will prove to the world that you are my disciples.
John 13:34-35

From an early age, my daughters learned that the horses came first and needed to be cared for before we could celebrate Christmas Eve and eat dinner. It was a routine they knew quite well. We would get home from Christmas Eve service and Dad would head out to the barn and top off the water buckets one last time to make sure all the horses were doing well. Then, he would turn off the lights and lock up the barn. It is something he does every evening, but on this special night, he knows we are all waiting to pray, eat dinner, and enjoy time together with family and friends.

My daughters have places of their own now, but as I reminisce about their childhood, as every mother does during the holidays, I get the sense that they were given an incredible gift that will stay with them for a lifetime. They have learned the true meaning of taking care of horses no matter the occasion, and even though they may have been impatient as little children because they were excited, as adults, they see the full picture of what love is all about. It taught them valuable lessons and responsibility for the animals entrusted to us and gave them a sense of stability.

As adults, they may not ride horses right now because they are busy doing the things young women do, but they will never forget their childhood. One day, they will share their stories with their children of what life was like growing up on a horse farm. They may not remember all the gifts they received on Christmas morning, but they will remember the horses and being a part of something bigger than themselves. And that is a wonderful gift.

~December 25~
The Perfect Day

For to us a child is born, to us a son is given;
and the government shall be upon his shoulder,
and his name shall be called Wonderful Counselor,
Mighty God, Everlasting Father, Prince of Peace.
Isaiah 9:6

There is something special about feeding the horses on Christmas morning. The truth is I would love to sleep in, but since I have been taking care of horses on our farm for twenty years, I have difficulty sleeping in, no matter the day.

When I wake up, grab a cup of coffee, and think about the day ahead, I am filled with joy and great anticipation because the kids will be coming home. Then I put my barn clothes on and head out to feed the horses, and the quietness of the morning is something to behold. There is calm in the air and the traffic from the highway has all but disappeared in the early morning. As I open the barn door, I hear the sound of nickers and instantly think about the birth of Christ and how he was born in a stable with animals surrounding him. He was wrapped in swaddling clothes and laid in a manager while Mary and Joseph gazed with loving eyes down at him, not knowing the impact this tiny baby would have on the world.

I can't help but feel emotional as I realize how special this day is and how blessed I am to be able to take care of such amazing animals. Christmas day will always be special for the believer and all I can do is praise God for the life he has given me on this earth.

Thank you, Lord, for sending your son as a baby to save this world. It truly is a perfect day.

~December 26~
The Day After

*For whoever has entered God's rest
has also rested from his works as God did from his.*
Hebrews 4:10

The presents have been opened and visiting with family has come to an end. Mom and dad are up early and trying to enjoy a cup of coffee together while the kids sleep in. It was a whirlwind day on Christmas and even though it was wonderful seeing family and eating too much good food, everyone is exhausted. It is time to rest and rejuvenate.

For the woman who loves horses, rejuvenation is found at the barn with her horse. No matter how hectic the rest of the world is, she finds peace and calm there and her exhaustion seems to disappear when she spends time with her beloved steed.

Every woman feels some weariness after the holidays, but today, I want to lift up the working women who care for horses and livestock even when they have entertained and fed a house full of people for the holidays. These women are wives and mothers and they know they won't get a day off from the chores that need to be done out in the barn. The horses still need to be fed and turned out, and their basic needs must be met like every other day. These women are strong and have gladly chosen this lifestyle, but sometimes they need to rest, which can be challenging on a working farm. Today, my prayer is for these incredible women who never stop.

Dear Lord, please lift up the women who care for horses daily. I ask that they be filled with energy to keep them going and to please keep them healthy and strong. I pray they will find time to rest after a busy holiday month with people and animals. God bless the hardworking horsewoman. She is a blessing to all who know her.

~December 27~
Waiting

The Lord is good to those who wait for him,
to the soul who seeks him.
Lamentations 3:25

This peaceful easy feeling comes over me whenever I walk into our old dairy barn to do the morning chores. I turn on the light, hear the nickers, and then I see all the hand-crafted wood beams around me that are well over a hundred years old. I often think about the men and women who walked through this same door over the last hundred years to feed the horses, milk the cows, and let the chickens out for the day. There is so much history in this old barn, and as I get older, the more emotional it becomes to me.

The woman who loves horses gets that same peaceful easy feeling when she drives by a field and sees the horses quietly grazing. She gazes out her window, and no matter how many times she drives by the same field, it still takes her breath away. She has her day job, but her heart longs for the day when her office is inside a barn and her clients are horses. She dreams quietly to herself and goes about her day but yearns for the day when her dream becomes a reality. She prays without ceasing and asks God what His will is for her life. Then, she shares her heart. She tells Him she feels like a fish out of water with her career and is waiting for the chance to change course. She wants to have a purpose in her life and she wants it to be God-honoring. So she waits patiently.

Dear Lord, today, my prayer is for the woman who feels like she is in the wrong place. She longs for the day when she can work with horses as a career but she is not sure how to make it happen. She has a heart for horses and for you, Lord. I pray that she finds the life she is longing for, and through her love of horses she will be able to share the love of Christ. Amen.

~December 28~
The Christmas Party

A worthy woman who can find?
For her price is far above rubies.
Proverbs 31:10

A woman who loves horses would do anything for them. We worry about their care and happiness, and we are not afraid to make noise if we see that a horse is being neglected or abused. Women in history have also done their part to help improve the horse's life—and sometimes, that involved throwing a Christmas party!

At the turn of the 20th century, horses were the engine that kept the cities going. They were considered work animals and most horses worked long days regardless of weather or season. In fact, very few horses actually got a day off to rest, and many died in the streets while still hooked up to the wagons they pulled.

The women who were part of the Humane Society saw how poorly the horses were treated and decided to throw a Christmas Party at Boston's Post Office to bring awareness of the inhumane treatment of horses. They put up a Christmas tree and banners that read "Massachusetts Society for the Prevention of Cruelty to Animals." There were bushels of oats and barrels of apples and carrots. Soon, horses were munching on the goodies and people began addressing the harsh treatment of the workhorses. Quickly these parties spread to most major cities and the lives of the horses began to change for the better. For the first time, horses were being appreciated for all the hard work they did daily.

Praise God for the women who decided decades ago to make a difference in the lives of the workhorses and, in the process, changed how people viewed and treated these animals for the better. These brave ladies helped pave the path to better treatment for the horse and all animals.

~December 29~
You Never Know

She opens her mouth with wisdom,
and the teaching of kindness is on her tongue.
Proverbs 31:26

When I think back through the years, there are several horsewomen who have shaped me without ever knowing about it. Some looked like perfection in the saddle, while others never rode a horse but were considered remarkable horsewomen. Some were young and beautiful with the clothes and boots to match their equine partner, while others rode in worn-out jeans and could handle even the most challenging horses. There were seasoned horsewomen aged from the sun, and the wrinkles they wore showed a long life full of ups and downs but they were the ladies to go to if you had a question and wanted an honest answer. Some horsewomen were unapproachable, while others gave you a hug and huge smile when you saw them and they had a way of making you feel like everything was going to be okay. All these women left a deep impression on me that has lasted my lifetime, and I find it funny how the people we meet when we are young often come back in a memory or thought just when we need it the most.

I realize now that the things I do and say could easily influence someone else when it comes to horses. You just never know who is watching, and as older women we have the awesome honor and privilege of helping others that are trying to figure out this crazy and wonderful life with horses.

Lord, I know that I have failed at times when I was short with someone who had a question about their horse. Help me to remember the patient women who greatly influenced me and teach me to walk in their footsteps. For there is no more excellent gift than to help someone in need.

~December 30~
New Goals

Therefore, if anyone is in Christ, he is a new creation.
The old has passed away; behold, the new has come.
Jeremiah 29:11

The new year is fast approaching and I am already thinking about my new goals. The weather outside is frigid so it gives me time to rest as well as the horses. But as women, our minds never really shut off. We are already making plans for when the weather gets warmer. Across the world, there are women everywhere thinking about trying new riding disciplines while others are thinking about buying their first horse. Some are deciding if they should buy a trailer and try horse camping, while other women plan to show their horses for the first time and are excited about finding the right show outfits to wear. Many women are thinking about breeding their mares and part of the fun is choosing the perfect stallion. And, of course, a newborn colt is always a joy!

For some of these incredible women the goals will be tough ones to obtain, but they will rise to the occasion and persevere no matter how they place. For others, the goals are smaller but every bit as important, for they are new horse owners and they want to do things right the first time. These ladies might all have different goals, but they have one thing in common. They love horses!

Today, I pray for each woman who is making plans for the goals and dreams she has with her horse. I ask for her safety in all she does in the coming year. I ask that she be surrounded by other women who will encourage and support her if her goals fall short and celebrate with her when she accomplishes what she set out to do.

Thank you, Lord, for the horsewoman who never stops dreaming. She is such an inspiration to all who know her.

~December 31~
Looking Back, Looking Forward

Therefore, if anyone is in Christ, he is a new creation.
The old has passed away; behold, the new has come.
II Corinthians 5:17

I could wallow in the mistakes of my youth and never forgive myself for everything I put my horse through, or I could forgive myself and make things much better for the horses in my life now. I could choose to only look back at the memories I have had with horses and never experience the complete joy of owning a horse as an adult. I could stick to what I learned as a young equestrian and never be open-minded to a new way of doing things that might be much better for my horse.

Owning a horse as an adult is even sweeter because we understand the cost and sacrifice involved, and we are willing to give up other material things that no longer mean anything to us for a life with horses. I love to share stories about my life as a teenager, but having horses as a grown woman and coming full circle makes it feel more complete. As grown horsewomen, we are less selfish than our younger selves and have gained incredible patience over time. We find joy in the simplest things and recognize how blessed we are. We may love looking back and reminiscing, but there is nothing better than looking forward with dreams to conquer.

Thank you, Lord, for the horses I was blessed to own in my youth. They taught me that I wasn't the center of the universe and that their needs came first. The lessons I learned growing up with horses were not easy at times, but they have shaped who I am today, and I will forever be grateful.

I am looking forward to a new year filled with horses, family and friends, with the Lord by my side. This is my prayer for every horsewoman. In Jesus' Name, Amen.

Made in United States
North Haven, CT
25 October 2024

59427224R00215